Duke Snider
with
Bill Gilbert
Introduction by Carl Erskine

CITADEL PRESS
Kensington Publishing Corp.
www.kensingtonbooks.com

CITADEL PRESS BOOKS are published by

Kensington Publishing Corp.
850 Third Avenue
New York, NY 10022

All Kensington titles, imprints, and distributed lines are available at special
quantity discounts for bulk purchases for sales promotions, premiums,
fund-raising, educational, or institutional use. Special book excerpts or
customized printings can also be created to fit specific needs. For details,
write or phone the office of the Kensington special sales manager:
Kensington Publishing Corp., 850 Third Avenue, New York, NY 10022,
attn: Special Sales Department, phone 1-800-221-2647.

First Citadel printing: May 2002

10   9   8   7   6   5   4   3   2   1

Printed in the United States of America

Library of Congress Control Number: 2001099900

ISBN 0-8065-2363-8

To Bev, my lovely and loving wife,
And the rest of our family —
Kevin, Pam, Kurt, and Dawna

A Note From the Publisher

This book was published in hardcover in 1988 and has enjoyed re-markable popularity since the beginning. It became a *New York Times* best seller that summer and was selected at the end of the year for the presti-gious list of that newspaper's "Notable Book of the Year." To this day it is one of the most popular baseball books ever written.

There are three reasons for its popularity:

- Duke Snider himself, a genuine folk hero in Brooklyn and elsewhere even today, 45 years after the Dodgers moved to Los Angeles.

- The Dodgers themselves, one of the favorite teams in the history of American sports.

- The delightful combination of Duke and Bill Gilbert, a baseball man himself who once represented the Washington Senators and who is one of America's most popular baseball authors.

Duke, like all other players of his era, still holds a special place in his heart for his sport and for his team, and Gilbert captures those sentiments to a fascinating and caring degree. That's why Citadel press decided to re-issue this enduring book. It has stood the test of time in telling the story of "The Duke of Flatbush" and the other players from his era, and in pre-serving the story of those special teams and those special times.

The Editors
Citadel Press

Don't worry about your individual numbers. Worry about the team. If the team is successful, each of you will be successful too.

—Branch Rickey, to the Brooklyn Dodgers

Some Thank You's

Before telling the story that will unfold on the following pages, we want to express our special gratitude to Becky Jackson for her help, especially her extensive research in gathering information from members of the Snider family. Becky is one of the family's closest friends. The professionally thorough quality of her excellent work and the valuable insights which she obtained from family members are major contributions in making this book complete.

●

We are also pleased to express our thanks to our editor at Zebra Books, Wallace Exman, and to our agent at the Scott Meredith Literary Agency, Russ Galen. Two photographers from the days in Brooklyn, Barney Stein and Herb Scharfman, are also due our thanks for supplying us with their priceless pictures.

Special thanks are also extended to Dave Gilbert and Lillian Gilbert for their editing, to Eileen Stubenrauch for manuscript preparation, and to our mutual good friend, Ed Liberatore, for performing the introduction which led to our partnership.

Duke Snider and Bill Gilbert

A Personal Note

This story mentions many baseball players who shared my career and my life with me, but eight people who were not players deserve particular recognition—our neighbors in Bay Ridge during my 11 seasons with the Dodgers in Brooklyn.

The people of Brooklyn were more than just neighbors. They were like family, especially the McKinneys, the Steiners, the Barwoods, and the Baumans.

Our friendship with Jack and Mildred McKinney began on a summer day in 1950 when their daughter Jeanne asked permission to take our son, Kevin, on a walk. It became a frequent routine for the two kids. Their other children, Jackie and Kathy, became our friends too. They, like the others, remain close friends of ours today, 30 years after we left Brooklyn.

Dr. Morris Steiner and his wife Martha were two other special people. Dr. Steiner was our pediatrician, as he was for all the Dodger children. He was never too busy to see us in his office, and he kept the children in good health with frequent checkups. He was also one of a vanishing breed—when a child was sick, he came to your house. The Steiners hosted many an enjoyable dinner, special occasions which always included spirited baseball discussions among the other Dodgers in the area—Pee Wee Reese, Carl Erskine, Rube Walker—and me, especially on the merits of right-handed hitters versus left-handers.

We met Dorothy and Gus Barwood in 1952. They lived only a short block away on Marine Avenue, and our children were close friends with their daughter Dorothy and their dog, "Happy Felton," named after one of the Dodgers' TV personalities. Our children were as much at home at the Barwood house as they were at our own. We adults felt the same way, especially because of many happy "block parties" hosted by Dorothy and Gus in their back yard.

Roz and Bob Bauman were another part of our Brooklyn family. We met them through Betty and Carl Erskine. They operated a large day camp in Oceanside, Long Island, and they'd send a van to Bay Ridge to pick up the children living there. They provided many a happy summer outing for us.

The Dodgers brought a lot of happiness to the people of Brooklyn, and the people of Brooklyn—especially the McKinneys, Steiners, Barwoods, and Baumans—brought an equal amount of happiness to my family and me.

D.S.
Fallbrook, California

Introduction

by Carl Erskine

Duke Snider and I became teammates and lifelong friends 40 years ago, 1948, at the Brooklyn Dodgers' new training camp in Vero Beach, Florida. We were a couple of kids trying our best to make it in the major leagues after service in World War II and a stretch in the minors.

We had different opinions of each other when we met. Duke hit against me in a practice game and asked me later how a little punk could throw a baseball so hard. I watched him play and knew immediately I was looking at one of the great talents in baseball. He had a grace and carriage which, like Joe DiMaggio, set him apart.

We became roommates and went through 12 unforgettable years together, of championships and defeats, of individual glory and despair, two guys making their way in a tough profession, two lives which seemed at times to be one.

Duke seems to remember everything about those days in this book—how unsure we were at the start, our magical year in 1955, his home runs and his worries about striking out, my good days and my worries about my chronic arm problems.

They say you can't go home again, but I did when I read Duke's book—the good times we had when we were on top of the world, the long talks in the dark quiet of our hotel room when one of us was struggling, and those special memories enjoyed by all of us who remember the 1940s and '50s.

I'm glad Duke asked me to write this introduction. I owe him a favor. As good as he was, he was even better when I was pitching. He always seemed to help me win—with a big hit or a game-saving catch. I'm glad to get this chance to do something in return.

For those of you who were not treated to the special skills of "The Duke of Flatbush," I should mention some things not in the stats. Duke Snider was the perfect player for his time and place. He balanced our heavy-hitting right-handed lineup and was the Dodgers' answer to the Giants' Mays and the Yankees' Mantle.

Duke always took excellent care of himself. He played every day and was seldom hurt enough to miss the lineup. He knew which players to needle and which ones to encourage, as he did me and the rest of our pitching staff. He often asked his own pitchers to watch for flaws in his swing. And he had good baseball savvy.

"The Dook," as he was called in Brooklyn, was the royalty which gave Brooklyn respectability. No player contributed more to our team both offensively and defensively. No player agonized more when he didn't perform well. Could he have been better? Some say yes. I say they didn't know him the way I did.

I always sensed Duke would be a Hall of Famer. I'm proud to have been his roomie, teammate, and close friend.

Special Time, Special Team

It was a tense situation for the Dodgers, and everyone knew it—the largest crowd ever to see a World Series game at Ebbets Field, and the millions listening on the radio or watching TV. But it was more than that for me. It was a personal crisis.

As I walked toward the plate from the on-deck circle to hit against Allie Reynolds, I was struggling against a challenge which would tell me, and the world, whether I really had what it took to be a major-league baseball player. Reynolds and the other Yankee pitchers had humiliated me in 1949, my first World Series. For three years I carried that monkey on my back. Now I had to get him off. I had to come through.

It was the first game of the 1952 World Series, the Brooklyn Dodgers versus the New York Yankees in another of their annual fall battles that captured America's attention on so many October afternoons in the 1940s and 1950s. Gladys Gooding was at the Ebbets Field organ, and the National Anthem was performed by Guy Lombardo and his Royal Canadians. If you weren't there, you listened in your office or your classroom (if you were lucky) to Red Barber and Mel Allen at the microphone of the Gillette Cavalcade of Sports. Or you watched on a ten-inch black-and-white TV set. In the end, the Yankees always won and their stars were always on the "Ed Sullivan Show" the following Sunday night. And the Dodger fans always defiantly said, "Wait till next year." It happened every October, or so it seemed.

The '49 Series was a nightmare for me, and the knowledge that I had driven home the run that won the pennant for the Dodgers in my first full season as a major-leaguer did nothing to ease my agony. Three hits, no runs driven in. And I tied Rogers Hornsby's record for the most strikeouts in a five-game World Series with eight. Hornsby's stature as one of the greatest hitters in the history of the game was of no comfort at all.

A lot of well-meaning friends and relatives back home in Compton, California, didn't help matters, either. They held a parade and organized a big banquet at the Veterans' Hall, honoring me as the first guy from Compton ever to play in a World Series. But I knew I was no hero—maybe to them, but certainly not to myself.

I was remembering all of this as I left the on-deck circle, with a pat on my backside from my friend and boyhood hero back in California, Jackie Robinson, who moved into the on-deck circle behind me. It was the sixth inning. The score was tied, 1-1. Two out. Pee Wee Reese on second.

Reynolds had every reason to be confident. He had gotten rid of me easily when we faced each other in '49—three strikeouts and a pop-up. In this game I was one for two, a fly ball to Mickey Mantle and a bases-empty double.

But now the game was on the line, and I was about to find out if

16

I had the most important requirement of all to be a major-leaguer in the true definition of that term—the ability to succeed under pressure.

Reynolds was a six-foot Cherokee Indian from Oklahoma and one of baseball's dominant pitchers. He won 20 games that year and was a consistent winner in World Series games. He owned a fastball that hummed with velocity and a good sweeping curve. He started me off with a curveball in the dirt. Ball one. I set myself for the next pitch. Everybody in the ball park knew what was coming.

He whistled his high fastball at me—his hummer. It might have been ball two, but it was close enough to my power zone, so I jumped on it. You usually know as soon as you hit a home run that it's gone. I knew it this time too. As I headed toward first, I watched the ball sail over the clock on top of the Schaefer Beer sign in right center field toward the promised land for every left-handed hitter—Bedford Avenue.

I never streaked around the bases on my homers, but I never "Cadillacked" either. This time I was air-lifted, floating on the magic of the moment, past the Yankee infielders—Joe Collins, Billy Martin, Phil Rizzuto, and Gil McDougald. I trotted past Yogi Berra to the plate, and Pee Wee and Jackie gave me an extra-enthusiastic reception. They knew what that home run meant to me—and my career. I finally belonged. I was a *real* major-leaguer.

I traveled a long, winding, uphill road to get to that moment. I always felt convinced I would make it in the majors, but I was fighting not just to make it, but to make it big. I was always reading and hearing about how great I was destined to be, how I had the potential to become one of the greatest baseball players of all time. That puts a lot of extra pressure on an athlete, and what pressure wasn't already on me I managed to add myself. I fought a lot of lonely battles with myself, telling myself that it wouldn't be enough just to be a major-leaguer—I had to be a great one, because everybody was saying I would be.

It started as early as spring training of my rookie year, when Tom Meany of the *New York World-Telegram* wrote a story under a headline that said:

DUKE COULD MEAN DODGER PENNANT

He wrote that I might become the key player who could take the team all the way to the World Series: "If young Snider does turn out to be that key man, he will be the player who will win the pennant for the Dodgers."

That's pretty heavy stuff to handle when you're just a rookie trying to make the team and you're still only 20 years old.

The year was 1947. It was a special time. Americans were beginning to enjoy life again after four years of World War II. The girls were wearing the "new look" dresses down to their ankles and the boys were sporting crew cuts. Perry Como was singing "Prisoner of Love," Elmo Tanner was whistling "Heartaches" accompanied by Ted Weems, and some guy in a novelty tune kept saying, "Open the Door, Richard." Detroit was turning out cars instead of tanks, and a lot of them had something new called automatic transmissions.

Ted Williams, Joe DiMaggio, Stan Musial, and the rest of the baseball stars were back from the war. The G.I. Bill was paying for college educations and new homes, and something called "the baby boom" was beginning. About the only TV most of us got to see was at some lucky friend's house or in a store window or a bar. And nobody was betting a plug nickel on Harry Truman's chances of staying in the White House after 1948.

*   *   *

I remember that year as a special time for the Brooklyn Dodgers, too. Branch Rickey, the Dodgers' president and one of the wisest executives in the history of baseball, was systematically putting together a team to rival our interborough neighbors, the New York Yankees and Giants. Mr. Rickey was so successful in the years immediately following the war that we came within two games of matching the Yankees' incredible achievement of winning their league's pennant for five straight years.

The Yankees won their consecutive pennants from 1949 through 1953. We came within two losses of doing the same thing in the very same years. We won the pennant in 1949, lost it on the last day of the season to the Phillies in 1950, lost in the last game of the 1951 playoffs on Bobby Thomson's home run, and won the pennant in 1952 and '53. That's how great we were as a team, and I would argue that such a record shows we were every bit as good as the Yankees over that same five-year stretch.

We were always the sentimental favorites too, and not just because it took us until 1955 to win our first World Series. The Yankees were admired, but the Dodgers were loved. The Yankees were the ultimate professionals—they even wore pinstripes. We were the colorful, scrappy underdogs. Somebody said, "Rooting for the Yankees is like rooting for General Motors," but the whole world had a great time rooting for the Dodgers. You had to love a team that had guys named Pee Wee, Oisk, Skoonj, Preacher, and—the name the writers gave me—the Duke of Flatbush. Later we picked up Campy and Big Newk. We even had some unique names on the management side with Branch, Buzzie, and Leo the Lip. Our batboy was "The Brow." We sounded like an assortment of characters straight out of Damon Runyon, and in many ways we were.

I'm going to enjoy telling you about those guys and those times, as remembered by one of them. I want to tell you about life as a Dodger, especially in Brooklyn, and my own career of peaks and valleys and my struggles to achieve the level of excellence that I knew was within my reach and expected of me. I want to tell you about our fans and our home, Ebbets Field. Most of all, I want to tell you about our closeness as a *team,* a group of young men mostly in our 20s who were destined to make history, some individually, but all of us as a team whose members genuinely cared for each other. The sports world has never again seen the likes of Brooklyn and its Dodgers in the 1940s and '50s.

People ask me today if I'm sorry I missed out on the big bucks they're paying athletes today. They say I'd be making a million dollars a year, maybe even two million. That would be great—I never made more than $42,000 a year as a player—but I wouldn't trade the biggest salary today for the fun we had then and the memories and friendships we have now. Today's players have a lot of money, but they'll never have what we had, and what we still have.

Times were simpler in 1947. I rented a room in the private home of Peg and Ben Chase on Bedford Avenue in the Flatbush section of Brooklyn, two and a half blocks from Ebbets Field. I used to walk to and from the ball park with my roommate, our third-string catcher, Gil Hodges. It's hard to imagine players, or even fans, walking to the ball park today, but Gil and I did it. Gil got into one game in 1943, and was back up for another shot at the big leagues in '47. I was up after getting out of the Navy the previous June and having a good two and a half months at Fort Worth in the Texas League.

We had all the anxieties that every kid has in that spot. Neither of us got to play much that year. Gil got into 28 games of the 154-game schedule as a catcher and a pinch hitter, and I made it into 40 games playing the outfield and pinch-hitting before and after playing on the Dodgers' farm team at St. Paul. Branch Rickey called us into his office at Ebbets Field one day and told us not to get discouraged. "You two young men are the Dodgers' power combination of the future," he told us. "I want you two gentlemen to be patient and to work hard to improve yourselves because you both have a bright future ahead of you."

After we left Mr. Rickey's office, Gil said with the spirit of a young player, "Hell, Duke—if we're so good, how come we're not playing more?"

Mr. Rickey knew what he was talking about, though. He always did. Neither of us hit a home run in 1947, but between us we hit exactly 777 home runs in the major leagues.

Not everyone gave me the same considerate treatment that Mr. Rickey did. I was being groomed to take Pete Reiser's place in center field, but I was playing right field in the early part of '47. One day in practice I went up to Dixie Walker, "the People's Cherce" among Dodger fans, who had played right field in Ebbets Field since 1940. The park had some tricky nooks and crannies along the outfield fence, and I was eager to learn how to play the ball when it would rattle around in those corners. I pointed to one spot and asked Dixie, "When the ball hits there, what does it do?"

The hero of Dodger fans everywhere said, "Find out for yourself, kid."

I understood. I was a threat to his job, and he wasn't going to give me a thing.

There was another rookie on that '47 team—Jackie Robinson. The day he became the first black man to play in the majors was a special thrill for me. I had been a Jackie Robinson fan long before most of the world heard about him, and there I was dressing just a few lockers away with both of us preparing to take the field as major-leaguers for the first time.

I knew what they were saying and writing about me so I could imagine how much pressure Jackie was feeling after all that had been said and written about him. I looked down the row of lockers and saw him quietly gird himself for what he knew waited outside the dressing room doors, knowing that what he did on that field starting in a few minutes and forever after would be matched in importance by what he did not do.

It was a long way, in more than mere miles, from the time I saw Jackie when he was in Pasadena Junior College and I was in junior high school. Five or six of us kids saw him play a baseball game, leave in the middle of it with his uniform still on to trot over and compete in the broad jump in a track meet, and then run back and finish the baseball game just as if nothing unusual had happened. That's how great and versatile he was, and how bright the fire of competition burned inside him.

I have another early memory of Jackie Robinson. I was in the eighth grade when he was playing football for Pasadena, the big rival of our own school, Compton Junior College. I was in the stands when he took a kickoff, reversed his field three times, and returned it for a touchdown. It was as dazzling a piece of broken-field running as you could ever hope to see, by the same guy I had seen play a baseball game and compete in a track meet on the same afternoon. No wonder he was my boyhood idol.

These memories were some of the reasons I refused to sign a petition that was circulated by several of the Dodger players, asking the Brooklyn management not to call Jackie up to the big club. But Jackie made that an impossibility. Branch Rickey had scheduled a seven-game series in spring training between Montreal, Jackie's minor-league club from the year before, and the Dodgers. He hit .625 in that series and stole seven bases in the seven games, against major-league pitchers and catchers. Combine that with his only year in the minors, when he led the International League in hitting, and how could you *not* bring him up?

In addition to his athletic greatness, there was that fire in his belly. His manager at Montreal, Clay Hopper, called him "the greatest competitor I ever saw." How competitive was he? He could beat you with his bat, his glove, his throwing arm, his legs, and his brain—and if he couldn't do it with any of those, he could beat you with his mouth.

A game in Chicago later in his career showed us that Jackie could literally yell his way to victory. I was hitting against Sam Jones— the guy who always had a toothpick sticking out of his mouth— when I heard some jabber coming from behind me. I looked and it was Jackie, in the on-deck circle, hollering at Jones.

"I'm going to get you, Sam! You just wait till I get in that batter's box!" I didn't know what effect he was having on Jones, but he certainly wasn't helping my concentration any. I went out on a fly ball and Jackie became the hitter.

He continued to give it to Jones from the batter's box. "C'mon, Sam—throw that thing in here so I can do something with it, unless you're afraid to." He kept that abuse up so long that Jones lost his control and, maybe accidentally, hit Jackie with a pitch.

Then Jackie took his lead off first base and stayed on Jones's case. "You better watch out, Sam. I'm going on this next pitch. I'm going to steal second and you're not going to be able to stop me."

He taunted Jones so much that Sam just had to throw over there, and when he did, naturally, he threw the ball past first, down the rightfield line, and Jackie was able to go all the way around to third base.

Then he started dancing down the line from third and yelling over to the mound, "Look out, Sam—I'm going to steal home. Get ready, because I'm coming!"

He didn't steal home, but only because he didn't have to. Poor Sam was so unnerved by this time that he threw the next pitch over the catcher's head. Jackie trotted home and we won the game by the margin of that one run. Jackie had yelled us to victory.

The world has known for a long time what Jackie endured in that 1947 season, so there is no need to repeat it here. I'll say this though: The man put up with far more than the rest of us could have. I was there on the field with him and I heard all the taunts and insults, and I saw the fans throw things at him, and other players go out of their way to spike him while he was playing first base. There were death threats too. Jackie played through it all and became Rookie of the Year, and the few Dodgers who circulated that petition weren't around for the next season. Once again, Branch Rickey had chosen the right man for an important job.

One of our teammates, Gene Hermanski, had a unique suggestion in view of the death threats: Give every player Jackie's number—42—so anybody thinking about trying something wouldn't be able to tell which one of us was Jackie. We let Gene take full credit for that one.

Roy Campanella came up to the Dodgers in '48 after playing in the minors in '47 under an unknown manager named Walter Alston. Don Newcombe was called up in '49. In the American League, the Cleveland Indians had signed Larry Doby in 1947 and Satchel Paige in '48. But even though Jackie wasn't the only black player in the game at that time, he still bore the brunt of the abuse.

The vast majority of the Dodgers tended to ignore the racial question, especially those of us not from the South. And the black players had the ability to laugh at the issue, especially Campy. He had come up the hard way. Like Jackie, he had spent a lot of years in the Negro National League in the days of segregation, where you played for starvation wages, and as often as you were told to. Campy once caught four games in one day—every pitch. Those experiences, plus his happy nature, made him able and willing to laugh at almost any problem, attributes which have helped him through the years after he was paralyzed in an automobile accident in 1958.

I remember one game we were playing against the Giants, and Willie Mays was the batter. Campy always tried to distract Mays by tossing dirt and pebbles on his shoes, anything to bother Mays so he wouldn't beat you with a hit. Newcombe was pitching, and he didn't mind brushing you back with his fastball just to let you know he was the boss—what players call "a pitch with a message."

Newk brushed Mays back and Mays told Campy he wished Newcombe wouldn't do that. Campy chuckled but Mays was serious. He wanted Campy to go to the mound and say something to Newk to make him stop throwing the inside pitch.

Campy said, "I could go out there and talk to him, Willie, but it wouldn't do any good."

Newcombe had that mean streak out on the mound that almost every good pitcher has, and when he saw a Giant uniform at the plate he got even meaner, just like the rest of us. So on the next pitch he makes, Mays jumps out of there again with another fastball high and tight. Now Mays is even more nervous.

"Hey, man," he says to Campy. "Go out there and talk to Newk! He's going to kill me!"

So Campy asks for time and trots out to the mound and he and Newcombe talk for a few seconds, then Campy trots back to the plate where Mays is anxiously waiting for some reassurance.

Willie asks, "What'd he say?"

Campy tells Mays, "He says to tell you he doesn't like black guys."

The truth, of course, was that Newk didn't like Giants. None of us did. They were our biggest rivals, even bigger than the Yankees. They were always an obstacle. Before we could hope to beat the Yankees in the World Series, we had to beat the Giants and six other teams in the National League, and the Giants were usually the team to beat.

We didn't just dislike them—we *hated* them. It wasn't anything personal. Their players were all right, but the Giants were the team we had to defeat. During the game we didn't like anything about the Giants—the players, the uniforms, the Polo Grounds, or the fans. They felt the same way about us. Girls who were baseball fans would compare pictures of their favorite players. The girls who rooted for Brooklyn were convinced the Dodgers were better-looking than the Giants. And vice versa.

All of us, Dodgers and Giants, still remember how deep that rivalry went. Like the time in 1956 when we picked up Sal Maglie from the Cleveland Indians. Maglie had had six great seasons with the Giants before going to Cleveland, and we had disliked him as much as we did his teammates. Maybe even more. Everybody called him "The Barber" because he shaved hitters so close with his pitches—"chin music," to use another term. Campy used to say, "Maglie's pitching tomorrow. Bring your football helmets."

On the day of Maglie's first start for us in '56, Campy walks out to the mound to go over the signals and he's talking to this guy he used to hate so much, standing there on the mound with his arm around him. Pee Wee told me after the game that when he saw that from his position at shortstop he said to himself, "Now I'll believe *anything*."

Even as recently as a few years ago, a quarter of a century later, that old Dodgers-Giants rivalry came back to mind. I had finished broadcasting a game on radio for the San Diego Padres in Chicago and I was looking for a cab outside Wrigley Field. A car came along. The driver stopped, honked his horn, and asked me where I was going. It was Alvin Dark inviting me to ride with him back to my hotel—one of the Giants' biggest stars back in those years of the great rivalry.

As were were riding along, Alvin pokes me and says, "You know something, Duke? I never thought I'd live to see the day when I'd be driving a Brooklyn Dodger back to his hotel."

These were the people and the times in my future on April 15, 1947, when Jackie Robinson made history and I started my major-league career in the background behind him. That was fine with me. He was baseball's biggest story in 1947, and he could keep the pressure off me as long as he wanted. It was Joe Hatten pitching for the Dodgers against Johnny Sain of the Boston Braves. The Dodgers won, 5-3, before 26,625 of what the writers called "the Flatbush Faithful."

The record book shows that Jackie went hitless that day, and no wonder—with all that pressure on him. From the bench I watched history being made.

The Picture
From My Radio

When I saw Ebbets Field for the first time as a Brooklyn Dodger, it was love at first sight. I loved that old ball park and everything about it, and that covered a lot. There was Hilda Chester with her cowbell in the outfield stands, bellowing out with leather lungs, "Hilda's here!" There was a fan named Eddie Battan who used to blow a tin whistle. The Sym-Phony band strolled through the stands playing Dixieland music, and from his seat Jack Pierce sent up balloons with Cookie Lavagetto's name on them, because Cookie was his favorite player. Before the game "Happy Felton's Knothole Gang," a TV show where kids got to meet the Dodger players, went on the air from the bullpen.

Tex Rickart, a film distributor who doubled as the public-address announcer, was another resident character. He'd sit on a chair next to our dugout on the first-base side and announce that "a little boy has been found lost." Or he'd ask, "Will the fans in the first row along the railing please remove their clothes?"

We played with only three umpires in those days, and the five fans in the Sym-Phony would strike up "Three Blind Mice" when a call went against us. An opposing player walking back to the dugout after making an out was accompanied by the tune "The Worms Crawl In, The Worms Crawl Out." As soon as his rear end touched the bench, the Sym-Phony's drummer hit his drum and cymbal. Occasionally an opposing player with a sense of humor would try to fake out the drummer and almost sit down, then bolt up and head for another spot on the bench, but the drummer never allowed himself to be fooled. When the player finally sat down, he always got the treatment. If a player went to the water fountain, the Sym-Phony played "How Dry I Am."

Ebbets Field was the smallest park in the league with only 32,000 seats. A sign said no more than 33,000, including people in the aisles, were permitted, but I think we broke that rule every time the Giants came to Brooklyn. Late in the 1947 season they squeezed 37,512 fans into the old park—for a Giants game.

The outfield fence had all sorts of advertising on it, something you don't see in today's new parks. The Ebbets Field's fence was a who's who of merchants and products—Griffin Microsheen Shoe Polish, the Brass Rail Restaurant, Van Heusen Shirts, Gem Razor Blades and the sign that everybody remembers:

HIT SIGN, WIN SUIT

It advertised a clothing store owned by a man named Abe Stark—and was at the bottom of the fence below the scoreboard, right behind Carl Furillo. Because it was at the base of the fence, 330 feet from home plate, and with Skoonj right in front of it, very few hitters were going to hit that sign on the fly. Abe Stark only lost about five suits, and he once gave Skoonj a suit for protecting the sign so well. There are those who say the name recognition

Abe Stark got from that sign over the years was a big factor when he was elected Borough President of Brooklyn years later.

The fans weren't the only characters there. The Dodgers had two of their own, our batboy, Charlie "The Brow," and our clubhouse attendant, John Griffin. The Brow, a man in his 20s like most of us, got his name from his thick, dark, bushy eyebrows. He was a man to be reckoned with. In addition to being an efficient batboy, he had influence in other important pursuits. He could get you a ride home, solve various problems for you, and sign your autograph better than you could. Sometimes The Brow would sign the team balls for us. I don't want to disillusion any fans who might have baseballs autographed by the Dodger teams in those years, but The Brow signed a lot of them—for all 25 players, the coaches, and the manager.

He could help you out of almost any jam, and he had some "boys" to do what he told them. One night three young men were really getting on me from the center-field bleachers, and after a while I'd had enough. The next time I was in the on-deck circle, with The Brow kneeling next to me the way the batboy always does, I said, "Hey, Brow—you got your boys here tonight?"

He says, "Sure, Duke. You need something done?"

I said, "Yeah. See those three guys in the bleachers, in the upper deck?" I nodded in their direction, being careful not to point.

"Yeah. Why?"

"They've been riding me pretty hard all night and now they're beginning to question my ancestry."

The Brow says, "You want me to do something about it?"

"Yeah. Send your boys up there and see if they can quiet them down, will you?"

The next inning while I was sitting in the dugout, I looked out at that spot in the bleachers. The three guys were gone. I never found out what The Brow had his boys do, and I never asked.

John Griffin was just as much of a character. He was big and heavy, smoked cigars, and had an endless collection of crazy hats and costumes and disguises. He'd be dressed as a monk one game, a baby the next, with a sheet for a diaper and wearing a baby bonnet. It was always anybody's guess what he would be for the next game. We called him "The Senator." He kept us entertained while performing the almost impossible job of keeping our equipment straight, making sure it was in the right city at the right time, and doing everything else an equipment manager, or clubhouse boy, has to do.

John was the one who gave me the number 4. When I was a rookie in 1947 at Ebbets Field, just before the season started, he told me some of the uniform numbers he had available. I asked him about number 4.

"I haven't given that to anybody since Dolf Camilli," he said. I knew why. Camilli was a Dodger favorite from the 1930s and early '40s, a home-run-hitting first baseman, and Griffin obviously felt some sentiment and loyalty about his number. He gave it to me anyhow, reminding me that Camilli was a long-ball hitter so John would be expecting me to hit a lot of home runs too.

I was thrilled to get the number. It was the number of my favorite baseball player of all time, then and now, and he wasn't a Dodger, he was a Yankee—Lou Gehrig. I had seen *Pride of the Yankees* several times with my high school sweetheart, Bev Null, and Gary Cooper made me cry every time I saw him as Gehrig making his famous farewell speech before 60,000 fans at Yankee Stadium on July 4, 1939. He was a dying man, the victim of Amyotrophic Lateral Sclerosis, which later became known as Lou Gehrig Disease, but he told the crowd, "Today, I consider myself the luckiest man on the face of the earth." Even today, when I see that scene on TV or play my video cassette of the movie, I still cry.

Getting to wear Lou Gehrig's number and play for the Brooklyn Dodgers was as much as a 20-year-old ex-sailor right out of the Navy and up from the Texas League could dare ask for. You hear people say that something is a boyhood dream come true, and in my case it was definitely so. I had always idolized Lou Gehrig, especially in view of his incredible feat of playing in 2,130 straight games, and I had been a devoted Brooklyn Dodger fan ever since Mickey Owen missed that third strike in the 1941 World Series that enabled the Yankees to come from behind and win the game and eventually the Series.

That was the Series that made me a Brooklyn Dodger fan. The Yankees were leading, two games to one, and the scores of the three games were 3-2, 3-2, and 2-1, and this one was 4-3. The Dodgers were about to tie the Series. It was the top of the ninth, two outs, when Tommy Henrich swung and missed for what should have been strike three, but Hugh Casey's pitch got away from Owen. Henrich reached first, the Yankees scored four runs, and the World Series was all but over.

I think everybody in America felt sorry for the Dodgers and Mickey Owen on that day in 1941, because everybody was tuned in to the game. Listening to the World Series on the radio in those days was just as much of a national pastime as baseball itself. You listened to it with your family at home over the weekend, and during the week if you were a kid like me, you listened every afternoon at school. You didn't have to worry about getting the teacher's permission—the teacher was usually the one who brought the radio. If you were a worker, it was the same thing. You listened in your office or your shop, and somebody always got up a pool. You'd draw a slip of paper and see what inning was yours in the pool and hope that the most runs of any inning were scored in the one you had so you would win the pool.

I'm not sure how much of that still goes on, especially with the World Series games being played at night. That's fine for television and for showcasing the Series and baseball, but the big drawback to that, remembering my own boyhood, is that a lot of kids don't get to see the games. Some parents won't let their kids sit up on a school night until 11 o'clock in the East to watch the World Series, and that part of it is too bad.

Telling me I couldn't sit close to my radio and listen to the World Series would have been a crushing blow. Back then, growing up in Compton, California, baseball was my world.

When I came along, my dad, Ward Snider, did what many fathers with a love of baseball do—he put a ball and a bat in my hands at the first opportunity. Even the way I was born had a certain baseball flair to it. It was a breech birth, so I entered the world by sliding home. The scene was my parents' apartment at the back of a grocery store in a blue-collar section of Los Angeles called Boyle Heights.

My struggles as a major-leaguer, when I would put too much pressure on myself to succeed, can be traced in part to my success as a schoolboy athlete. The whole time I was growing up, my parents assured me they wouldn't ask me to get a job while I was engaged in athletics—as long as I did the dishes every night, mowed the lawn, and did other household chores. From the time I started playing softball in the fourth grade at George Washington Elementary School, I rarely experienced any frustration or failure. There were five junior high schools, grades seven through ten, that played sports, and I had no trouble competing against four of them—Lynwood (Bev's school), Roosevelt, Willowbrook, and Clearwater—while playing for the fifth one, Enterprise. After graduation we all went to Compton Junior College, grades eleven through fourteen, covering the last two years of high school in the lower division of the school and the first two years of college in its upper division. It sounds complicated, and it's since been revised, but I was able to compete successfully in athletics regardless of the opposition.

I threw a pass 63 yards in the air for a touchdown with 40 seconds left to win a game for the Compton Tarbabes, and we won the school's first championship in 15 years. I pitched a no-hitter in the first high school baseball game I ever played in, struck out 15 batters, and got three hits. I was one of our leading scorers in basketball. I was voted to All-Star teams in every sport, and I won

16 letters in four years of school. All of that was fine, but it was no preparation for handling some difficult days ahead.

I have to confess that I didn't make those All-Star teams without some help. A classmate, who was also my teammate in high school basketball, wrote high school sports stories for the *Long Beach Press-Telegram*. He plugged me in his own articles and sent letters to the sports editors of the other papers telling them that this guy Snider at Compton was worth writing about. His ploy worked. I made the All-Star teams, and then we both went on to bigger things. His name is Pete Rozelle, the Commissioner of the National Football League. His column in the *Press-Telegram* was called "Pete's Repetes." Honest. When he got the NFL job, our paper back home ran a big story about Pete with the headline:

DUKE SNIDER'S PRESS AGENT NAMED NFL CHIEF

His uncle, Joe Rozelle, was my first baseball coach. When I was inducted into the Baseball Hall of Fame 36 years later, Pete and his uncle were in the crowd at Cooperstown.

The only hard part about being a scholastic athlete in those days was being able to afford it. Ward and Florence Snider never had a surplus of cash in those years of the Depression, even with only one child. Dad didn't make much money working in the pits of the Goodyear Tire & Rubber Company, handling hot molding equipment. He used to come home with his hands burned and blistered from handling that equipment, but he was always willing to go right back outside and play ball with his son. And Mom somehow was always able to find another couple of pieces of cardboard to stick into my sneakers until she could save enough to buy another pair. Her cardboard, plus her ability to mend worn-out T-shirts and long-sleeved shirts, helped keep expenses down.

My whole life was sports, especially baseball. When I wasn't playing, I was lying in bed at night listening to the Los Angeles Angels and the Hollywood Stars games on my small table radio.

When Dad and Mom could save enough money, they'd take me to Wrigley Field to see the Angels, the Cubs' minor-league team in the Pacific Coast League. They had my first baseball hero on their team, one Jigger Statz. Most kids want to grow up to be Babe Ruth or Mickey Mantle or Reggie Jackson, but I wanted to grow up to be Jigger Statz. He was the Angels' center fielder and their leadoff man. I never was a leadoff man, but I did get to be a center fielder.

My enthusiasm for baseball even led to good nutrition habits. My favorite radio program was "Jack Armstrong, the All-American Boy." The sponsor was Wheaties, the breakfast cereal that called itself (and still does) "The Breakfast of Champions." Every day in the middle of our hero's adventures the announcer would tell us kids, "Remember to eat your Wheaties so you can grow up to be an All-American like Jack Armstrong." Every time I heard the announcer say that, I'd hustle out to the kitchen and gobble up another bowl of Wheaties.

The Wheaties must have helped. While I was still going to Enterprise Junior High, I started playing summer baseball for Coach Pop Powers, and one year I led both the junior and senior divisions in home runs. I had a .611 batting average, which won me a five-dollar bat from Kimball Stores. My seven home runs won another bat from Sierra Sports Shop. They were the first two items I earned as an athlete.

Joe Rozelle and another coach at Enterprise, Chet Crain, were a great help to me. Along the way, I was always blessed with people who cared enough about me to help. Jake Pitler, who later was our first-base coach in Brooklyn, was my first manager in the minor leagues, at Newport News in 1944, the last full year of the war. His baseball savvy and his fatherly guidance in those first months away from home for a 17-year-old kid got me off on the right foot. Branch Rickey made me a major-league hitter with a series of lessons that bordered on genius. Teammates like Gil Hodges and Pee Wee Reese and my roomie Carl Erskine helped me keep my balance, or regain it after I would lose it. Managers like Burt Shotton, Charlie Dressen, and Walter Alston—especially Dressen—were an immense help.

The one who did me my first big favor, though, was my father; in fact he did two of them. He forced me to hit left-handed, even though I am naturally right-handed, because he knew that would put me a step or two closer to first base—and the outfield fences in most major-league ball parks in those days were shorter in right field than in left, thus favoring left-handed hitters. We argued about the switch loud, long, and often because it was awkward at first, but he insisted. When our backyard arguments reached their loudest, Mom would call out, "You two children behave out there!"

The other favor Dad did was to call me Duke, right from my arrival. To this day I don't know why he picked that name, but it sure went over better with the fans in Brooklyn than Edwin would have. My full name is Edwin Donald Snider, but Dad never called me anything but Duke, and Mom never called me anything but Edwin. Terry Cashman's smash song hit a few years ago would not have sounded the same: "Talkin' Baseball—Willie, Mickey, and Edwin." "The Ed of Flatbush" doesn't have much of a ring to it, either.

Pete Rozelle wasn't the only one beating the drum for me in Southern California in the early 1940s. My high school baseball coach, Bill Schleibaum, who later made that trip to Cooperstown with Joe and Pete Rozelle, wrote a letter about me to Branch Rickey. The Dodgers picked up my trail and scouted me all through my junior year at Compton High. Scouts have their own grapevine like any other business, so before I knew it, other big-league teams had scouts following me too. One of them wrote a report in my junior year that said, "Snider has steel springs in his legs and dynamite in his bat."

I graduated early, in February, and by that time I had to make a decision, and it wasn't easy. Mom knew little about baseball and nothing about the business side of it. Dad was thousands of miles away in the Navy fighting in the South Pacific. I didn't have any older brothers or sisters to advise me either. I had to decide whether to sign a professional contract—and if so, with what team—or join the service or go to college. The first choice was easy: baseball.

Which offer to accept was more complicated. Tom Downey of the Dodgers, Hollis Thurston of the Pittsburgh Pirates, and Pat Patterson of the Cincinnati Reds had been watching me not only in my games for Compton, but also with the Montebello Merchants, a semipro team, which gave me a chance to show my hitting ability against a higher level of pitching. The Pirates dropped out of the chase when Thurston saw me smile on my way back to the dugout after striking out. He didn't think I took striking out seriously enough. Little did he know that strikeouts were one of my biggest problems. I guess he thought I should have broken the bat in half, too.

Then it was between Mr. Downey of the Dodgers and Mr. Patterson of the Reds. They made separate visits to the house to talk with my mother and me. Then another scout joined the bidding, Jay Kelschner of the St. Louis Cardinals. They all wanted to sign me, but they also played it close to the vest, each saying he wouldn't offer any money at that moment, but promising to top whatever the other teams might offer.

The Dodgers got me simply because they outhustled the competition. Tom Downey made another visit to our house one morning in March 1944, and he brought his wife, Elda, and a typewriter. When I asked him what the typewriter was for, he said, "You're going to sign today." The typewriter was for preparing the contract.

Mom wasn't sure it was the best thing to do and said, "I wish your father were here." But he wasn't, so we had to decide for ourselves. I took her aside and said, "Don't worry, Mom. If I had any money, I'd give it to *them* just for the chance to be a professional ball player."

Mr. Downey typed while we talked, filling in the numbers on a contract with Montreal, the Dodgers' top farm team. I signed it and then Mom did too, because I was still only 17 years old. The contract gave me a bonus of $750 for signing, and a salary of $250 a month. I thought everything about the deal was fair. I knew the Dodgers were aware they were taking a chance. There was a war on, and if you could hear thunder and see lightning, you were in the service at age 18. The Dodgers knew I was good for only one season before military duty, and nobody, including them, had any guarantee I'd come back.

The next day Pat Patterson came by the house and said, "I'm ready to offer you some money."

I said, "I'm sorry, Mr. Patterson, but I signed with the Dodgers yesterday."

He asked what the Dodgers gave me and I said, "It doesn't matter Mr. Patterson. I signed, and you're just too late."

"Whatever it was," he said, "I would have given you more." That was easy for him to say, 24 hours after the fact. If he had said that one day earlier and been willing to mention figures, which Mr. Downey was willing to do, I might have spent my 18 years in the major leagues with the Cincinnati Reds.

Leaving home for the first time was easier for me than most other teenage guys. I wasn't going off to war, not yet. I was still 17. I knew I'd be back after the '44 baseball season, for more good times around Compton and L.A. and some more dates.

There would be time after the season for seeing movies like *The More the Merrier, Cabin in the Sky,* and *The Major and the Minor* with Ginger Rogers. And I might be able to see *Pride of the Yankees* again. I had a '33 Chevy, with a rumble seat, that I bought for $200 with savings from working as a laborer at the Shell Oil refinery in the summer of '43. I'd have time for hopping in the Chevy and going to The Clock, a drive-in restaurant in South Gate, to get a giant malted drink for a dime or a Coke for a nickel. For a dollar I could really have a blast. And I could hear the hit tunes on the car radio, "Tiger Rag," Duke Ellington's "Take the A Train," "Sentimental Journey," and "Black Magic," or the songs about the war, like "Comin' In on a Wing and a Prayer" and "Praise the Lord and Pass the Ammunition." We could listen to Jack Benny and Fred Allen and to the mystery shows like "The Shadow," "Inner Sanctum," and "The Whistler."

There would be some time for all that between the end of the season and whatever military fate awaited me. In the spring of '44, though, there was only one item on my list of priorities: baseball—*professional* baseball.

Minor-league baseball in wartime is a way of living which just can't be compared to anything else. It was a thrill at the time, but when I look back on my first season as a professional player—my only full season in the minors—I wonder how any of us kept going. The answer, of course, was that we knew what the option was—going to war. We'd take baseball, gratefully, for as long as our luck could hold out.

The Dodgers assigned one of their players who lived in our area, Hal Gregg, to chaperone several of us kids who were told to report to the Dodgers' spring training camp in Bear Mountain, New York. Just my luck—spring training was held near the major-league cities during the war because of the restrictions against unnecessary travel. No Florida training camp for me. When we stepped off the train at Bear Mountain, I could see that this kid from southern California was going to have to do it the hard way. It was snowing. I had never seen snow and didn't own a topcoat, so I did a lot of running whenever I ventured outside.

The highlight of the trip came when we stayed overnight at the New Yorker Hotel before catching the train to Bear Mountain. I was taking the elevator down to the lobby when it stopped and the world's favorite sports celebrity got on—Babe Ruth. It was just the two of us—Babe Ruth and me. He was dressed exactly the way we always saw him in newspaper photographs: a camel's-hair coat and matching camel's-hair cap, what a lot of us now call "a Babe Ruth cap." In awe I managed to say, "Hi, Mr. Ruth."

His response was as familiar as his clothes. He grinned at me and said, "Whatta ya say, kid?"

The Dodger favorite, Dixie Walker, was one of the few legitimate players in our training camp that year, with most of the stars off to war. Howie Schultz, the six-foot, six-inch first baseman, was there, and the Waner brothers, Paul and Lloyd—"Big Poison" and "Little Poison." Between them they played 38 years in the major leagues, with Paul hitting .333 for his career and Lloyd .316. They're both in the Hall of Fame. I had some talented hitters to watch.

I got my first rave New York notice in a newspaper article by Red Patterson, who wrote, "There's a 17-year-old, Duke Snider of Compton, California, who takes his cut at the plate a la Pete Reiser and is causing more than a slight ripple among the scouts and coaches." Our early games were intra-squad games and a few games against West Point, whose lineup included the Army football star Glenn Davis.

My first real test came when the Dodgers decided to take me with their regulars to Atlantic City for a game against the Yankees. I was delighted—in camp only a couple of weeks and already getting a taste of what it would be like if I made it in the big leagues and got to play against the Yankees. It was only a practice game, but it was important to me. I got into the game in the sixth inning, taking Dixie Walker's place in right field. I got a base hit off one of the good Yankee pitchers, Hank Borowy, in my first time at bat. Borowy won 17 games for the Yankees that year and 21 the next season, so I wasn't hitting against any slouch. The hit gave me a shot of self-confidence, making me feel more than ever that eventually I would be able to hit big league pitching consistently.

But the important thing for me was to get to play every day, and I wasn't going to do that on the Dodgers, even with wartime personnel, not as a 17-year-old kid right out of high school. They farmed me out to their Class B team in the Piedmont League at Newport News, Virginia, where the main industry was building warships for the Navy. We had some crazy times there, but we were serious enough about our baseball that five players from that team made the bigs—Clem Labine, Bobby Morgan, Leroy Jarvis, Tommy Brown, and me.

Life in "the bushes" is worth a book all by itself, and if nobody has written a book about it yet, somebody certainly should. In our case, home was Shipbuilders Park, an ancient wooden grandstand with a rickety dressing room, two showers, and an open-air toilet. The outfield had a wooden fence all the way around and one of the ground rules entitled the batter to a home run on a batted ball that went *through* the fence. Still, to a high school kid, it could have been a lot worse.

Baseball was a big draw during the war years. When some people started talking about suspending baseball for the duration of the war so the nation could concentrate its resources on the war effort, President Roosevelt stepped in and said baseball would be allowed to continue. Pro football and pro basketball weren't developed to the extent they are today, so baseball was king. FDR, who used to go to the Washington Senators' games at Griffith Stadium and always threw out the first ball on Opening Day, said baseball was too important to the national morale to be discontinued.

Even minor-league teams, with players who were either 4-F or too young, drew good crowds. Night baseball was becoming popular. It was great fun for the war workers to get off their jobs and still be able to go out to the ball park and see a baseball game for fifty cents or a dollar.

We used to draw 1,200 or 1,500 to our games, workers from the shipyard and Navy personnel from the base at Norfolk, plus vacationers from Virginia Beach. Our shortstop, Tommy Brown, made it to the Dodgers later that year and spent nine years in the National League, but his arm left something to be desired that season. Tommy was prone to scattering his throws all over the

40

first-base side of Shipbuilders Park, and he quickly earned the name "Buckshot." The sailors behind first used to bring their baseball gloves to the game to catch Tommy's errant throws, then keep them as souvenirs. They used to cheer every time the ball was hit to him.

The playing field was less than major-league. A player slid into third base one night and tore up his leg. They found a brick just below the surface, and he had caught his knee on it. In another game, a visiting outfielder slammed into the wooden fence and the whole thing teetered dangerously back and forth before finally returning to a comparatively upright position.

Our manager was Jake Pitler, and Jarvis, Morgan, and I gave him fits. We were the Three Musketeers, all 17 years old and all sowing some wild oats. We needled him, joked with him, scared him a time or two, and sent him from one pack of cigarettes a day to two. They broke us up before Jake had to be fitted for a straitjacket. Bobby Morgan was leading the Piedmont League with a .382 batting average, but they shipped him off to Olean, New York, and they sent Leroy Jarvis to Trenton. They kept me at Newport News.

We had a jack-of-all-trades there named Curly, who acted as groundskeeper, driver of the team bus, and trainer of dubious skills. He once rubbed down the arm of one of our pitchers before a game and when he was finished asked with obvious pride, "How does that feel?"

The pitcher said, "It feels just great, Curly. My right arm, that is. But I'm a left-hander."

We traveled in an old, beat-up school bus, and slept, or tried to, on our equipment bags as we bounced along the roads in Virginia. Curly had an alarming tendency to fall asleep behind the wheel when he was driving us to our next city, so one of us made a point of sitting right behind him and talking to him. Once he began to nod off as we approached a fork in the road. There was an old house right in the middle of the fork and we were heading straight for the living room. I began to fear Curly was dozing again, and I said in a loud voice, "Curly are you awake?" He didn't respond. That house was suddenly getting closer and bigger so I hollered, *"CURLY!"* He woke up just in time to veer to the left. The people in that house never knew how close they came to having a whole baseball team drop in on them that night.

On our longer road trips to Lynchburg and Roanoke in the Blue Ridge Mountains of Virginia we were given the grand sum of $1.75 per diem for meals. I don't care how long ago this was—a buck-75 for meals was never enough money. It was even worse than that on shorter hauls to towns like Portsmouth and nearby Norfolk. On those trips we got only a dollar a day.

We arrived at the ball park one day for a trip to Portsmouth, and Jake told us the game had been postponed because of wet grounds. One of our players asked, "What about our meal money?"

Jake said simply, "No play, no pay."

That really made me sizzle so I said, with all the authority that a 17-year-old has, "You cheapsake! For a measly dollar? You can't give us a dollar to eat on?"

Not only did he not give me a dollar, he fined me 25 more dollars for popping off.

Later in the season Jake invited me to dinner. He said, "Duke, I'm taking you out to dinner, but you're not going to get your twenty-five dollars back. You have to learn a lesson some times."

I asked him, "What did you do with my twenty-five bucks?"

He said, "The ball club's got it. I haven't got it."

I didn't know any better.

It wasn't my last argument with a manager, and it wasn't even my last argument with a manager about meal money. With the Dodgers in 1951, Chuck Dressen had a team meeting one day to caution us against running up the tab too much when charging our meals on the road. We didn't have a specific allowance, but were allowed to sign the hotel check, as long as we kept the amount reasonable.

Dressen was lecturing us, presumably on orders from above, and I was getting itchy to get out onto the field and start warming up for the game. But Dressen kept droning on and on about our food checks, and then he started harping on Dick Williams, who was a rookie that year, about a side order of creamed cauliflower he had the night before with his dinner at the Warwick Hotel in Philadelphia. It cost an extra 75 cents.

I kept shifting my weight from one foot to the other, clearing my throat and doing anything else I could think of to let Dressen know he was making too much out of a side order of creamed cauliflower. Finally I couldn't take any more of it.

"Cripes, Charley," I said. "What the hell is the big deal? If it's so important, take it out of my allowance for last night. I didn't even eat at the hotel. I ate at a restaurant at my own expense. Deduct the damn seventy-five cents from what you saved on me. Let's go out and warm up."

Dressen exploded. It was like the scene in *The Caine Mutiny* when Commander Queeg conducts an investigation to see who ate the missing strawberries. "Who the hell do you think you are, Snider?" Dressen yelled. "Are you trying to tell me how to run my ball club?"

I told him no.

"I'm the manager here," he went on, "and don't you ever forget it! Don't you *ever* try to tell me how to manage my ball club!"

All that over a side dish of creamed cauliflower.

By the time the '44 season in the minors was over we had a manpower shortage. We had only nine players, and three of them were pitchers. I played center field with a pitcher on either side of me. By the last game, my tongue was hanging out. We used recovered baseballs that were hard as rocks and your hands stung when you hit them with your bat. This wasn't the majors and it wasn't peacetime, and nobody had to tell us.

I won the home run championship of the Piedmont League,

and I may be the first player since the dead-ball era to lead a league in home runs with nine. With those re-covered baseballs you couldn't get the ball out of the park if you fired it with a cannon. I also led the league in doubles with 33, finished second with 149 hits and 50 runs batted in, and had a .293 batting average.

It was a successful first year for me, but the question was whether it would be my *only* year. When the season ended, none of us on that team, or on any other team, knew if we'd ever play ball again. There was still a war on, but it was going much better for our side. Eisenhower's forces had invaded Europe, and in the Pacific we were recapturing the islands one by one, with my Dad in the thick of several invasions. It was encouraging for America as a nation, but if you were a 17-year-old boy, you knew you were about to become a man.

I made the trip back to the West Coast with my Newport News roomie, Buddy Hicks, who was from a California town called Downey, which I assume was not named after the scout who signed me. We didn't need to be reminded there was a war on; the evidence was all around us. The train was filled with uniformed servicemen and women traveling home on leave or returning to camp or—worst of all—being shipped overseas.

Buddy and I got a chair car from Virginia to Chicago, but from there to Los Angeles we had a Pullman berth—one. Military priorities had taken all the other berths, so Buddy and I had to share the only one left.

I was looking forward to a few more months of good times, but the Selective Service System didn't fool around in those days. With more than ten million people in uniform and the manpower needs growing all the time, your friendly neighborhood draft board had a way of letting you know you were always in its thoughts.

I got home in early September, turned 18 on September 19, and received my greetings only a few days later. They came in the form of a telegram directing me to report to the pre-induction center in the Watts section of Los Angeles on October 19 for my physical. Worse yet, I was informed I had to be there at 7:15 A.M. For someone who had been playing night games for a whole season, that hour of the morning was cruel and unusual punishment.

When I got there, everything was what I'd expected. They checked us just enough to make sure we were warm and upright, and a guy handed me some papers I didn't want to know about and screamed "NAVY!" in my face at the top of his lungs. I was headed for the high seas. I wondered why they took me if they thought I was deaf. After boot camp I was shipped to Guam, where to my delight, I managed to squeeze in some baseball between my duties on the submarine tender USS *Sperry*. I was playing for the *Sperry* team against a Marine team, and I was stinging the ball so hard the Marines asked me to play for them when they took on some of the other teams on Guam. So I played for both the Navy and the Marines, doing what I could to help unify the services. In one of the games when I was masquerading as a Marine, I got to hit against Johnny (Double No-Hit) Vander Meer, the Cincinnati Red left-hander who had pitched consecutive no-hit games in 1938. I reached him for two hits in the game. Remembering back to my hit off Hank Borowy in Atlantic City in the spring-training game, I began believing more and more I could make it in the big leagues.

The Navy lost money on me. In one of those wild coincidences that always pop up in the military service, I discovered that one of the guys from Compton High, Ralph Hawley, was also a member of the *Sperry* crew. Seeing how talented we were in the really important things, the powers that be assigned us to permanent dishwashing detail. We were the only two, and that's where the Navy made its mistake. There was a porthole behind the sink and any time we came across a chipped glass or a dish that wouldn't come clean in less than a second, we fired the sucker into the Pacific Ocean.

While the Navy was losing money on Ralph and me, we were

45

picking up extra pocket money, thanks to our own little con game. Any time a new sub would tie up at Guam, members of the *Sperry* crew would break out their balls and gloves and start playing catch. The new crew would eventually join in. It all looked innocent enough, and so typically American. Norman Rockwell would have loved the scene. Then our guys would start talking about this sailor on the *Sperry* who could throw a baseball so far he might even be able to throw one the length of their sub. The crew members of the incoming ship knew their sub was over 300 feet long, so they always took the bait and bet this guy couldn't do it.

What they didn't know was that the crew member in question was a professional baseball player. After the betting reached a sufficient volume, I'd throw the ball the length of their sub, my crewmates would win $300 or so, and I'd pick up my guarantee—$50. We did it over and over. What the heck, $50 in those days was a month's pay. I could always throw a ball over 400 feet. I used to throw balls over the scoreboard at old Shibe Park in Philadelphia. And I helped my popularity among the Flatbush Faithful by throwing balls from home plate into the center-field bleachers at Ebbets Field, 405 feet away and behind a ten-foot wall.

But my number-one priority at all times during the war was to survive it. Our ship did not get into the heat of combat, but the Pacific Ocean on the way to Japan was no place to be in 1945 for a guy who wanted to grow up and play baseball for the Brooklyn Dodgers. Actually Dad was the one in danger, seeing more combat than the Snider family preferred in supporting various island invasions in the South Pacific. Poor Mom—only three people in the family and two of us, her husband and her only son, were in the Navy in the Pacific. I worried about her probably as much as she worried about Dad and me.

There was one close call when it looked as if I was going to find myself in combat after all. I was on watch duty on the number one 5-inch gun when we sighted an unidentified ship ahead. The command came down from the bridge to load the gun with a star shell that would be fired if the ship did not respond to our signal requesting identification.

No World Series moment ever scared me as much. I was no authority on loading or firing shells. All I had been told in our drills was that you press this lever, a shell comes up, you put it in and press another lever, and the shell goes "Boom!" I pressed the first lever, the shell came up, and I put it into the loading chamber. I was actually shaking while waiting for the command to fire. Two ships might start firing at each other in the middle of the Pacific Ocean as a small part of World War II, and I was going to be the one to start the firing.

Seconds before the command to fire would have come, the other ship identified itself as friendly. I needed an immediate change of underwear.

Throughout those months of playing ball, winning bets, throwing dishes out the galley porthole, and managing to survive, other people were helping my cause. The Allies had what managers and coaches call momentum. Eisenhower finished the job in Europe and the world celebrated with V-E Day on May 8, 1945. The atomic bomb accomplished the same result in the Pacific in August, with all of us whooping it up on V-J Day, August 14.

The day the war ended, I was in another one of my unique Navy positions—dangling over the side of the ship chipping off paint and putting on a fresh coat, chipping and painting, chipping and painting. I was only slightly less scared than on the day I loaded the 5-inch gun. Two of us were sitting on a wooden platform, suspended by ropes with pulleys to move us up and down, 40 and 50 feet above water at our dock on Guam. The experience convinced me I was afraid of heights, especially when my buddy and I had to push our feet against the ship's bow in order to swing out and then in to reach the curvature of the ship. We'd swing in, take a swipe at the side of the ship with our brushes, push off, dip our brushes again, and swing in for another swipe.

We were engaged in this hazardous duty when all kinds of

sirens, guns, and ships' whistles started going off. I said to the guy I was working with, "The Japanese have surrendered! See you later!"

I climbed hand-over-hand up the rope, crawled on deck, and was met by the chief boatswain, who asked, "What the hell are you doin' up here?"

I answered with a question of my own: "Does all that noise mean the Japanese have surrendered?"

"Yeah."

"Well, I want to tell you something. I'm a professional baseball player—"

"Yeah, I know that."

"—and I'm deathly afraid of heights. I'm dyin' down there worrying about falling. I'll clean the latrines, anything. But the war is over. Please don't put me down there again."

The chief said, "You got it." So I cleaned latrines. I didn't enjoy that work either, but I worried a lot less.

And I survived. On June 26, 1946, three months ahead of schedule, I was discharged from the Navy in Long Beach as a fireman third class, the same rank I started with. Once again luck was playing on my team—the Dodgers were holding a tryout camp in Long Beach and Branch Rickey, Jr., was there looking over prospects in his role as his father's assistant.

I had notified the Dodgers I was getting out of the Navy early, and was told to go to the tryout camp, where 300 other guys were working out hoping to get minor-league contracts, and let Branch, Jr., see how I looked and performed after my hitch in the Navy. He saw that I had gotten bigger, faster, stronger, and all in all, had a more mature body.

Dad was with me at the camp, and Branch, Jr., called us aside and gave us his analysis: "Duke, you have two choices. We can send you back to Newport News, or we can send you up to our Double-A team at Fort Worth. From what I've seen here, I think you can play in that Texas League." The Texas League was much stronger than the Piedmont League, in which Newport News played. The decision was easy.

I joined the Fort Worth Cats in Dallas on the Fourth of July, 1946. The Cats were strong, with a lot of returning veterans and an outstanding manager, Ray Hayworth. Success did not come quickly for me, though. The pitchers were at their peak, and I was still going through my own "spring training" trying to catch up.

Hayworth came over one day during practice and gave me the word. "Duke," he said, "I know your timing hasn't had much of a chance to come around, and I haven't been able to play you too often, but I'll tell you what: I'll play you as a starter in our next series in Houston, and we'll see what you can do. I'm not trying to put pressure on you, but it might be better for you to go back to Newport News and play every day."

I got that sinking feeling in my stomach. Those were the words I had dreaded. Newport News would be a demotion, and a delay, and I couldn't afford either. I had to make the big leagues, and going backward wasn't going to get me there. I had to do something.

The series in Houston opened with a doubleheader. I hit two home runs that night, both of them against a strong wind. That was it—the break I needed to snap out of my slump and start hitting consistently. So much of hitting depends on confidence and the ability to relax. If you don't feel confident and relaxed when you step into the batter's box, the pitcher has you right where he wants you.

That's why baseball people, including knowledgeable fans, know that just one hit often will be all that's needed to snap a hitter out of a slump. If you're up there with your body rigid and your hands are squeezing sawdust out of the bat, you're not going to do a thing. But once you get a hit, you're loosey-goosey and can start having fun again.

That's exactly what happened. All of a sudden, those Texas League pitchers couldn't get me out. In late July, Mr. Rickey, Sr., came down to look at his Fort Worth team. The first night he was there, I hit one over the clock in the outfield, also against a wind, well over 400 feet. The next night I did the same thing, to the same spot. Now I knew I had his attention.

By the end of the season I was playing every day, batting in the cleanup position, and the Cats won the league championship. We whipped Tulsa four straight in the playoffs, but lost to Dallas in the finals—but nobody was stopping me. I tore the cover off the ball throughout the playoffs and hit seven home runs. I was applying my own philosophy of hitting: "Always swing hard, in case you happen to hit the ball." On the "scout report card" which minor-league managers fill out about their players at the end of the season, Jake Pitler had written in 1944, "Must improve on hitting curveball. Has lots of ability. Might go all the way." Mr. Rickey told a reporter, "The Dodgers wouldn't take one hundred thousand dollars for Duke Snider," and that was in 1946 prices.

They couldn't stop me now. Could they?

The Captain
And The Rest

Over the winter of 1946-47, I got what I had hoped for and worked for—an invitation from the Dodgers to report to their training camp in Havana. That wasn't a guarantee that I'd make the team, but at least it meant I would get the chance to impress a lot of people and *maybe* get to start the season with Brooklyn.

The good folks of Compton, the ones who threw the big bash for me in '49 after my miserable World Series, were always good for a party, and 1947 was no exception. Ray Gonzales, who managed a local team I played for during the off season, threw a party for me, attended by the team players and members of my family. We loaded up on all the food we could find, and managed to find some beer to wash it down with. In the shank of the night, one of the players asked my grandmother, "Don't you think

Duke's having too many beers for someone who has to fly to Cuba tonight?''

Grandma was born two generations before the rest of us and was blessed with the wisdom of her years. "Young man," she explained, "Edwin doesn't have to fly that airplane. He just has to sit in it."

In Havana I revisited the world of my boyhood. There I was, not only seeing the guys whose plays had thrilled me over the radio in 1941—Pee Wee Reese, Dixie Walker, Pete Reiser, and Hugh Casey—I was even playing with them. I was a Brooklyn Dodger, something I found hard to believe even when I looked down at the blue script lettering across the shirt of my flannel uniform. I had accomplished the third goal on my way up the baseball ladder. I had become a professional player, I had been successful in the minors, and now I was a Brooklyn Dodger, at least in spring training.

Knowing Pee Wee Reese and playing on the same team with him have been two of the blessings in my life. Reese was our captain, and to this day, 40 years after those magical times began, we still address him by that title. He was our unquestioned leader. He led by his example, making so many big plays and getting so many big hits over his 16 years in the majors, all of them with the Dodgers. Without Pee Wee, we wouldn't have won as many pennants as we did. And when we finally won our first World Series, beating the Yankees in 1955, it was only right that the last out of the Series, a ground ball by Elston Howard, was hit to Pee Wee.

Pee Wee was our leader in other ways, too. He helped me tremendously with the mental approach to the game. So much of baseball is the mental alertness and anticipation to make the right play. And you had to sustain that level of mental sharpness over a season of 154 games. That's not easy even if you have the physical tools, and that's why Pee Wee was so important to the Dodgers as a team and to so many of us individually. That's why we called him "Captain," and why there was a captain's chair, one with arms, in front of his locker, while the rest of us sat on stools.

I remember one time early in my career when I was at the plate and I fell behind in the count, with two quick strikes against me. I had been striking out too much, and here I was only one strike away from doing it again. To avoid a strikeout this time, I choked up on the bat and tried to punch the ball to left, with a "Punch and Judy swing." I hit a weak ground ball and was an easy out.

When I got back to the dugout, Pee Wee called me over to sit next to him. Then he said, "What were you doing up there? Giving up?"

I said, "What are you talking about?"

He said, "That wasn't your swing."

I said, "I was just trying to punch one to left."

Pee Wee said, "Look, I'm the guy who's supposed to punch the ball and move it around. That's because I'm the leadoff hitter. I'm supposed to get on base any way I can. But you're not supposed to do that. You're supposed to drive me in."

I gave Pee Wee fits from time to time on a lot of things, but the thing that bothered him most was my play on ground balls. That may surprise people, because ground balls to the outfield seem routine, but those ground balls were the weakest part of my game. I didn't always charge them as hard as I should have, and when I didn't, Pee Wee was quick to let me know it.

In one game I nonchalanted my way in to pick up a base hit over second base, and when we got back to the dugout after the inning, Pee Wee got on me. "C'mon, Duke," he said. "Charge those balls. Be aggressive out there."

I'd heard it from him before, so I decided it was time to explain things. "Let me tell you, Pee Wee. When I was a kid in junior high, about fourteen years old, they stuck me at third base. After three or four innings the coach decided to get me out of there for my own safety. He moved me to the outfield—and I *still* hate those ground balls."

At least Pee Wee got an explanation.

I had some laughs at his expense. I worked hard to learn the habits and tendencies of the opposing players, and I soon got to know where to play a particular hitter against a certain pitcher.

53

Every once in a while, though, Pee Wee would turn around from his spot at shortstop and wave me more toward left or right. Outfielders have been told too often that infielders are smarter than they are, and a couple of times I decided to get cute. Pee Wee would gesture with his hands to move to the right or left and I would take a giant step and holler, *"Is that far enough?"* He always ignored me, which is what I deserved.

From time to time he'd get upset with me about pop-ups, too. I was never afraid to go after any batted ball, and I think my reputation as an outfielder proves that, but Pee Wee was unequalled at the infielder's art of getting back quickly on a pop-up to the shallow part of the outfield. Occasionally I'd slow up, holler "Lotta room, Pee Wee, lotta room!" and let him make the catch even though I could have made the play. I loved to watch his grace and surefootedness in turning around, getting back there, turning around again, and making a difficult play look routine, the hallmark of every outstanding athlete.

On one of those occasions, we came trotting in toward the dugout after Pee Wee had made the catch and he said, "Dammit it, Duke. That was your ball."

I said, "I know, Pee Wee, but you look so good on pop flies that I just love to watch you catch them."

He said, "Gol dang it, Duke, you're gonna wear my legs out. I want to play a few more years."

Pee Wee was typical of all the great athletes—he was highly competitive, excelled in all sports, and didn't know how to spell the word lose. He knew how to win, he knew the sacrifices you had to make to win, and he led by example.

Jackie Robinson was also in the '47 training camp, still on the Montreal roster but obviously ready for the big leagues; he'd led the International League in hitting and had been one of the dominant players in that league. We both made the club, which meant they had to keep me on the roster until the Fourth of July, because of the baseball rule protecting returning servicemen. I was beside myself with joy. I was getting closer to achieving my goals, and to make things even greater, my boyhood sports idol was now my teammate in the major leagues.

Jackie was another Dodger who was quick to tell people that Pee Wee Reese helped him more than any other player. In later years he said that if it hadn't been for Pee Wee, he might never have made it through those first seasons of torment. "Torment" seems almost too mild a word to describe what Jackie went through. "Torture" would be more like it. He had promised Mr. Rickey there would be no incidents, after Mr. Rickey told him he wanted a black player who had the courage not to fight back. Right from the start of his rookie season all the way through his first year, and for years after that, Jackie endured what no other mere mortal could or should.

The opposing players and fans got on him without mercy and without letup. They called Jackie "shoe-shine boy" and a "nigger" and a "black S.O.B.," and they filled in the initials. They hollered at him that he wasn't good enough to play major-league baseball and that the only reason he was on the Dodgers was to attract black fans to Ebbets Field.

The Philadelphia Phillies were especially harsh, egged on by their manager, Ben Chapman. They climbed all over him during our first series against them, and this was still only April; the season was just a few games old. Eddie Stanky, from Mobile, Alabama, was the first Dodger to stick up for Jackie. "Listen, you cowards," he hollered into the Phillies dugout, "why don't you yell at somebody who can fight back?"

Pee Wee literally stepped to Jackie's defense, early in the season when he went over to Jackie, put his arm around Jackie's shoulders, and stared into our opponents' dugout. The message was clear and it was intended for not just the other team but the whole National League. From that day on, Pee Wee and Jackie were the best of friends.

It was a vicious and explosive situation. Jackie was our first baseman in his rookie season, and he had to tag that bag faster than any other first baseman in history because if he didn't, he'd get his foot cut off.

Jackie made us better because of his ability and he made us closer because of his suffering. The Dodgers helped to make him a major-leaguer, and he helped to make us champions.

The man I played beside for the next eleven years was in the 1947 training camp in Havana too—Carl Furillo, the one we called "Skoonj" because he led the league in eating his favorite Italian dish, scungilli. I always thought he was the most underrated of all the Dodgers, and Buzzie Bavasi, our general manager in those years, told me not long ago that he agreed. Carl did more things to win games for us than he ever got credit for. He played the tricky right-field wall in Ebbets Field with precision. I'd always been told that Dixie Walker played it well, but I don't see how he could have played it any better than Skoonj. And I know Walker never had the arm that Furillo had. We called him the "Reading Rifle" because of his throwing arm and his hometown. Carl was a private person who never socialized much with the rest of us. But when there was a game to be played, Carl was right there ready to do whatever it took to win.

No two outfielders ever communicated better than we did. Skoonj would take anything in right center that was hit deep and I would take anything that wasn't. Films of those years show Carl gliding in back of me and me running a few feet in front of him, still leaving plenty of room to prevent a collision. You see other plays where I'm going for a ball hit to right center and he's hustling over in case he's needed, but we're nowhere near running into each other. It was a pleasure playing alongside him.

In addition to all of his strengths as an outfielder, he was a hitter to be feared. He won the National League batting championship in 1953.

Despite all of his ability and everyone's appreciation of it,

Skoonj almost didn't get to be an everyday player for the Dodgers. It might never have happened if Leo Durocher hadn't left us in the middle of the '48 season to become the manager of the hated Giants. Leo never fully appreciated Carl's tremendous talents and always platooned him, playing him only against left-handed pitchers. Carl detested that, and it showed in his feelings toward Leo.

Durocher, of course, was never the most lovable of men on a baseball field anyhow, and Carl Furillo was certainly not the only man in the National League, player or umpire, who felt the way he did about Durocher.

Leo was always going after the umpires with a vengeance. He wasn't called "Leo the Lip" without reason. Early in '48 he married the beautiful and talented movie actress Laraine Day. Laraine and Leo had a lot of class. Off the field Leo was one of the ten best-dressed men in the U.S. He could charm you right out of your shoes. But on the baseball field he was a different man.

Durocher wanted to win through any means possible, legal or illegal. He stole signals. He screamed obscenities at opposing hitters from the dugout. Occasionally he ordered our pitchers to throw at the opposing hitters. "Stick it in his ear!" he'd scream from the dugout. "Let's see how he hits flat on his back!"

Branch Rickey had the best description of Leo. He said, "Leo is the only person I ever met who can walk into an impossible situation and immediately make it worse."

I remember one game when Pee Wee Reese was called out on a close play at first base. Pee Wee argued with the umpire so long he got himself thrown out of the game. That brought Leo charging from the dugout demanding to know why his shortstop had been given the thumb. The umpire said, "Because he called me a blind S.O.B."

Leo said, "Take the blind part out and how wrong was he?" Leo was thrown out too.

*　　*　　*

57

After Leo defected to the enemy and became the manager of the Giants, he ran into two problems at the same time, Carl Furillo and Babe Pinelli. Babe was the most mild-mannered umpire you'd ever see, so mild he was almost meek. He'd call a borderline strike and then apologize. "Gee, Duke," he'd say, "I'm sorry about that last one. I guess I just missed it." He was as nice as Durocher was arrogant. And he was another Durocher hater.

During one game Durocher's pitcher, Ruben Gomez, hit Carl, and as Furillo, still not a Durocher fan, was standing on first base, he looked into the Giants' dugout and saw that Durocher seemed to be beckoning to Carl with his index finger. That was all Carl needed. He asks the umpire, Pinelli, for time and then bolts toward the New York bench. Durocher, who never ducked a fight, comes charging out—behind Monte Irvin and Jim Hearn. But Furillo simply bowls those two over, grabs Durocher, and body-slams him to the ground.

Both benches emptied, as they always do, and I was on the fringes making sure I didn't do anything stupid like getting hurt. Furillo is on top of Durocher with his fingers around Leo's throat and he's choking him. Leo is turning white; I'm afraid the guy is going to die. And there's Babe Pinelli, Mr. Nice Guy—in all his umpire's neutrality—yelling, "Kill him, Carl! Kill him!"

The other special person I met in Havana in '47 was Gil Hodges, my roommate that first year and my friend forever. Gil was one of a kind, a quiet ex-Marine who kept his feelings and emotions inside, but was a tower of strength for the whole team. He was a fine catcher, and he might have played there the rest of his career, but the Dodgers already had Bruce Edwards and a guy in the minors named Roy Campanella. So Gil ended up at first base, where he eventually made it big.

He was like a magnet around the bag, handling almost any kind of throw that came his way. His power was awesome, as they say today, and like Campy he was a guess hitter. There's a difference between guessing and anticipating. If you're a guess hitter, you decide what the next pitch is going to be and just "sit on it," confident it's going to be what you've guessed. If you anticipate, you say to yourself it's going to be a certain pitch, but you're going to be ready for anything just in case you anticipated wrong. Gil was not only able to guess *what* the pitch would be, but *where* it would be, and that's hard to do.

Through his years as a Dodger, Gil remained a quiet leader, never showing his emotions. One day, though, I got a glimpse of those emotions. Gil smoked a lot. It wasn't unusual for him to sneak a cigarette on the bench even though it's against major-league rules. I saw him this particular day light up on the bench during a close game, and his hands were shaking so much he could hardly light the cigarette. After that, I watched him every time he would light up, and it was always the same. His hands were shaking. That told me there was a lot more going on inside Gil than he was willing to show.

Gil was a fun guy to be with. He and Don Hoak, our third baseman and another ex-Marine, used to ride each other. Hoak, who later reached stardom with the Pittsburgh Pirates, loved to needle Hodges. They'd race their cars on the way home from Ebbets Field, two Marines trying to beat each other, Hoak in his Packard and Gil in his big white and black Chrysler. One day some of us followed behind them to see who won. Three or four blocks from the ball park we saw Gil run Hoak up over the curb and into Prospect Park. Hoak jumped out of his car and raised his clenched fist, but Gil just tooted his horn and kept right on going, one more victory for the quiet man.

His strikeouts were almost as many as mine because we were both big swingers. But absolutely the worst slump I ever saw anybody have was the one Gil had in the '52 World Series, the one in which I fortunately found myself. Gil's Series was exactly the opposite experience. He went 0-for-21. The slump even extended into the 1953 season, and by late spring he was having so much trouble that his pastor at St. Francix Xavier Church in Brooklyn,

Father Redmond, said one Sunday morning, "It's too hot for a sermon, so I suggest that you go home, keep the commandments, and say a prayer for Gil Hodges."

The power of prayer is a wonderful thing. Gil caught fire right after that and stayed hot the rest of the year. He finished with a .302 batting average, 31 home runs, and 122 runs batted in. His pastor made a believer out of all of us.

There was another rookie in camp that year who is worth mentioning, even though many fans won't remember him today. He was knuckleballer Willie Ramsdell. "Willie the Knuck" wasn't the greatest pitcher who ever came down the pike—he was only in the big leagues five years and ended his career with the Cubs in 1952—but he was a fun guy to have around. He liked to hoist a cold one every now and then, and I did too in those days.

Then, as so often happens in professional athletics, he was gone, traded first to Cincinnati and then to the Cubs. The Dodgers were in Chicago in 1952 and Willie invited Erv Palica and me to come out to his house for dinner. While we were eating he told me he was pitching against us the next day. I said, "Willie, you wouldn't throw me that nickel curve of yours, would you? I bet you'll just give me that knuckler. You wouldn't have the guts to show me that rinky-dink curveball, would you?"

Sure enough, the next afternoon he dared me with his curveball and I hit it out of the park. As I was rounding second base, I was laughing hard and he hollered, "You S.O.B.! That whole damn conversation last night was just a setup!" He was beside himself with anger, and the more he shouted the harder I laughed.

The next day I felt terrible when I heard that the Cubs had sent Willie down to the minors, farmed out to the Los Angeles Angels, who were then in the Pacific Coast League. I tried to help make amends by renting him our house while we both finished our baseball seasons. That may have made *me* feel better, but it didn't change Willie's feelings. I arranged for Mom and Dad, who were living in nearby Lakewood, to meet Willie at our house to give him the key. They had met Willie in 1946 when we were teammates at Fort Worth. Mom was talking old times with Willie and she said, in her innocence of baseball matters, "Willie, you took care of Edwin, didn't you?"

Willie said, "Listen, Mom, it was Duke who took care of me! If it wasn't for that son of yours I wouldn't be standing out here today in California!"

Those were the Brooklyn Dodgers as we started the 1947 season, my rookie year as a major-leaguer. I was making the major leagues' minimum salary—$5,000—minus several hundred dollars to help start the pension plan, the first ever for players. It still exists today. Jackie, Gil, Willie, and I were hoping against hope to make it in the company of the heroes of Brooklyn—Reese, Walker, Casey, Reiser, and the rest. There was a world of talent on that team, more than anyone realized at the time.

There was something else on that team, an ingredient that would typify the great Brooklyn teams of the next ten years—it was an attitude, what Vince Lombardi used to call the will to excel. We weren't the only team who had it. The Yankees had it, the Giants and Cardinals had it, all the good teams of those years had it. There are other important things in life besides baseball— being a good husband and father, setting a good example for the kids and the rest of the fans—but when you're a professional athlete you must have a strong commitment to your career and to your success. You won't be a great ball player, or a great anything else, just by wanting it. You have to work hard at it, devoting your mind and body to becoming the greatest player your ability will allow.

That's something you don't see as much of in the professional players of today. I remember the case of Wes Parker, an excellent first baseman for the Dodgers after the franchise was moved to Los Angeles. Wes was a highly intelligent man and a gifted player, but

61

he had trouble with his willingness, or his unwillingness, to pay the price. "I have trouble devoting myself one hundred per cent to baseball," he told me once. "I have my investments in the stock market to think about. I like to date. I enter bridge tournaments with my father. I just can't seem to give myself completely, day in and day out, to baseball."

A few years later he told me he was going to give himself one hundred percent to baseball. He did, too. He didn't date as much, and cut down on the other outside distractions, and—you guessed it—he had his best year ever. But the next spring he told me, "I can't do that again." So he didn't, and he never equalled that one stellar year when he had forced himself to concentrate on his profession.

That's who we were and the way we were in 1947, and our leader without question was Pee Wee Reese, the guy we would follow into combat without flinching. A small but significant incident much later might give an insight into the esteem we all had for Pee Wee. Bev and I went to the major league winter meetings in Hawaii several years ago, and we met up with Pee Wee and Don Zimmer and their wives, Dottie and Soot, and a mutual friend, Rex Bradley and his wife, Maggie. The eight of us decided to go to dinner, and we picked a Polynesian restaurant with all of the South Seas furniture and decor, including a long table for each group, headed by one big high-backed chair made of bamboo. Zimmer turned to Pee Wee, motioned toward the chair, and said with genuine respect, "Captain, that big chair is yours."

Brooklyn, Branch, Burt, And Bev

Even 40 years later, I remember the sights and sensations of my first trip to Ebbets Field and my first game as a major-league baseball player, at the tender age of 20. It was an exhibition game with the Yankees just before the start of the '47 season. Some of us younger players were staying at the St. George Hotel, and we didn't even know how to get to the ball park. After asking directions, we took the subway and got off at Prospect Park, and there it was two and a half blocks in front of us. Ebbets Field—the place I had dreamed about and worked so hard to reach. I half walked and half ran those two and a half blocks.

I went through the players' entrance and into the clubhouse, and found my locker. I dressed with the excitement of a kid on

63

Christmas morning, nearly jumping out of my skin to see the playing field, where I hoped to perform for years to come.

I walked down the runway leading to the dugouts. It was only a dirt runway, but to me it was a magic carpet. I climbed the eight or so wooden steps, and there I was—Duke Snider of the Brooklyn Dodgers, wearing Number 4 on my back and standing in the Dodger dugout at Ebbets Field.

I stepped onto the field I had seen so vividly in my imagination when I listened to Red Barber and Mel Allen broadcast the 1941 World Series over the radio in my room back home in Compton six years before. Red was a part of my life now as the Dodgers' radio announcer with his sidekick, Connie Desmond. Red Barber was, and still is, a Brooklyn institution with his colorful descriptions, telling his listeners, "They're tearin' up the pea patch!" after we made a great play or got a big hit. We were "sittin' in the catbird seat" when we were playing well, and when we lost it was, "Ohhh, *doctor!*"

The field was even greener than my boy's mind had pictured it. In later years, friends of ours visited Ireland and said the grass there was plenty green all right, but that not even the Emerald Isle itself was as green as the grass that grew in Ebbets Field.

The right-field fence was the thing I looked at first. It was 297 feet down the foul line, a cozy distance for a left-handed hitter, and I was more grateful than ever that Dad had made me hit left-handed. But the fence was 40 feet high. The distance grew to 335 feet in right center and 393 in center, then 343 down the left-field line, to a wall nine feet, ten and a half inches high.

It was a picturesque setting, with all the intimacy of those old ball parks where the fans sit close enough to the field to feel a part of the game. The new stadiums are beautiful structures. The seats are wider, the aisles roomier, and the scoreboards do everything except serve you dinner. I'm sure they offer a big improvement in fan comfort. But for atmosphere and the sheer joy of baseball in God's fresh air and the thrill of feeling a part of it all as a player or even as a fan, give me Tiger Stadium or Wrigley Field or Fenway Park. Better yet, give me back Ebbets Field.

As big a story as Jackie Robinson was at the start of the '47 season, Leo Durocher was almost as big himself. Happy Chandler, the former governor of Kentucky and United States Senator who had become Commissioner of Baseball only two years earlier when Kenesaw Mountain Landis died, shocked the baseball world by suspending Leo for the entire 1947 season. Leo had long been known to circulate with certain characters of "unsavory reputation." Chandler, exercising the wide authority he had as Commissioner, declared Leo's social life to be "detrimental to baseball" and ordered him to sit out the whole season.

The Dodgers were more shocked than anyone else. Here we were at the start of the season, a team Branch Rickey had expressly assembled to compete successfully against the other two New York teams, the Giants and the Yankees, at the starting gate ready and raring to go—and all of a sudden we had to find a manager! Chandler's action may have been intended to help the sport of baseball, but at the moment it didn't seem like a big help to the Dodgers. The success the Dodgers achieved that year was a convincing tribute to Rickey—and to the man who took over the manager's job, Burt Shotton.

Clyde Sukeforth from the coaching staff was designated to be the Dodger manager for the opening game of the season when we beat the Braves. Shotton arrived to take control of the club for the second game of the season. Sukey had just finished a ten-year playing career as a catcher with the Reds and the Dodgers, the only 155-pound catcher I ever heard of. His last year as a player was 1945. He became a coach with the Dodgers in '46. The record books will forever show that as a manager in the major leagues he never lost a game—one win, no defeats.

Shotton was a Rickey man. He was 62 years old, and had been

an outfielder in the big leagues for 14 years and a manager for seven years with the Phillies and the Reds. He looked more like a businessman than a baseball manager because he never wore a uniform. Instead of suiting up like every other manager, coach, and player, he wore a shirt and tie. He wore a Dodger jacket over his shirt and a Dodger cap, the only man I ever heard of except for Connie Mack who was allowed to sit in a major-league dugout without being in uniform. He never went onto the field for anything. He dispatched his coaches to change pitchers and argue with the umpires. If he wanted to challenge an umpire's call Sukey went out, and then the umpire would walk over to the Brooklyn dugout, where Burt would argue his case.

I didn't get to do much for Shotton and the Dodgers in 1947. Furillo had come up the year before and hit .284 in 117 games, so he was being used in center with Pete Reiser in left and Dixie Walker in right. But the betting was that the Dodgers regarded me as the center fielder of the near future and that at some point Skoonj would be moved to right and I would play center as the permanent successor to Reiser.

In fact, it happened the next season, and it wouldn't be the only time I succeeded Pistol Pete. After my playing career ended, I followed him as manager of the Dodgers' team in Spokane after he had a heart attack. His was a special story—a man with more talent for the game than anyone else around, but also a man who refused to admit he couldn't run through an outfield wall. He took on every center-field wall in the league, and lost every challenge he made, suffering numerous concussions, broken bones, and even a fractured skull. He never made any attempt to see where he was when he went back on a fly ball, and we didn't have padded walls or warning tracks in front of the walls in those days. Pete simply knocked himself out of his baseball career.

How good was Pistol Pete Reiser? People who saw him when he came up before the war say he was a future Hall of Famer if anyone ever was. In his first full season in 1941 he hit .343 and won the National League batting championship. He also led the league in doubles, triples, runs scored, and slugging average. In 1942 he was fourth with a .310 average and led the league in stolen bases. He lost three seasons because of the war, and a lot of people will tell you that with all those full-speed collisions into outfield fences, he never approached the level of performance he achieved in his first two full seasons. He came back to the Dodgers after the war and played for them in '46 and '47. He hit .309 in 1947, but his average dropped to .236 in '48, and then he was gone, traded to the Boston Braves for another outfielder, Mike McCormick, who had hit .303 that year as the center fielder on the Braves' pennant-winning team.

On July 4th of my rookie season, I was farmed out to St. Paul. It was one of the top Dodger farm teams and it meant I would be playing every day instead of picking up splinters on the bench. I knew I had to go down to the minors again and play my way back up to the big club for the '48 season.

That's what happened. In September, with Brooklyn winning the pennant under Burt Shotton, I was recalled in time to finish the season as a member of the Dodgers. But I wasn't eligible for the World Series, so when the first game was played in Yankee Stadium before 73,000 spectators, I was one of them. I could have gone straight home after the last game of the season, but I wanted to see Yankee Stadium at World Series time. I still had my dream—to play against the best, the Yankees, and beat them in a World Series. So I was determined to see the first two games, the ones at Yankee Stadium before the Series moved to Brooklyn.

I took in the whole scene—the red, white, and blue bunting, the band, the introductions of the players—and thought to myself, "Someday I'm going to be out on that field, playing against the Yankees in a World Series just like this." I watched Spec Shea pitch five strong innings and then give way to the best relief pitcher in baseball that year, Joe Page, who pitched the final four against my teammates. The Yankees won, 5-3, but it wasn't exactly a display of Yankee power. Ralph Branca breezed through the first four innings, retiring all 12 Yankee batters. But in the fifth inning he gave up three hits and three walks and hit a batter. It was a five-run inning, enough for the Yanks to beat us even though we outhit them, six to four. In the second game, the Yankees got 15 hits off four Brooklyn pitchers, scored in every inning but two, and won easily, 10-3. Allie Reynolds struck out 12 Dodger hitters. It was my first view of Allie Reynolds in World Series competition. The next time I would see him, two years later, I would have a different view of both him and of myself.

The Series went seven games, but the Yanks did it again. It was a typical Yankee-Dodger "subway Series." Hugh Casey shut the door in relief for the Dodgers in the third and fourth games, and the outcome seesawed through the next three games. It was the Series in which Bill Bevens was on the verge of the first no-hitter in World Series history when Cookie Lavagetto hit a two-out pinch-hit double off the right-field wall in Ebbets Field to drive in two runs and win the game for Brooklyn. A newspaper picture showed fans still clustered around the right-field wall long after the game, pointing to the spot where Cookie's ball hit. It was the Series in which Al Gionfriddo backed up against the low fence of the left-field bullpen in Yankee Stadium and made his historic catch of Joe DiMaggio's 415-foot drive to save the win for the Dodgers in the sixth game. And it was the Series in which Joe Page pitched in four of the seven games, topping his performance by holding the Dodgers to only one hit over the last five innings in the deciding seventh game. Tommy Henrich drove in the winning run with a single, the third time in the Series he delivered a key hit, showing why he was known as "Old Reliable."

That was the kind of player I wanted to be, the guy who came through with the game-saving catch or the big hit that would win it. I had done it in high school and in the minors. I was confident I could do it in the majors too. When I got my chance two years later, Reynolds and Henrich would play significant roles in that story.

By the time the Series ended on October 6, I was back home in California doing what I used to do as a kid, listening to the Series on the radio.

I also had a date with Bev—to marry her, the girl I'd met in high school. She sat near the front of the class. She was a cute little girl, and one day she happened to turn around just as I was looking her way. I winked at her, and she whipped her head back around to the front of the room. She was shy, and so was I, so I had my buddy, a kid named Elmer, ask her if she'd go out with me. I hid around the corner of the school building waiting for her answer, which was yes. We soon became steady patrons of the movie theaters, and I went with her on her baby-sitting jobs and we listened to the radio shows. I'd borrow the family Hudson and drive her to school. I was able to work this into my schedule while still concentrating on athletics, especially baseball.

When I got back from the Pacific we made up for lost time. I was stationed in San Diego and I made it home for as many weekends as possible to see Bev and to play a Sunday doubleheader for the Montebello Merchants. We became engaged on Valentine's Day of 1946 with a ring that had a story behind it. Dad told me about a friend of his who had won a diamond ring on a radio show that he was willing to sell—cheap. I bought it at a bargain price, and for the next 18 months Bev was engaged to a minor-league baseball player who had no money in the bank, whose future in baseball would not be determined for another two years, and who operated a jackhammer on county roads and delivered mail for the Compton Post Office during the winter to keep from going broke.

We were married the same month that the '47 Series ended, on October 25, in the Lynwood Methodist Church. I was slicked up in a rented tux, but Bev was what the bride is supposed to be—the radiant star of the show. We had the reception at the church, and after it was over Bev's father, who was known to have a short fuse on occasion, came over to me and said, "I have to talk to you for a minute." Coming from the father of the bride, that would shake up any groom.

69

He guided me into a corner of the room and said, "I don't know if anyone ever told you, but Bev inherited my temper."

I said, "Well, gee, Cliff—thanks for waiting until *after* the wedding to tell me."

In 1948, the Berlin Airlift started, Harry Truman upset Tom Dewey, I became a Brooklyn Dodger again, and Bev and I set up housekeeping in Flatbush. We rented a second-floor apartment in a private home on East 18th Street between Beverly Road and Church Avenue. The apartment was in the back of the house and we had a lovely view of an eight-story apartment building. The only sky we saw was a narrow slit of blue almost straight up.

Two notable people came back into my baseball career in 1948, as well as two new and lasting friends. The notables were Branch Rickey and Leo Durocher. The friends were Carl Erskine and Roy Campanella.

Mr. Rickey was a genius, but that's not news to anyone who knew him. The Rickey touch showed itself in so many different ways. He always emphasized the importance of team attitude, and the Dodgers probably had the strongest feeling of commitment of any team in either league. His genius was evident in historic ways, such as his selection of Jackie Robinson as the man to break baseball's color barrier. It was especially evident in his knowledge of how the game should be played and in his ability to teach it to others.

Rickey had been a catcher with the Yankees (for which we forgave him) and the St. Louis Browns for four years. After retiring as a player he managed the Browns and then their city rivals, the Cardinals, for ten years, and then turned to a career as a baseball executive.

Branch Rickey knew the game more than most and taught it

better than any. He was a stickler for the proper techniques and execution of the individual elements of the sport—hitting, pitching, and fielding—and the proper ways of performing assignments in game situations. "Dodgertown" at Vero Beach was a baseball academy. The Dodgers had 28 farm teams and 800 baseball players, and we were all there to learn about the game from one teacher, Branch Rickey.

He conducted half-hour lectures—and that's the right word for them—every day, Monday through Friday, for the first week of spring training. But unlike other classes, students couldn't doze through Rickey's sessions or mutter wisecracks under their breath. And he'd give examinations. Test papers were passed out that had to be turned in the next day. During class he'd give detailed instructions on the fundamentals—cutoff plays, relays, bunt situations, squeeze plays on offense and defense. He drew diagrams on a chalk board. And he preached intangibles: the responsibility for staying in shape, getting enough rest, a proper diet, and above all else, a strong commitment to the team. He was a man of strong religious convictions, who brought an almost evangelical fervor to his spring-training lectures.

Branch Rickey was the one who taught me the strike zone, and how to lay off bad pitches. He knew from reading Jake Pitler's scouting report after my 1944 season that I had trouble with the curveball, although what young hitter doesn't? He also knew I was a power hitter, and power hitters can often be tamed with the high fastball because it looks so tempting.

They say that there are three strike zones—the one in the rule book, the umpire's, and your own. Mr. Rickey taught me mine. It sounds elementary if you've never played the game, but it's far more difficult than it sounds, and the fact is that many players who come up to the big leagues but don't stay are failures because they never learn the strike zone.

I had a frustrating habit of trying to hit the ball too far out in front of the plate instead of waiting for it to reach my power area.

You still have to hit the ball before it gets to the plate or you'll never get any body into your swing, but I was swinging far too early, and as a result striking out way too much.

Mr. Rickey made me his personal project in the spring of '48. The Dodgers trained in the Dominican Republic that year. I spent three weeks with them there and then was sent to Vero Beach for special hitting instruction. Every day at Vero Beach, long before any of the other hopefuls were on the field, Mr. Rickey had John Carey, one of our instructors and scouts, pitch to me. The team's hitting coach, George Sisler, would also be instructing me.

Sisler was qualified on any subject that had to do with hitting a baseball. He was a Hall of Famer with a lifetime batting average of .340 for 15 seasons in the majors. He hit .400 twice, including .420 in 1922, the third highest season's batting average in this century. I was grateful that Mr. Rickey thought enough of my abilities to have George Sisler working with me.

My individual sessions with Mr. Rickey and George Sisler lasted an hour each day, and that was in addition to the regular schedule for the rest of the day, which included more batting practice and a game in the afternoon.

Those private morning sessions were vintage Rickey. For the first 15 minutes, he had me stand at the plate and call each pitch, with my bat on my shoulder. I had to tell him where it was and whether it was a strike or a ball. I was often wrong. In the second 15-minute segment, I would swing at every pitch I thought was a strike. I had to tell Mr. Rickey where each pitch was, whether I swung at it or not. Then he would ask each of the others where the pitch was—the pitcher, the catcher, and George Sisler. Mr. Rickey would do all the talking, sitting off to the side on a stool, with his bow tie and chewed but unlighted cigar.

In the third 15 minutes, Mr. Rickey set up a hitting tee with the ball placed in the strike zone and watched me hit it off the tee. In the final 15 minutes, I got to swing the bat again, but with two conditions: The pitcher was allowed to throw only curves and change-ups, and I was not allowed to hit the ball to the right side of second base.

He was teaching me my strike zone, but he was also teaching me the secret of waiting on the pitch. Ted Williams used to tell the Washington Senators when he was their manager, "It's wait-wait-wait and then quick-quick-quick." That's what Mr. Rickey was training me to do, in addition to teaching me my strike zone. He was also training me how to hit to the opposite field, and I soon was able to hit the ball 400 feet to left center.

The man knew what he was doing. During my career I drew 80 or more walks four years and I hit .300 seven times, so I must have learned something from him. But I still struck out a lot, as all long-ball hitters do, and reporters began calling me "the swinging gate." Strikeouts were more of a mental problem for me than they should have been, but Mr. Rickey made it possible for me to become a major-league hitter. Of all the people I have to thank, I'd say Mr. Rickey is the one most responsible for my being in the Hall of Fame today.

And then there was Leo, the only manager with four words in his name—Leo "The Lip" Durocher. He sat out his suspension during the '47 season, and the word was the Dodgers paid his full salary. He was back managing the Dodgers in '48. We would play for him only half a season before he switched over to the hated Giants. But you didn't need a half season, or even half a month, to discover what a firebrand Durocher was.

Durocher would do anything, and I mean *anything,* to win, legal or illegal, and he wanted us to be the same way. To the fans he was most famous for his run-ins with umpires. He disliked them and the feeling was mutual. He baited them from the dugout with his loud, penetrating voice, and when he dashed out on the field to argue a call he would show them up by carrying on too much, and that's a no-no to an umpire.

Tom Gorman was the umpire who seemed to handle Durocher best. Gorman, who passed away not long ago, was an entertaining after-dinner speaker following his retirement, and Leo made it possible for Tom to make a handsome living telling Durocher stories. One of the ones he loved to tell most happened when Leo was managing the Chicago Cubs.

"It was getting late," Gorman would reminisce, "and in the late innings, unless it's a close game, any close play at first base is going to be an out, at least if I'm umpiring there, and I was in this game. Well, it's the ninth inning and Leo's team is pretty far behind when his leadoff hitter tops one down the first-base line. It's a bang-bang play—bang you hear the ball land in the first baseman's glove and bang you see the runner's foot hit the bag and you have to know which bang came first.

"Last inning. The game's not close. I made my call: 'He's *out!*'

"Now Durocher is in the dugout all the way across the infield on the third-base side, but I'm supposed to believe he's got a better view of the play than I did right there at first, so he comes out screaming bloody murder. I did what an umpire is supposed to do in that situation. I turned my back and started walking down the right-field foul line. By the time Leo caught up with me, I was almost at the fence.

"He's yelling his usual abuse and I wait him out and then tell him, very calmly, 'Leo, it doesn't make any difference whether your runner beat the throw. He tagged the bag with the wrong foot.'

"'Oh,' Leo says politely, and he goes back to the dugout.

"Well, the game ends, the Cubs lose, and I'm in the umpire's dressing room and I suddenly hear Durocher outside, yelling and screaming and trying to knock the door down with his bare hands. When I finally get the courage to go out the door and look for a cab to the hotel, Leo is right in my path and in my face too.

"With all that angry defiance he used to show umpires on the field, he screamed, 'I got news for you, Gorman! The runner can tag the bag with *either* foot!'"

In another game involving the Cubs when Gorman was umpiring at first base, there was a collision on a play at the bag and Gorman was knocked to the ground and broke his arm. Durocher came charging out of the Cubs' dugout. He didn't bother to ask Gorman whether he was okay or not, which as it turned out he wasn't. Durocher just wanted to know about the Cub runner.

Gorman is rolling on the ground wincing with pain and Durocher leans over him and says, "Is my runner safe or out?"

Gorman, his eyes squeezed shut in agony, says, "Who is that?"

Leo says, "This is Durocher."

Gorman says, "He's out."

Despite his personality conflicts with most of the world at one time or another, Leo Durocher belongs in the Baseball Hall of Fame. I'm convinced that the only reason he wasn't elected years ago is that one-year suspension he received from Happy Chandler. I think it was an unfair suspension.

There are only 14 managers in the Hall of Fame, and Leo won more games than nine of them. He ranks fifth in games managed and sixth in games won. He won three pennants and a World Series and was a major-league manager for 24 years. His teams won 84 more games than Casey Stengel's did even though Leo managed 72 fewer games. Any manager whose teams won over 2,000 games belongs in the Hall of Fame, and no excuse should be good enough to keep him out.

Carl Erskine joined the Dodgers in July of '48. The fans, in their best Brooklynese, pronounced his name "Oiskin" and nicknamed him "Oisk," a name that stuck with him throughout his career. Carl Erskine is just about the classiest guy you could ever hope to meet. Today he's a bank president in his hometown of Anderson, Indiana, a devoted husband and father, and as much a friend of mine now as when we were teammates. You get an idea of how special he is when I tell you he put up with me as his roommate for over ten years.

Carl was not a big guy as professional athletes go—5-10, 165 pounds—but he could throw a baseball. The first time I saw him was at Vero when I was getting that extra hitting instruction. Erskine was a pitcher for the Dodgers' Fort Worth team and he struck me out in a practice game. I met up with him afterwards, and my first words to him were: "How can a runt like you make that baseball go so fast?"

Erskine pitched in the major leagues for 12 years, all for the Dodgers, and he would have pitched many more years except for one thing: He pitched in constant pain. He had a knot on his right shoulder the size of a golf ball. He took frequent treatments in the training room at Ebbets Field. On the road he would be examined and treated by various doctors in cities around the league, but he never told the Dodgers about the doctor visits because he didn't want them to know how much he always hurt.

Including 41 innings in five World Series, Carl pitched 1,760 innings. If you assume an average of 12 pitches an inning, and that's low, that means Carl threw more than 20,000 pitches in his major-league career—every one of them in pain.

He won 122 games for the Dodgers, including a lot of pressure games, two no-hitters, and a record-breaking World Series game in 1953 when he struck out 14 batters in a pitching duel against Vic Raschi. He owned Mickey Mantle and Joe Collins that day, striking out each four times.

Carl was "sneaky fast." His fast ball didn't look that fast, but it sneaked up on you. He combined that with an excellent overhand curve, the kind that seems to drop off a table just before it reaches the plate. He also had an outstanding change-of-pace.

In '48, neither of us played the first part of the season with the Dodgers. Then fate stepped in. In midsummer we were called back up from the minors within a few days of each other. Carl was the starting pitcher in my first game back. I pulled a double down the right-field line to drive in the winning run. That's a good way to make friends with a pitcher in a hurry. I didn't exactly burn up the National League in August and September. I hit only .244, but I showed some power with 17 extra-base hits. Maybe I had them thinking.

Roy Campanella—Campy—came along in that '48 spring training season too. He was 26 years old, one of the first black players to follow Jackie Robinson into the majors. Many people feel Campy could have been the man to break baseball's color barrier, but Branch Rickey knew his personnel. The reason people give for saying Campy could have been the first—his easygoing, happy-go-lucky disposition—is the very reason he couldn't have done it. Jackie was absolutely militant in his determination to show the world a black man could, and should, play major-league baseball. He knew history had placed him in a special role, and he never ducked it and never removed himself from that role, even long after there were many black players in both the National and American leagues. Campy could never have done that because his personality just wasn't built that way.

However, Campy could well have become the first black manager, something I don't think Jackie could have handled. Jackie could have been a good general manager. But Campy had a thorough knowledge of the game, and outstanding attitude, and he got along with the press.

Campy was a roly-poly guy who showed up every day in a Panama hat, chomping on a big stogie and telling us in his squeaky voice, as he came into the dressing room after a win the day before, "Same team that won yesterday is gonna win today." His durability was unquestioned, proved by catching those four games in one day in the old Negro League. Only a few guys in the history of the sport have ever won the Most Valuable Player Award for their league, but Campy did it three times, and he had a habit of doing it every other year—1951, 1953, and 1955. The pitchers on the other teams feared him, especially after he drove in 142 runs in 1953.

But the pitchers on our team loved him. He knew the habits and weaknesses of the opposing hitters, he had a strong throwing arm, and he knew how to run a game from behind the plate. And, like all great leaders, he had confidence. Erskine remembers that Campy used to tell our pitchers, "You guys listen to me. Do what I say and you'll be okay. Ol' Campy knows how to get the hitters out. You just watch what I signal and then throw it."

Erskine had the same faith in Campy that our other pitchers did, but one day he let Campy know he was not infallible. He was looking at the box score of the previous day's game, which Carl lost, and was giving Roy a hard time, claiming Campy's selection of pitches was the reason we lost. Then Carl pointed to the line in the box score that said: "Losing pitcher: Erskine," and said to Campanella, "Shouldn't there be a line for losing *catcher?*"

On the day that Erskine made World Series history by striking out 14 batters in one game, Campanella made a bit of history of his own. Edward R. Murrow was beginning a new kind of television show, interviewing celebrities in their homes. It was to be called "Person to Person," and Campy was going to be on the first show. Three weeks before, Murrow's producer, Fred Friendly, called Campy to make the arrangements. Then he said, "Roy, you'll probably be playing in the World Series against the Yankees the week that Ed's show premiers. Hit a home run in the late innings to win the game, will you? It'll help the show."

That's exactly what Campy did, to help his teammate Carl Erskine—and to help Ed Murrow too.

The Dodgers, in their wisdom, decided in the spring of 1948 that I still wasn't quite ready to play every day in the major leagues. Once again I was sent down to the minors, to their farm team at Montreal. Before I left, Mr. Rickey called me into his office and said, "Show me some big numbers up there, son. Make me bring you back."

As always, Mr. Rickey was displaying the wisdom of Solomon. I went to Montreal, posted those "big numbers," and on the afternoon of August 3, sure enough, there was Branch Rickey in the dugout as we got ready for a night game. I walked over to him and said, "Mr. Rickey, don't you think that twenty-one home runs, a batting average over .300, and more than seventy RBIs in seventy-six games are big enough numbers to bring me back to the major leagues?"

He said, "Duke, play this game tonight and then pack your bags. You'll be on a plane tomorrow morning, and tomorrow night you'll be the center fielder for the Brooklyn Dodgers."

An athlete knows when he's ready for the highest professional level, and I knew I was. My attitude by the middle of that season was, "I've proven myself in every league I've ever played in except one. And there's only one league left."

On that last night in Montreal, I hit two home runs, just for good measure.

Brooklyn At Last

The smell known to baseball fans everywhere—that heavenly aroma from hot dogs and peanuts—wasn't the only thing in the air over Ebbets Field when the 1949 season started. Changes were in the air too, as the Dodger management solidified the team into one that would be a contender for the National League pennant for years to come.

Burt Shotton told the press something he had told me privately near the end of the '48 season: that I was the Brooklyn center fielder. It was music to my ears, because once again I was being nagged by doubt. Despite what I thought of my .244 average, the Dodgers must have seen something. In 47 starts and six pinch-hit appearances, I hit six doubles, six triples, and five home runs. The six triples showed I had some speed to go along with my power.

Furillo was shifted from center to right, I was assigned to center, and Pete Reiser was taken out of the lineup. Reiser got into only 64 games that year, 21 as a pinch hitter, and then was traded to the Boston Braves for Mike McCormick. In 12 months, two men who to this day are legends in the folklore of the Brooklyn Dodgers were gone. The winter before, the Dodgers had traded Dixie Walker to the Pittsburgh Pirates, along with pitchers Hal Gregg and Vic Lombardi, in return for two men who would be important to the Dodgers in the 1950s—Preacher Roe and Billy Cox.

Two other moves in 1949 were just as important to the team's future. Jackie Robinson was shifted from first base to second, and Gil Hodges was brought out from behind the plate, and from behind Campy, and was made Brooklyn's first baseman. Two years after the "new look" was introduced into women's fashions, the Dodgers had introduced a new look of their own—a new first baseman, a new second baseman, a new third baseman (Cox), a new center fielder, a new right fielder, and several new pitchers.

Mr. Rickey had the team he wanted out on the field. It was a team that would win six pennants and two World Series over the next 11 years.

When Shotton gave me that public vote of confidence by telling the press I was his center fielder, it did wonders for me. I became a consistent major-league hitter that year, with a batting average of .292, 23 home runs, 100 runs scored, and 92 batted in.

I would make the grade, even in the face of a barrage of pre-season publicity and the pressure that always brings. One story said, "The big question has to be Snider, the big, good-looking fellow who has been extravagantly touted for two years." Another article said, "Brooklyn's crying need is power, the fellows who can blast the ball into the seats and win a game with one punch. Snider is such a prospect." One team official was quoted as saying, "If Snider clicks, we'll win the pennant." The headlines said the same kind of things:

DODGERS: CHAMPS OR CHUMPS?
SNIDER'S BAT HOLDS ANSWER

SNIDER FINALLY FINDS STRIKE ZONE
AND BROOKS FIND THEIR CENTER FIELDER

MEET THE DUKE OF FLATBUSH—
THE DODGERS' SLUGGING DUKE SNIDER

I was 22 years old.

The whole team clicked that year. Jackie won the National League batting championship with a .342 average, Furillo hit .322, Gene Hermanski missed .300 by one point, and Gil and Campy hit .285 and .287, respectively. That's six of the eight positions, not counting the pitcher, with batting averages of .285 or better. Jackie also won the Most Valuable Player Award, only two years after being voted Rookie of the Year. He was doing everybody a lot of good, us most of all.

The result was what you'd expect: We won the pennant. We beat out the St. Louis Cardinals by one game. That's when we knew we really had something. When you beat the Cards of that era you were beating a team that fielded Stan Musial, Red Schoendienst, Marty Marion, Enos Slaughter—and a future TV star named Joe Garagiola.

Mr. Rickey's batting instructions from the spring before were paying off. I was hitting the ball hard and often, and the customers at Dodger Dodge on Bedford Avenue behind Ebbets Field's right-field fence were beginning to pick up some souvenir baseballs on my home runs.

Still, I continued to strike out—92 times in '49, too often in my opinion, and this kept gnawing at me. Maybe I was too competitive. I wanted to help the team win so badly that when I struck out, I felt it was not only a personal defeat, but that I had let my teammates down. I would be twice as determined on the next trip to the plate—and twice as uptight—and kept on digging myself into a deeper hole.

So much of hitting is mental and self-control. The K's on the scorekeeper's scorecard continued to haunt me. It was like that for too many seasons in the early part of my career, and years later my teammates still remember how I kept fighting myself.

I tried for a positive attitude, though, remembering the hit song by Johnny Mercer of a few years before that advised, "Accentuate the positive, eliminate the negative." There was plenty to remember on the positive side, with the .292 average and 23 homers. Almost any major-leaguer will be happy with those stats, especially one playing his first full season in the bigs. The fact was I had made it to stay, and that knowledge did wonders for my confidence, strikeouts or no strikeouts.

The frosting on the cake came when we were in Philadelphia for the last game of the season. We were neck-and-neck with the Cardinals in the standings and the game with the Phils could not have been more dramatic. After nine innings we were tied, 7-7. Ken Heintzelman was pitching for Philadelphia and Pee Wee was on second when I came to bat in the top of the tenth. I hit a shot up the middle past Heintzelman into center field scoring Pee Wee while I took second on the throw to the plate. Then Louis Olmo drove me in with a single to left. We clinched the pennant, and I had driven in the winning run. There was just one more piece to make the dream complete.

The scene on our train heading back to New York was one of screaming good times. We had our own railroad car and we managed to pack a full day of celebrating into the hour and a half it took to get back to New York.

When we pulled into Penn Station we were in for the shock of our lives—25,000 cheering, jumping Dodger fans were there to greet Train 229, and 75 extra police officers were on duty. The crowd went so bonkers when they saw Jackie, their new batting champion, that he became separated from his wife Rachel and the police had to rescue him from the mob. Erv Palica and I took the subway home to Brooklyn without being bothered, and that was fine with us after surviving the Battle of Penn Station.

The scene at the train station shocked everyone, even the veteran players, but it had a special impact on me. I was finally going to live my boyhood dream. I was going to play in the World Series and against the Yankees. I was going to get a chance to beat them in Yankee Stadium, my fantasy stadium, wearing Lou Gehrig's number on my back.

The borough of Brooklyn paid tribute to us the next day, an open date before the Series started. There was a parade, the players chauffeured in convertibles, and a ceremony in front of Borough Hall. The dizzying atmosphere was even more astounding than the mob scene at Penn Station, even to the *New York Daily News.* Its front page headline said:

900,000 ROARING
FANS HAIL BUMS
Hysterical Crowd Lines 2-Mi. Route

I received many good-luck messages as I prepared for my first World Series, but my favorite was a Western Union telegram that said:

GOOD LUCK DUKE. WE HOPE YOU WIN BUT WIN OR LOSE YOU CAN ALWAYS COME BACK TO WORK IN COMPTON POST OFFICE.

CLARK WALLACE, POSTMASTER

The memory of the crowd of 25,000 roaring a welcome home at Penn Station, coupled with the sight of 900,000 cheering people in the parade, began to have an impact on me. The troubles which lay ahead in my first World Series, my humiliating failures

85

against Allie Reynolds and the rest of the Yankees, may well have had their start not on the playing field but in all the hoopla before.

The frenzied sights and sounds suddenly made it clear what a big thing the World Series was for everyone, not just for me. It seemed the world had stopped turning on its axis and that everyone's attention was riveted on the Dodgers and the Yankees. I slid, without knowing it, into my old habit of thinking too much. I read all the stories in the papers and heard what they were saying on radio. People stopped us everywhere we went, and the only thing they wanted to talk about was the World Series.

By the morning of the first game, I was doing a good job of turning myself into a basket case. In addition to all the hoopla, Bev was back home in California, with our first child due in November, and that didn't help to relax my nerves either. I shared a room at a hotel with Palica. As we got ready to leave for the ball park for the first game, the inside of my mouth felt like cotton. My hands were clammy. I was short of breath. And I hadn't even left the hotel!

When I walked out onto the field at Yankee Stadium and gazed up at "the house that Ruth built," my blood pressure took another spurt upward. There it was in all its baseball majesty— the towering doubledeck stadium, the green fence-like trim hanging from the roof, the red, white, and blue bunting, the famous monuments in center field—where I would be playing— to Babe Ruth, Miller Huggins, and my hero, Lou Gehrig. When they introduced the players and we took our spot along the foul line near home plate, my knees felt like rubber. But I felt confident I would perform well. I had always had success in pressure situations, always seemed able to make the big play, from that 63-yard touchdown pass for Compton High to the base hit that won the pennant for the Dodgers just a few days earlier. Now I was ready to take that one last step in my boyhood dream. I was ready to help beat the Yankees in the World Series. I wanted it badly—I wanted it too badly.

History has recorded that the Yankees defeated us in five games, but it doesn't record the agony I went through. I had insured my own failure by putting too much pressure on myself. Reynolds tied me up completely in that first game and set me down on three strikeouts and a pop-up. It shouldn't have bothered me as much as it did because nobody else on the team did a thing against Reynolds either. But I wasn't worried about anybody else. I was worried about myself. It was only the first game, but the nerves and insecurity of not knowing how I'd do in the next game sealed my fate for the rest of the Series. It may have taken the Yankees five games to defeat the Dodgers, but it took them only one game to beat me.

Don Newcombe lost the first game, and if ever there was a heartbreaker, that game was it. Newk, a rookie responding to the pressure that I didn't respond to, pitched a masterpiece. He held the Yankees to five hits and shut them out through the first eight innings. Our problem was that Reynolds held us to only two hits. Tommy Henrich broke up a 0-0 tie by leading off the bottom of the ninth with a home run.

Believe it or not, the score the next day was the same. This time we were the winners. Preacher Roe beat Vic Raschi, and the only run of the game came in the second inning when Gil scored Jackie with a single. It was our only win.

After the second game I was tied up in knots. Pee Wee and Jackie could see I was becoming a candidate for a straitjacket but nothing they said helped me relax. By the time the Series was over, I wanted to pack my .143 batting average and get out of town as fast as I could.

I finally showed some life in the fifth game with a single and a double, two of my three hits for the whole Series. But it was too late. I had let my team down. I had let the people of Brooklyn down. I was the goat of the Series with that batting average, zero runs batted in, and eight strikeouts in only five games—all this from your number-three hitter in the lineup, from the guy with the big, bright future who was going to make the difference. I didn't know how I was going to overcome this awful setback, or even if I could.

Erv Palica and I drove home to California together but it was the loneliest cross-country trip I ever took. I tried as hard as I could to put the Series out of my mind, but how could you forget something like that? I didn't know anymore if I was the "clutch" player I had thought I was, the guy you could count on to come up with the big play on defense or the key hit when all the chips were on the table. Sure, I got some important hits during the season, including the one that won the pennant, but when it was for all the marbles, I hadn't come through.

The one guy I was happy for was Preacher Roe, who won our only game with that great pitching job in the second game. One newspaper's page one headline said:

SERMON ON THE MOUND: PREACHER 1, YANKS 0

Preacher was a tall, skinny left-hander, the pride of Ashflat, Arkansas. We called him Preacher because of the down-home stories he always told. He wasn't just a character either. The guy could pitch. He led the National League in strikeouts one year and won 127 games in 12 years, seven with us. He was just about unbeatable in 1951 when we tied the Giants. He won 22 games that year and lost only three. Over three seasons beginning in '51, his combined record was 44 wins and only eight losses.

People may remember Preacher more for his colorful personality than his exceptional pitching skills. When he came to us in the Pittsburgh trade he told me, "You cost me my slider. I threw you a slider one time and you hit a double off the scoreboard and Frisch wouldn't let me throw it any more."

Then he told me that Frankie Frisch, the Pirates' manager during Preach's four seasons there, took away most of his pitches, one by one. "He took away my curveball because it got hit once in a while. Then he took away my change-up. The only thing Frisch

88

left me with was my fastball. But I solved that problem—I learned how to throw the spitter."

Preacher was the kind of pitcher you liked to play for because he had good control and was always in or near the strike zone. With that kind of pitcher, the infielders and outfielders must stay alert because they know the hitter is going to be swinging. When you're playing behind a pitcher who has trouble throwing strikes, you tend to get out of the flow of the game, and pretty soon you're not getting that quick jump on the ball when it's hit.

Preacher also had a definite idea where he wanted the fielders to play because he knew his good control would enable him to put the pitch in a certain spot and thus he knew where the batter was likely to hit it. He'd wave his outfielders to the left or right and then set up the hitter accordingly.

In one game we had a big lead at Ebbets Field by the middle of the game, but Preacher had given up four home runs, all with the bases empty. Then he gave up another homer, his fifth of the night, into the upper deck in dead center field. After the umpire threw him a new baseball, he walked two thirds of the way from the pitcher's mound to second base and hollered out to me in his Arkansas twang, "Hey, *Duke*! Play a little *higher*!"

Erv and I made the trip across the country in my new Pontiac. We had each earned $4,272.73 for playing in the World Series, which meant Bev and I could put a down payment on a new house. We drove straight through, day and night, and made it in three days, back when the speed limits were 75 and 80 miles an hour.

Shortly after we got to California my friends threw the banquet hailing me as a hero for being the first person from Compton to play in the World Series. I didn't feel like any hero, but you can't very well boycott something like that when the people are trying to be nice to you.

They gave me a wristwatch, and the mayor, Harry Laugharn,

gave me the key to the city. Tickets were two dollars. They read some nice messages including a telegram that said:

SAW ENOUGH OF SNIDER DURING THE WORLD SERIES. WISH HE HAD LOST HIS FIELDER'S GLOVE BEFORE THE SERIES.

CASEY STENGEL

Casey couldn't find anything in the hitting department to compliment me about, so he mentioned my defensive performance. Pretty smart. No wonder they called him "The Old Professor."

When it was time for me to speak I told the audience I was afraid nobody would talk to me after I got home from the Series, and I wouldn't have blamed them. I ended by telling Bev and Mom and Dad and the rest of the people, "You really have to be loyal fans and friends to honor a guy who had the type of World Series I had. I promise you that if I ever get into another one, it will be a different story."

My depression was relieved the best way a young married man could hope for—I became a father. On November 4 Bev delivered Kevin. He was the most important of three arrivals that day. The stove and refrigerator for our new house arrived too. The house was only 960 square feet, but it was ours.

There was one comment made during that World Series by a man I admired greatly that stuck with me and helped me three years later when I got my second chance in the World Series. Nobody else heard it except me.

I got a walk my first time up in the third game. I trotted down the line to first and said to the Yankees' first baseman, Tommy Henrich, "Gee, I thought I was never going to get here."

Henrich looked at me and said, "Well, I wasn't going to pick you up and *carry* you down here."

He was telling me I had to do it on my own. Nobody was going to give me a thing. The rest of the message was that if I couldn't perform in a World Series, I didn't belong there anyhow.

Coming from the one they called "Old Reliable" because of his dependability in pressure situations, the comment had added meaning. He was what I wasn't, not yet anyhow—someone you could turn to for the big hit or the important catch in the World Series. He'd won the first game with his ninth-inning homer off Newk, and he had performed the same heroics in three other World Series before '49. He was the batter who hustled down the line to first base on what would have been a strikeout when Mickey Owen dropped Hugh Casey's pitch in the '41 Series.

Henrich was one who made things happen. I knew after the '49 Series I was going to have to be more like Tommy Henrich to make my dream come true. Somehow I had to become reliable too.

The First Near Miss

Burt Shotton had me pegged right, and he proved it three times. At the start of the 1950 season, people were still talking and writing about the floperoo I pulled in the Series, but Shotton showed the wisdom of his years by saying, "I believe those games against the Yankees will benefit Snider. Sure he looked awful striking out so much, but it was worth it for the future. Nothing will seem tough to him after that."

It may be a sports cliche to say you have to be able to rise above adversity, but like most cliches, it's true. I had to put that failure behind me and go on to other opportunities for future success. Teams have to do that too. Failure was something the Dodgers learned and profited from three times in my 16 years with them.

Our white-haired manager in his white shirt and tie got on my case once in '49 for not putting forth 100 percent. Then he explained to reporters, "Snider needs a kick in the pants about every third day." He had me pegged.

The third time involved something as simple as a bunt. It was early in a game in 1950 and there were two on and no outs when I came up. I was off to a good start, hitting around .320, but Shotton gave me the bunt sign. I popped up my attempt and the catcher caught it. When I got back to the dugout I slammed my bat against the bat rack and made some crack about the stupidity of having a .320 hitter laying down a bunt. Shotton heard me and said within earshot of the rest of the guys on the bench, "That'll cost you fifty." It wouldn't be the last time a bunt figured in my career, and it wouldn't be the last time I was fined.

After the game Shotton called me into his office in the clubhouse and said, "I fined you fifty dollars but I'll take it off if you apologize in front of the team tomorrow."

I said, "No. I'll pay the fifty."

Shotton said it was up to me, but he didn't let it go at that. "I'm your manager," he said in a stern voice. "When I tell you to bunt, *you bunt.*"

I told him I knew he was right but I was upset at myself for blowing the play. He said he understood. The air was clear again. Then he added, "But it still cost you fifty dollars."

The 1950 season was one of those two years in the stretch from 1949 through 1953 when we went down to the last day of the regular season before losing the pennant. The 1950 loss was enough to make grown men cry, and the next year, which was even more of a crushing blow, some did.

One of my career highlights occurred in 1950. I hit three home runs in one game and came within two feet of being the only player except my idol, Lou Gehrig, and Ed Delahanty to hit four home runs in four straight times at bat.

It happened in the second game of the Memorial Day

doubleheader at Ebbets Field. I went 0-for-5 in the first game, a morning game, and had only a doughnut and a glass of milk in the clubhouse between games. Then I went out in the second game and connected twice off Russ Meyer and a third time against Blix Donnelly. Then, in the seventh inning against Bob Miller, I hit my hardest shot of the game, to right field. The ball hit the screen two feet from the top.

Not only did I miss out on a home run that would have put me in the record book right next to Gehrig and Delahanty, I didn't even get an extra-base hit out of it. The ball got out there so fast, and Dick Whitman did such a quick job of fielding it, that I had to settle for a single. But I did get a standing ovation from the sellout crowd of 34,000 Flatbush faithful.

Looking back on it almost 40 years later with the benefit of 20/20 hindsight, I think that game was a decisive point in my career. Those three home runs and my close call trying for my fourth caused a big stir in Brooklyn. The fans weren't used to seeing that kind of long-ball hitting. Suddenly the reporters and fans were talking about my home runs and my power. I developed a large following. A Duke Snider Fan Club was formed. I was catching on with the public, and my miseries after the World Series the previous October began to fade.

It was my first All-Star year, and controversy even dogged me there too. Burt Shotton, as manager of the pennant winner the previous season, was the National League's manager for the game. He felt he had no center fielder among the three outfielders elected to the starting lineup so he wanted to put me there, moving me up from my spot as a substitute. To do that, he would have to take Hank Sauer, the star of the Chicago Cubs, out of the starting lineup. It happened that the game was in Chicago, and the Cub fans raised such a fuss that he relented and started Sauer in the outfield along with Ralph Kiner and Enos Slaughter. Slaughter was in center, and I was on the bench.

When the lineups were introduced, I was booed. Can you imagine that, getting booed at an All-Star Game? I eventually got into the game as a pinch hitter, but I had a better time of it than Ted Williams. He broke his elbow making a catch against the outfield wall in the first inning and his 1950 season was over. That was the game that some people still remember because it went 14 innings. I wasn't sure either team was ever going to win, until Red Schoendienst ended the endurance contest with a home run.

Red's homer was a called shot. Late in the game, with the score tied, 3-3, Red turned to me on the bench and said, "Looks as if you or I will have to win this game with a home run."

I said, "Okay, you pick out your spot and I'll pick out mine." I chose a spot in the upper deck in Comiskey Park's right-field stands. Red picked out one in the lower stands, and because he was a switch hitter he made a prediction in case he batted right-handed: "See that guy in the red shirt in the third row of the upper deck in left field? If I have to bat righthanded, that's where I'm going to put it."

His home run landed two seats from that guy in the red shirt.

The year 1950 saw many firsts for me: the first year I hit .300—.321, the first year I drove in more than 100 runs—107, the first year I scored over 100 runs—109, and the first year I hit over 30 home runs—31. And I lowered my strikeouts from 92 to 79. I had the third highest batting average in the league, behind Stan Musial and Jackie. Combined with my decent season in 1949—until that World Series experience—I had put two good years back to back, just what management, the reporters, and the fans expected from me.

The 1950 season came down to a showdown on the last day of the season. We were one game behind the Phillies, the "Whiz Kids" with Robin Roberts, Curt Simmons, and Jim Konstanty plus Richie Ashburn, Del Ennis, and Dick Sisler, the son of the man who helped Branch Rickey to teach me hitting two springs before.

If we beat the Phillies, we'd force a playoff. The drama was there at the start of the game and it grew throughout the innings. In the ninth, the score was tied. Cal Abrams and Pee Wee got on base to lead off our ninth, and then I came up. I didn't see any signals being flashed so apparently I was on my own to swing away. But the stakes were too high to take chances, and I asked the umpire for time out. I had learned my lesson when Burt Shotton fined me earlier in the season. I walked over to our dugout and asked, "Do you want me to bunt them over?"

Shotton never hesitated. "No," he said, "I want you to get a base hit and win the game so we'll be able to beat them in a playoff."

I went back up to the plate and hit the first pitch for a single. Fate stepped in, though. Abrams was thrown out at the plate. Pee Wee and I both took an extra base on the throw to the plate, so the Dodgers were still in great shape: score tied, men on second and third, only one out, Jackie Robinson and Carl Furillo coming up. Just a simple fly ball would win the game.

The Phillies manager, Eddie Sawyer, ordered Jackie walked intentionally to set up the possibility of a double play. Now we have the bases loaded with one out, Furillo and Hodges coming up. We were confident that we would do it right here—win the game, then win the playoff and be in the World Series again.

But we didn't win. Furillo popped up and Hodges flew out to deep right. Then Sisler, my hitting instructor's son, hit a home run for the Phillies.

For the Brooklyn Dodgers, 1950 was over.

Bev and I had Kevin now, and when we left for spring training at the beginning of the '50 season, Kevin was not even four months old. Traveling across the country from California to Florida and then up the East Coast from Florida to live in New York with an infant, and with the father gone half the days from April to October, certainly made things different.

If you've never driven 2,500 miles from California to Florida with a baby and no air-conditioning and it takes three days and three nights just to get through Texas—don't. We made frequent stops for gas, changing diapers, and warming up a new bottle of baby formula. After that, Bev had the long drive north from Vero Beach to Brooklyn, another 1,200 miles, this time alone except for the infant on the seat beside her. I had to travel with the team.

For Bev this was the start of an entirely new kind of life, filled with automobile trips thousands of miles long with only the children for company, and the two-week stretches in Brooklyn alone with the kids while I was away on road trips in my own role as the family breadwinner.

A baseball player's wife makes a contribution to her husband's career that never shows up in the statistics, but it's just as real as it would be if she hit some of those home runs herself. She's helping with work at home, driving to Little League games and Girl Scouts. She's the parent in the audience at the school play, and the shoulder that's always there when the kids need one to cry on. And she provides the athlete with the peace of mind which is essential to his performance on the field. When he calls home during a road trip and she says, "Everything's fine," the player knows not to ask any questions beyond that. The two-word response means now you can concentrate on the next game.

Bev was and still is a homemaker, and the family home was wherever I was playing. She pulled a 15-foot trailer to New York in 1963, San Francisco in 1964, and Spokane in 1965, when I managed in the minor leagues after my playing career. In 1972, while I was managing in Alexandria, Louisiana, we upgraded the vehicle to a 25-foot motor home. By then there were only two children at home—Kurt and Dawna—and Kurt could help with the driving. Bev loved the adventure and wanted to show the children a type of camping life as opposed to motel living.

They made a game of things. The children made one up in Brooklyn while going through the tunnels. The guards would wave the cars on, and the children would wave too, just to see if the guards would wave back. They decided those who did were Dodger fans. Those who didn't were Yankee fans. They carried this game over to the ride back to California. They would wave at the truck drivers, hoping to get them to blow their horns. The same standards applied: Those who did were Dodger fans.

Bev took over-the-counter stay-awake pills to keep from getting mesmerized by the road. She would stay with the kids in the less expensive motels, and thought nothing of parking overnight at a gas station when they were pulling the trailer and no campground was available. The service-station attendants were always helpful when they saw her pulling the trailer and handling the children by herself.

The attendant at one station in Tuxedo Junction, New York, gave her the restroom key to use overnight, and had a police officer come by to make sure Bev and the children were okay.

If there were a Hall of Fame somewhere for baseball wives, Bev would belong in it.

I had some driving adventures of my own in those years. We lived in Bay Ridge in the 1950s, with the Reeses, the Erskines, and the Rube Walkers as our neighbors. The four of us sometimes car-pooled to Ebbets Field, and to the Polo Grounds if we were playing the Giants.

After we learned some tricks about our commuting route, we got so we could make great time after our night games by zooming through Prospect Park. We learned to be more careful after Pee Wee and I were stopped one night by a swarm of police cars. Several cops leaped from their cars and ran toward us with drawn guns. It turned out that some of the residents had reported cars zipping through the park every night at about the same time. The cops thought we were a gang of car thieves.

Pee Wee and I had a couple of other memorable encounters with the law. We were stopped for speeding one night when Pee Wee was driving, and as the police officer was walking from his car toward ours, I said, "Well, Captain, let's see how you handle this one."

The cop gets to the window and Pee Wee, ever the smoothie, says, "Gee, officer. I'm really sorry. I'm Pee Wee Reese of the Dodgers, and this is Duke Snider . . . Carl Erskine . . . and Rube Walker."

The officer is genuinely thrilled. "Geez, it sure is. Say, take it easy, Pee Wee. We don't want any of you guys to get hurt."

Then he waves us on without a ticket.

The next night, in almost the same spot, I'm driving and the same thing happens. Another cop pulls us over. Pee Wee remembers how I needled him the day before and says, "Your turn, Duke."

The cop walks up to my car and I decide to use Pee Wee's strategy. "Hi, officer," I said. "I'm Duke Snider of the Dodgers and this is—"

He cuts me off in mid-sentence and growls, "I hate baseball."

For the second straight year I had come through with one of the season's most important hits—driving in the run that won the '49 pennant for us and getting the hit that would have forced a playoff in '50 if Abrams hadn't been thrown out at the plate. But I still had an occasional crisis in confidence. During one of those periods Dick Young began a column in the *New York Daily News* with a headline I would remember for a long time:

ALL SURE SNIDER HAS IT
—ALL EXCEPT SNIDER

He'll Think
Of Something

Charlie Dressen walked into our lives in 1951, and things weren't the same for the next three seasons. Burt Shotton was relieved of his responsibilities after too many people, including Dick Young in his columns, became convinced he was too old for the demands of the job as a big-league manager. Dressen, who was in our organization before as a coach, got the job.

He brought with him a vast knowledge of the game in general and our personnel in particular, a shrewd ability to make the right moves in games, and the world's biggest ego.

He had a definite liking for the word "I" and almost wore it out in his conversations. He had supreme confidence in his knowledge and ability. Before a crucial series he would tell us in our team meetings, "Just hang close 'til the seventh inning—I'll think of something."

We were playing the Giants one day when Walker Cooper, the old catcher for the Cards and Cubs who was finishing up his career, came up to the plate before the game to meet with Dressen and the umpires and exchange lineup cards. But he hands Dressen a little present first. It's a book, and the title on it is:

WHAT I KNOW ABOUT BASEBALL

By Charlie Dressen

Inside, on every page, there was only one thing—a big, bold capital letter "I." Dressen brought it back to the dugout and laughed louder than his players about the Giants' gag.

Dressen knew to expect something like that from Cooper, one of the characters of those times. Cooper called me "third-of-a-dozen" because I wore number 4, and he once showed me the extra padding he used in his catcher's mitt: not the usual sponge or handkerchief—a woman's falsie.

Dressen was a real pepper pot, and he was a manager worth watching during a game. When we played the Giants, it was Dressen vs. Durocher, and Dressen almost always won their battle of wits. They went a long way back together, not just with the Dodgers but all the way back to the time Durocher was a shortstop with the Yankees and Dressen was a Yankee coach.

When Charlie would make a move during a Giant game, changing pitchers or putting a play on, he'd say, to anyone willing to benefit from his genius, "Now when I do this, Durocher is going to come back with such-and-such, and then I'll do so-and-so." He was almost always right. He was our manager for three years, and it's not just a coincidence that in that time we won two pennants and tied for another.

The man would do anything to win, and he didn't care whose feelings he might hurt. He once took Pee Wee out for a pinch hitter, a first for Pee Wee, and he was plenty upset about it. He slammed his bat against the bat rack, something I never thought I'd see Pee Wee do because of what his manager said or did. But Dressen could have that effect on you. He once took me out of a game for a pinch hitter in the first inning. I was just as upset as Pee Wee, but I was in a slump at the time and I figured I was in no position to make a Federal case out of it.

Dressen had a run-in at one time or another with just about every player on the team, but he also knew how to get the most out of each individual. He knew which ones to pat on the back and which ones to kick in the rear, and I was in the second category. He was certainly successful with me. I had three of my best years in the three seasons he was our skipper. You might not have loved him, but you had to admit he won. Of all the managers I played for in the big leagues—Durocher, Shotton, Dressen, Alston, Stengel, and Dark—Chuck Dressen was the smartest manager of them all.

He even knew how to outsmart the umpires. He was thrown out of a game at Ebbets Field one afternoon in only the third or fourth inning. He went into the dressing room, as he was supposed to, but about an inning later I noticed a member of the ground crew standing in the middle of the dugout, near the steps coming up from the clubhouse. Nothing unusual about that. Guys from the ground crew frequently stood there, in their blue uniforms and blue caps. Only I knew all the guys on the ground crew, most of them on a first-name basis, and this guy didn't look familiar.

You guessed it. It was Dressen, wearing a groundskeeper's uniform, and a pair of fake glasses with one of those big noses and a thick black mustache. The umpires never caught on. The game ran another five or six innings, and Dressen managed every pitch of it in the dugout, as a member of the ground crew.

I knew I was going to be successful in 1951 long before the season, as soon as I found out Buzzie Bavasi was our new general manager. He'd been the GM when I played in Montreal, and when Branch Rickey moved on to the Pittsburgh Pirates and Buzzie was brought up to take his place, I knew I was going to be all right. The reason I was so sure of myself was a conversation I had with Buzzie in Montreal when I was on a baseball exhibition tour after the '50 season. He complimented me on the year I had and gave me some advice for my contract talks. "You had a great year, Duke," he said, "so make sure you get paid for it in your new contract. Don't settle for anything less than double your 1950 salary. Stick it to 'em!"

Shortly after Buzzie became the Dodgers' GM, contracts went out and when mine arrived, it showed a figure less than double the previous year's salary. I sent it back to Buzzie unsigned with a note that said, "This doesn't look like double my salary to me."

Buzzie sent me another contract, with the figure that was double my salary. He attached a note saying, "You have a great memory, you rat."

The fans' love affair with us, which started right before World War II, was in full bloom now. I remember all those war movies about the fighting in the South Pacific, and you almost always saw at least one scene with John Wayne or William Bendix near a foxhole with an arrow next to it that said:

EBBETS FIELD, 10,000 MILES

Our characters were always out in force, including the leather-lunged guy who started yelling, "Oh dem Bums! How I love dem Bums!" The fans helped us in more ways than just cheering for us. They could intimidate opposing players, and even umpires.

We were playing the Phillies at Ebbets Field one afternoon when Granny Hamner hit a shot up the alley which I fielded quickly in case he tried to make it to second base for a double. Sure enough, he did try for two, so I cut loose a throw to Reese, covering second, and Pee Wee put the tag on him.

Beans Reardon was umpiring that day and he hollers, "Safe!"—but he gives the signal with the thumb which in those days was the umpire's signal that the runner was out.

Pee Wee says, "Beans. Do you know what you just did?"

Reardon says, "Yeah. I know."

Granny is now up and standing on the bag and he says, "Well, what am I?"

Beans says, "Well, Granny, there are only three of us who heard me. I *called* you safe, but there are 35,000 Brooklyn fans who saw me *signal* you were out."

"So what am I?"

"You're out."

I found myself playing on the same team with another one of my boyhood heroes in 1951—Andy Pafko. I saw Andy play for the Los Angeles Angels when I was growing up, and I liked his smooth, hustling style of play.

Andy had already been playing big league ball for eight years when he came to us in the middle of the 1951 season with Johnny Schmitz, Wayne Terwilliger, and Rube Walker in exchange for Bruce Edwards, Joe Hatten, Eddie Miksis and Gene Hermanski in a trade with the Cubs. It was a big deal which caused a lot of comment, and most of the comments were that it gave us the left fielder we needed to win the pennant. The Dodger players felt the same way, and when our lead grew to 13 and a half games in August, the whole world was sure we had a lock on the 1951 National League pennant.

Now I was playing behind one of my boyhood idols, Pee Wee, and next to another, although playing next to Pafko didn't last long. He was a Dodger for only two seasons, before the Boston Braves got him from us for Roy Hartsfield and $50,000. He didn't stop there, though. He went on to play another seven seasons for the Braves and ended up with 17 years in the National League, four World Series, and a lifetime batting average of .285.

Dodger management had not been completely happy with left field, which is why there was so much elation when we got Pafko. Now we had an outfield that was solid defensively from foul line to foul line, and Andy also made us stronger offensively. In that season, the three of us, Andy, Carl, and I, hit 75 home runs. When it came to the outfield, we didn't have to take a back seat to anybody in either league.

The same was true in the infield the year before when we picked up Billy Cox to play third base and join Pee Wee, Jackie, and Gil. Cox was an exceptional infielder, a shortstop, with the Pirates, but until he came over to us with Preacher Roe in the Dixie Walker deal, most people didn't know how good he was..

Cox and I were good friends despite our first experience with each other. When he was with the Pirates he got a hit to the outfield and was trying to get a double out of it when I threw in to second and hit him in the head. My throw knocked him out. They had to carry him off the field.

He had the quick, soft hands of an infielder, plus a throwing arm that seemed unable to make an inaccurate throw. He may have made a bad throw sometime during his years with us, but if he did, I sure don't remember it. He and Preach were roomies with us and they played a lot of poker, and one night they almost played one hand too many. Billy was running shy when the betting got heavy late in the evening. One hand went on forever, the table was covered with dollar bills, and Billy was having trouble staying in. When his money ran out, darn if he didn't write a check to cover the next bet. Then he called his opponent's hand, and Billy won the pot.

The first thing he picked up from the top of that pile, before any of the bills, was that check he'd just written for two hundred dollars. "Boy," he said, "it's a good thing I won that hand. If my wife had seen a cancelled check for that much money, she'd have killed me."

Billy Cox once figured in an incident with the Yankees during a World Series game that illustrates the special closeness we had as a team. Bob Cerv, a big strong outfielder with the Yanks, came charging into third base well ahead of the throw, safe by plenty. But instead of just making a conventional slide, he went right into Billy and knocked him all the way into the third-base coach's box where Frank Crosetti coached the Yankee runners. Cox and Cerv exchanged some hot words, but that was the extent of it—except where Pee Wee was concerned.

Our captain filed that little piece of information back in his memory. The next spring we were playing the Yankees in a spring-training game and Cerv was on first base. Pee Wee called over to Jackie at second from his position at short and says, "If you get a ground ball, give it to me in plenty of time, because we've got some getting even to do."

Jackie answers, "I gotcha."

We got lucky. The batter hit a ground ball to Jackie and he got it to Pee Wee early. Pee Wee stepped on the bag and threw the ball straight at Cerv's head as he was sliding into the bag. The ball missed him by inches. Cerv stood up, dusted himself off, looked straight at Pee Wee, and said, "I guess we're even." Then he turned and trotted back to the Yankee dugout.

With Pafko and Cox making us so much stronger in 1951, we knew it would be a special year, and for the Sniders that came true early. Pam, our first daughter, was born in June, but not until Bev learned about life in the big city.

In the spring, Bev drove north a few days ahead of the team because we were playing exhibitions on the way up the coast. She stayed in Brooklyn at the St. George Hotel and ate at the Plymouth Cafe near the hotel. When the team arrived in Brooklyn to start the season, Bev and I went to dinner at the Plymouth and it didn't take me long to get irritated at the slow service. I told Bev I didn't know why she kept eating in a place if the service was always that slow, and she said it always was.

As we were getting ready to leave after paying the check, Bev left the tip—a quarter. I looked at it and said, "Is that all you ever leave for a tip?"

She said, "Yes, why?"

I told her, "Now I know why the service is so slow."

Things were going great guns for the Dodgers in mid-August, so much so that Charlie Dressen told the writers, "The Giants is dead." The quote was picked up all over the country and Charlie became as famous for his prediction as he was for his grammar.

But it doesn't take much for a team to lose that precision that has been winning games. An injury here, a short slump there, and all of a sudden the machine that had been breezing toward a championship is beginning to cough and sputter. If another team gets hot at that same time, the whole world can turn upside down. And that's exactly what happened in 1951.

The Giants started coming on like gangbusters, and at that same time, Pee Wee and I both started to slump. When a baseball team has its leadoff hitter and its number-three hitter in slumps at the same time, it's not going to score many runs. The leadoff hitter, the man who's supposed to get on base so those behind him can drive him in, wasn't getting on; and the three hitter, the guy who's supposed to drive others in, wasn't doing that either.

The world knows what happened. The Giants caught us and did what we hadn't been able to do the season before with the Phillies—they forced a playoff series. A lot of familiar thoughts were going through my mind again. "Here you are," I would say to myself. "It's clutch time again. The team had a big lead, and now it's not so big any more, and you're going 0-for-4 and leaving a lot of runners on base." I lost my confidence again, started trying too hard again, and ended up making the same old mistakes.

Pee Wee and I both had bad Septembers, but mine was as hard on Bev as it was on me. She had Kevin, who was not quite two, and Pam only a couple of months old, and a husband struggling in his job and not saying much around the house. In the following season, during a mini-slump of mine, she went down to Vinnie's Meat Market in Brooklyn and bought me a club steak. I had a great dinner at three in the afternoon that day, then went out that night and hit two home runs.

When I got home after the game, Bev said, "Maybe the steak did it." Every time after that, whenever I started to slump, Bev headed for Vinnie's Meat Market.

But that was in '52 and this was '51. There were no steak cures or magic potions to get me out of my slump, and the Dodgers kept sliding, and the Giants kept closing the gap.

Then came the classic three-game playoff between the Dodgers and the Giants, a fantastic showcase for major-league baseball in front of the whole nation, two outstanding teams slugging away at each other in the drama of a playoff necessitated by a tie for first place after a 154-game season.

The idea that the Dodgers were psyched out by the Giants in August and September and choked up to lose the pennant just isn't so. We thought we would win it all, right up to the moment Bobby Thomson hit his home run. We were confident, we knew we were good, and we knew we were better than the Giants, just as we knew we were better than the Phillies the year before. There was no reason for us to shake in our boots, so we didn't. Our attitude was, "Okay, bring on the Giants. Let's have that playoff. Then we can knock off the Yankees for the first time in the World Series."

We split the first two games of the playoff, and the whole season came down to that third playoff game. It was Don Newcombe vs. Sal Maglie, a matchup of two outstanding pitchers with the National League pennant on the line. We went out and got a 4-1 lead, and the way Big Newk was pitching the lead looked like money in the bank. Newk was always a hard worker, his big 6-4 body shedding some of its 220 pounds as he pitched, the sweat streaming off his forehead, running across the beak of his cap and down his nose. He was an imposing figure out there on the hill only 60 feet, six inches from the batter, and I'm sure he was even more imposing than usual to the Giant hitters that day. In the eighth inning, Newk threw the ball as well as he had all afternoon, and he looked as strong as he did in the first inning.

I trotted out to center field for the last of the ninth inning confident that we were about to enter the World Series and I would get a chance to atone for 1949. The Giants scored a run and had a couple of men on base but I still wasn't worried. Then Dressen decided Newk was tired—he'd pitched his heart out all afternoon—so Dressen calls the bullpen from the dugout telephone. He had three guys warming up down there, and Clyde Sukeforth was sizing them up to see who had the best stuff to come in and put out the fire.

Sukey tells Dressen, "Preacher can't get loose, Erskine just bounced a curveball into the dirt, but Branca's throwing pretty good."

Dressen says, "Gimme Branca."

Erskine joked to me later, "That's the best curveball I ever threw."

It might have been a different story if we knew then what we learned over the next few years. Clem Labine, my teammate at Newport News in 1944, had beaten the Giants the day before, so everyone assumed he couldn't pitch the next day. Labine proved in the next few seasons that he had a rubber arm—he could pitch every day and never feel the effects that other pitchers do, but nobody knew it then. Fate was stepping in and taking over.

Dressen asked for time and then walked to the mound and took the ball from Newk. The dressing rooms in the Polo Grounds were beyond the center-field fence so I got to say something both to Branca on his way into the game and Newcombe on his way out. I always called Newk "Tiger" and I'd tell him, "Roar, Tiger," and he let out a bellow that would shake the walls. When he came trudging out toward the dressing room, I called over to him, "Nice going, Tiger." He thanked me and kept on going. It was inadequate, but what else can you say to a guy like that? He was a hero, and yet we didn't even know if we were going to win the game.

As Branca walked by on his way into the game, there was no hint of any rubbery knees on his part. He was full of confidence, even though he had given up a home run to Thomson in the first game. We called Branca "Honker" because of an oversized nose. I called out to him, "Go get 'em, Honk," and he said, "I will." As he approached the infield, Pee Wee and Jackie stopped him and gave him a few more words of encouragement. Then Ralph continued toward the mound. He expected to get the side out and we'd be the National League champions. I expected him to do it too. I still was not worried. But then something happened—or didn't happen—and suddenly I was worried.

Charlie Dressen was the kind of manager who was in complete control at all times. Whenever he took a pitcher out, he'd take the ball and hold it until his relief pitcher reached the mound. Then he'd talk to him, explain the situation—the score, runners on base and where, how many outs, the hitter and his tendencies—then hand him the ball, pat him on the butt, and trot back to the Dodger dugout. Most managers followed the same routine.

Only this time Dressen didn't do that. When Branca got about five feet from Charlie, Dressen flipped the ball to him and said, "Get 'em out," and headed back to the dugout. That left Ralph and Rube Walker, who was catching that day because Campy was injured, by themselves on the mound to discuss how they were going to pitch to the next hitter—Bobby Thomson. I noticed

Dressen's absence, and I'm sure some other Dodger players did too, and I thought to myself, "Oh-oh. Charlie's worried." That made me worry too.

When Thomson hit his now-famous home run, "the Miracle of Coogan's Bluff," I didn't think it was going out. It headed toward the wall in left center, and Pafko was quickly up against the wall to make the catch if humanly possible. I dashed over to play it off the wall and hold the runners to two bases. That way it would still be only 4-3. But all of a sudden the ball was too high for either one of us, and then it disappeared over the wall.

I didn't break stride. I saw the umpire circle the index finger of one hand over his head meaning "home run." I took a right turn and headed toward the clubhouse. Our season was over, in an even crueler ending than our extra-inning defeat to the Phillies the year before.

There were only a couple of players in the dressing room when I got there, Newk and one or two others. Some of the reporters were there and the TV cameramen. All of a sudden they start picking everything up—cameras, refreshments, the champagne—and start hauling all of it over to the Giants' dressing room. The celebration had been transferred. I watched in silence, stunned by it all. A few more players straggled in, first the guys from the bullpen, followed by the ones from the dugout.

Then Branca came in, took off his shirt with number 13 on the back, and draped himself on the steps of the clubhouse, which was a split-level room, and started to cry and moan, "Why me? Why me?" I forgot about our loss because all I could think of was sympathy for this pitiful figure on the steps in front of us. Jackie came in and fired his glove into his locker. Dressen took his shirt off without unbuttoning it—just ripped it off, buttons popping everywhere. Walter O'Malley, our president since the departure of Mr. Rickey, and Buzzie Bavasi came in and said a few words of comfort to us and then left. I showered and left, with most of us still silent.

Bev and I went out to dinner that night because Mom and Dad had come all the way from California in mid-September in hopes of seeing their son play in the World Series a second time and get a chance to redeem himself. There would be no World Series for the Snider family in 1951.

I was quiet at dinner, for reasons I think were understandable, but they weren't understandable to Mom. Late in the meal she looked across at me and said, "What's the matter with you?" I wasn't very cordial. "We just lost the National League pennant—that's what's the matter with me."

It wasn't a nice way for a son to answer his mother, regardless of the circumstances, and I regretted it immediately.

In Brooklyn that night, on my way home from the Polo Grounds and on our way back from dinner, I passed eight or ten stuffed figures hanging from light poles and telephone poles, figures wearing baseball shirts and Dodger caps.

The baseball shirt in every case had a number on the back—13.

Next Year...
Next Year...

Today's baseball players are walking conglomerates. They have fantastic salaries, multiple investments, and that unbelievably lucrative pension plan that we started for them in 1947, but we had one thing they don't have today—the train ride. We didn't always like it, but those rides kept us close as a team and as friends, something you can't get on a two-hour plane ride that used to take 15 hours on a train.

Athletes often talk about "camaraderie" in athletics, what *McCall's* magazine used to call "togetherness." We got that on those train rides, when we were brought closer together by the circumstances of our travels. When you spend 20 hours sitting in a coach car or sleeping in a Pullman berth going from New York to St. Louis, you're either going to become better friends or you're going to start slugging each other. We became closer, all of us on all the baseball teams. People still in baseball today who were around in the 1940s and early 1950s will tell you that today's players are not nearly as close to each other as we were then, and the introduction of jet air travel is one of the main reasons.

The camaraderie may have been great, but the travel conditions were not. We had upper and lower berths to sleep in, and I never slept well in either one. If Carl Erskine was going to be pitching when we got to our destination, he got the lower berth because it was roomier and easier to sleep in. The trains made so many stops during the night that sleeping was even more difficult. You had to keep the windows open at least a little bit because there were no air-conditioned railroad cars in those days. That, of course, brought in the soot from the engine or the ground around the tracks. The trains would switch tracks frequently, and the jarring and backing up and lurching forward would be another way of interrupting your sleep. The thump-thump-thump and the clickety-clack along the railroad tracks may have helped songwriters with their lyrics, but they didn't do much for professional athletes trying to get some rest en route to their next city.

When we got to our next town, the hotels weren't any cooler than the train because they weren't air-conditioned either. You'd sleep with the window open and the city dirt would float in and darken your pillow. The Schenley Hotel in Pittsburgh was the worst in that department. There was rejoicing around both leagues when the Chase Hotel in St. Louis became one of the first hotels in the country with air-conditioning. The National League teams playing the Cards, and the American Leaguers going to play the Browns, knew that St. Louis, which was always the hottest and stickiest city in either league, now offered cool comfort.

Some of the dugouts today are air-conditioned in the newer stadiums, and some teams even play in domed stadiums— Houston, Montreal, Seattle, and Minnesota. Toronto will have

116

one soon. In the days before those advancements, we just had to suffer. We sprinkled ourselves with ammonia water, and Campy wore a wet cabbage leaf under his cap like the old-timers did. And we did all that traveling in those hot, stuffy railroad cars and spent all those hours together in those hot, stuffy hotel rooms without something else the modern player has—spray deodorants.

Ebbets Field could get just as uncomfortable as anyplace else in the summer time. We were still playing a lot of afternoon games in those days, although the number of night games was on the rise, and in afternoon games following a night game we always seemed to start out on the sluggish side. With the temperatures often in the 90s and the humidity about the same, it often took the Dodgers a few innings to get going. If you were to run our games of those years through a computer, you might find we didn't start scoring our runs until the middle innings of most of our games, or until the hitters were coming up for their second time.

Harold Parrott, our traveling secretary, who was in charge of all travel arrangements and the man who got all the blame and none of the credit for getting us around the nation every year, used to arrange special outings for us if we had an open date on the road. The most memorable outing happened in St. Louis.

Harold and Tom Valenti, who was in charge of our broadcasts, made reservations for us at a golf course and we went out and played 27 holes in the St. Louis summer heat. On the way home we were still feeling strong, so we stopped off and bowled some games just to have some more fun. Then Rube Walker and Valenti challenged each other to a 100-yard dash in a nearby park.

Valenti said he was so sure he could beat Rube that he'd spot him a lead of ten yards. Don Zimmer was at the finish line, and I was the starter. We were still in our golf clothes and golf caps, standing there in that park, with this broadcast producer and this member of the Brooklyn Dodgers about to race each other. I was to signal the start of the race by dropping my golf cap. I told Rube I'd wink at him just before dropping my cap so he could get another step or two on Valenti. We all put bets down on the outcome, but the fix was in. There was no way our teammate was going to lose that race. We could have saved ourselves the trouble. Valenti quit after 50 yards.

We played poker, gin rummy, and bridge on those train rides, and we read and talked baseball, something else today's players don't do to the extent that we did. We talked about other things too, but we had such a love for our sport that we naturally talked about it often, with enthusiasm and an eagerness to hear the latest about the other teams and our friends on them, as well as swapping more yarns than you could ever imagine.

"The Boys of Summer," as Roger Kahn described us—sometimes accurately and sometimes not—in his book about our team in 1952 and 1953, approached the '52 season with nothing but a positive attitude following the crushing loss to the Giants in the playoffs. Rather than feeling down and out, we felt we were better than any other team in the National League. We had won the pennant in 1947 and 1949, had lost to the Phillies on the last day of the 1950 season and to the Giants in the last game of '51. No other team in the league was figuring so consistently in the pennant fight year in, year out. Our attitude as a team after the '51 loss was that we just had to go out and prove ourselves again—knowing we were better than the other teams—win the pennant, and then get our revenge against the Yankees.

Walter O'Malley, our president, and Buzzie Bavasi, our new general manager, congratulated us in the dressing room in the first moments following our loss to the Giants. They told us we'd had a great year, and that other great years were ahead of us. We believed it then, although we were too down at the time to respond, and we still believed it six months later as the 1952 season started.

We were right in our assessment of ourselves and the rest of the National League. In effect, it was only a four-team league. We beat the Giants by four and a half games—how sweet it was!—and the Cardinals by eight and a half, with the Phillies a game behind the Cards.

One of the high points of the season was provided by my roomie. Carl Erskine pitched a no-hitter. To show it was no fluke, he pitched another one in 1956.

His first masterpiece was a 3-0 win over the Cubs at Ebbets Field. It was one of those days when the weather was threatening and you're just hoping to get the game in. It started raining in the third inning, the umpires called time, and we hustled into the clubhouse. Somebody yelled, "Deal 'em!" and the daily bridge game, introduced to us by our pitcher Clyde King, was under way six innings early.

I restricted myself to occasional kibitzing. Just as Carl made four hearts, the umpires sent word that they were going to resume play. By the late innings, the only Cub baserunner was our old knuckleballing buddy, Willie Ramsdell. "Willie the Knuck," who had just been traded to Chicago, was the Cubs' relief pitcher, and he had drawn a walk as a batter in the third inning, after relieving Warren Hacker. As the no-hitter began to take shape, Happy Felton went into the Cubs' dressing room to get Willie, who had been lifted in the late innings, for his post-game TV show, "Talk to the Stars."

Happy told Willie, "Don't take off your uniform. If Erskine ends up with a no-hitter, I'm going to want you on my show as the Cubs' player of the game because there isn't anybody else." Willie knew he might be the losing pitcher, but he might also pick up 50 dollars for being on Happy's show.

With two outs in the ninth, Eddie Miksis was the Cubs' hitter. Happy was in the TV room with Willie watching the game on the TV monitor. Willie was hollering at it, "All right, Miksis, you dirty &!!**! You've popped up for me enough times, so don't go getting a hit now!"

Carl took care of Miksis and got himself a no-hitter—and Willie got an extra 50 dollars for drawing a walk.

The next day, Carl got a phone call in the clubhouse from

Charles Goren, the internationally famous bridge expert, who wrote a daily column, "Goren On Bridge," which appeared in hundreds of newspapers. Goren had heard about the bridge game during the rain delay. He reconstructed Carl's bridge hand from the day before and used it as the subject of his column a few days later.

My strikeout problem seemed to be under control, thanks to some advice from Pee Wee. He could see how much those K's kept eating away at me, so he came over to me one day and said, "Why do you let those strikeouts bother you so much? You're a power hitter, and any power hitter is going to strike out a lot because of the big swings you guys take. Why not just accept the fact that you're going to strike out ninety or even a hundred times a year, especially when you know you're also going to get a lot of home runs and drive in a mess of runs for us? When you strike out, instead of getting yourself all mixed up in your head, just say to yourself, 'I still have another eighty-five.' Shrug 'em off like that."

It was sound advice from the captain, and it helped to bring me the stability I needed in coping with those strikeouts. After 92 strikeouts in my first full season in '49, I cut the number to 79 in 1950. I shot back up to 97 in '51, but with Pee Wee's advice I went from that highest figure to my lowest, 77 in 1952. My homer total dropped from 29 to 21, still a respectable number, and my RBIs dropped slightly from 101 to 92, but I raised my batting average 26 points to .303, my second .300 season in three years.

Wally Moses was another one who helped me that year. I was slumping toward the end of the season, and Wally, who was a coach with the Phillies after ending his 17-year career as a player the season before, came over to me after our last game of the season with the Phillies. He said he'd noticed I was doing something different from the last time they'd played us. Wally hit .300 seven years in a row in the majors and finished with a lifetime average in the .290s, so I listened.

"The last time we played you," he said, "and you were hitting so well, your front shoulder was pointed to the shortstop side of second base. This time it was pointed toward the other side, the second base side. Try to keep your front shoulder pointing toward the shortstop side."

He was telling me that I was probably pulling up in my swing, pulling myself away from the pitch instead of striding into it. I never forgot Wally's advice.

I was beginning to feel that I was headed toward a successful career as a major-league baseball player. I knew we would get in the Series again. Everybody knew the Yankees would be in it for the American League.

For the Dodgers, the outcome was the same as in other World Series. We lost to the Yankees, taking them to the maximum of seven games in another one of our seesaw matchups. But this was the Series of my deliverance. I hit a home run off Allie Reynolds in the first game that gave us the lead, and we were never behind. I hit another one in the fifth game and two more in the sixth. The World Series monkey was off my back.

From the second the ball left my Louisville Slugger bat on that first home run, things were different. I had always performed well in every other kind of pressure situation, including those tense end-of-the-season battles against the Phillies and the Giants, and now I had finally proven my ability to play up to the challenge in the biggest pressure cooker of them all, the World Series.

I became the only player except Babe Ruth and Lou Gehrig to hit four home runs in one World Series, and later I became the first man ever to do it twice. With the help of God and a lot of people—Bev, my parents, and my teammates—I was able to play in a total of six World Series. With all that help, I became the player with the fourth highest number of home runs in World Series history, the sixth highest number of doubles, tenth in runs scored, and seventh in runs batted in.

Following that first game in the Series, we thought 1952 was the year we would finally do it, and that the Dodger fans could store

121

their famous slogan "Wait till next year" up in the attic. One of the reasons for our optimism, in addition to my home run, was the pitching of one of our rookies, Joe Black. Joe was a relief pitcher for us that year. He started only two games all year, but he pitched 142 innings and had 15 saves. Chuck Dressen, with that great baseball instinct of his, tapped Joe to be our starter in that first game.

Black responded with a six-hitter and we beat Reynolds and the Yankees, 4-2. With Carl and Preach ready to start the next two games, we had a bring-'em-on attitude, ready to show the world that the Brooklyn Dodgers really could win the World Series, and what's more, we could do it against the Yankees.

Even though it didn't happen, we had no reason to feel embarrassed and every reason to consider ourselves the Yankees' equal. One game in particular proved that point, the fifth game, one of the most memorable, tension-filled games I ever played in.

There were a lot of fives floating around that day—the fifth day of October, the fifth game of the Series, Erskine's fifth wedding anniversary, the five runs he gave up in the fifth inning, and the score of 5-5 at the end of ten. If there had been a state lottery in those days, nobody would have bet any other number.

Ewell Blackwell started for the Yanks, but Johnny Sain came on in the sixth after New York took the lead in its half of the fifth with that five-run inning. I had hit my second World Series home run earlier, with one on, but Johnny Mize trumped that in the Yankee fifth by hitting a homer with two on.

Erskine was superb. With that great assortment of pitches he had, and despite the pain he felt on every pitch, he shut the Yanks down after the fifth. They never got another man on base. Starting with the out that ended the New York fifth, Carl retired all 19 batters who followed.

We got a quick run off Sain in the sixth, but then both teams stopped scoring. We had a chance to win it in the top of the ninth when Sain plunked me in the ribs with a pitch. I went down because he hit me solid, but all my parts were still in one piece, so no damage was done. But we weren't able to take advantage of the opportunity, and went into extra innings. World Series drama was building.

I made two catches that Carl later thanked me for, and I got another chance at bat in the 11th inning, when I came up with Cox on third and Pee Wee on first. I had always been successful hitting against Sain when he was with the Braves, and I was having a great World Series this time around, so I stepped into the batter's box with complete confidence and fully relaxed.

I hit the ball unusually hard to right center field, and for a moment I thought I had another home run, but it was a double to the bullpen fence. Cox scored, Pee Wee went to third, and I went to second. One of the most dramatic games in World Series memory ended with the Dodgers winning, 6-5. My roomie went the full 11 innings, and I helped win it for him with my hit and a total of four runs batted in. We took the lead in the Series, three games to two. Things were definitely getting better.

The memorable game wasn't the first major development involving Carl in his first World Series. Dressen had named him to be our starting pitcher in the second game, opposing the Yankees' Vic Raschi. It had been another threatening day, so Carl stood on a stool in the trainer's room to look out the window and see if it was raining. As he stepped down, he hit his knee, already tender from ligaments torn in a high school basketball game, on the corner of a heater. The pain was so intense he passed out.

At this point, Dressen came into the trainer's room and saw his starting pitcher lying on the floor, face down, out cold. Somebody cracked the smelling salts and brought Carl around, and then they patched up the cut on his chin. He went out and pitched his way into the sixth inning before running into trouble. The Yankees won, 7-1.

That was the background when my roomie was our starting pitcher in that 11-inning game of fives. Carl, who is the most modest guy in the world, says, "I have a lot of stories about things that happened to me in my baseball career, and they're all true." He doesn't have to say that. Carl couldn't tell a falsehood if his life depended on it. So you can believe him when he talks about the Yankees' five-run fifth inning in that fifth game on the 5th of October, his fifth wedding anniversary:

"I was pitching well through four innings and had a 4-0 lead. Then, a few fluke hits, a walk, and a Johnny Mize home run and the Yankees had five runs. Dressen calls time out and comes out to the mound. I was sure he was coming out to change pitchers, especially after he took the ball from my hand. Dressen's rule was, 'No conversation unless I ask for it.' He said they had hit the ball well only once, Mize's homer—so he wasn't upset with me.

"Then, right out of the blue, he says, 'Is this really your fifth wedding anniversary?'

"He'd heard it from somebody. I told him yes. He asked if I was taking Betty out to dinner, and I said yes to that too. I knew what he was doing. He was stalling, giving somebody in the bullpen time to get loose.

"Then, to my astonishment, he took my gloved hand with his empty hand, turned my glove so the pocket was facing up, and put the ball in it. Then he said, 'See if you can get the side out before it gets dark.' Then he walked back to the dugout."

While he was still in a state of shock, Carl got Yogi Berra on a soft line drive to Carl Furillo in right and we were out of the inning.

Carl has another story about that game:

"The Yankees had two outs in the last half of the eleventh. Only one more out and we'd be leading the Series, three games to two. The hitter was Berra again.

"On my first pitch, I felt a sting on the tip of the middle finger of my pitching hand. I looked down and saw a white circle. I was developing a blister. I threw a curve and got another sting. I looked and saw the skin on the tip of that finger flipped over on its back. I flipped it back over and tried to tuck it into place over the new, red raw skin underneath. I was ahead in the count, no balls and two strikes. I threw another curve. Berra took it for strike three. The fantastic game was over.

"I looked at my finger. The skin had been torn all the way off with that last strike to Berra. I couldn't have thrown one more pitch. It was the only blister I ever had. And who knows? That blister might have affected the movement of my curveball just enough to help me strike out Berra."

The world knows that the Yanks won the Series anyhow, but they didn't exactly dominate us. We lost the sixth game, 3-2, even though I hit two home runs. I had the misfortune to hit them with the bases empty, and Vic Raschi and Reynolds combined to hold us scoreless except for those hits.

Game seven had another dramatic moment, the famous Billy Martin catch, but that catch of a pop-up by Jackie Robinson would have been forgotten if I hadn't popped up right before Jackie.

The Yanks were leading, 4-2, in the bottom of the seventh when I came up with the bases loaded and one out. Stengel waved in a left-hander, Bob Kuzava, from the bullpen, which was all right with me. I had always hit Kuzava well when we played against each other in the minors and the few times we had faced each other in the majors.

I walked back to the on-deck circle while Kuzava was taking his warmup pitches and said to Jackie, "Well, Jack, we've been waiting for this for a long time, and it's up to you and me, and I'd just as soon get it over with."

Jackie said, "Yeah, I'd like to see you get it over with too. Whack one and get us two or three runs."

We were both relaxed and confident. As Kuzava threw his last couple of warmups, I said, "I know one thing, Jack. I'm not going to overswing against this guy. I'm just going to try to hit one hard somewhere. I don't care where it goes."

He gave me a pat on the rear and said, "That's the way to approach it." Then I strolled up to the plate, confident I would get a hit and drive in two runs, and if I didn't, confident Jackie would.

Kuzava and I battled our way to a full count. I fouled off several pitches which I should have hit, but I just nicked them. Kuzava was doing a good job, battling me every pitch, determined not to let the lead and the Series get away from his team. He wasn't blessed with an overpowering fastball or an exceptional curve, so he relied on control and just enough movement on his pitches to throw you off.

When he came back in with still another 3-2 pitch, I popped it up to the left side of the infield. Two outs. Even with my vastly improved performance in this World Series and my new confidence, I wasn't going to be able to do it every time. I went back to the bench disappointed but confident that Jackie was about to tie up the game.

Kuzava jammed Jackie with an inside fastball, and he popped it up just like me, only to the other side of the infield. Kuzava looked at Joe Collins, his first baseman, and Collins looked at him. Billy Martin, playing second, saw the indecisiveness between the two so he took off at full speed toward "no-man's-land" just to the right of the pitcher's mound and made a shoestring catch with the ball about six inches off the ground. With two outs, the runners were going on anything so if Martin hadn't made that saving catch, we would have tied the game.

I thought about my disappointment after the game, but I had come to realize that I was as capable as anyone else of performing in the World Series. I had shown the world—but more importantly, I had shown myself. I knew from my experience as an athlete that not even the greatest player who ever lived, Ruth or Cobb or anyone else, can deliver every time. But I had performed well. In addition to my four home runs, I drove in eight runs, leading all players on both teams in those two departments. I tied Mickey Mantle in runs scored with five, and tied Pee Wee and Mickey with the highest batting average, .345. I wasn't going to walk around with my chin on the floor after a World Series like that. It was time to go home and prepare for 1953 and another shot at the Yankees—after winning the pennant first.

The fans felt that way too. I took Kevin, who was now three, with me to Ebbets Field to clean out my locker, after the season ended. At the exit gate a fan had tied up a hand-lettered sign, hanging from a piece of string, that said:

GOODBYE DODGERS,

THANKS FOR A *WONDERFUL* SEASON WHICH MADE YOUR FANS SO HAPPY.

NO REGRETS!

Oh, how we all loved this place—Brooklyn's fabled Ebbets Field.

This is what I looked like in my first season with the Dodgers.

This one's headed for Bedford Avenue.

The welcoming committee
at home plate after
one of my home runs: Pee
Wee Reese (1), Jim Gilliam
(19), and our bat boy,
Charley "The Brow."

Happy days in the Dodger clubhouse.
(*Above*) Preacher Roe shows his winning grip
to Roy Campanella and me.
(*Right*) Sandy Amoros and I laugh it up after
helping to win one for home team.
(*Below*) Campy plants one on me while Gil
Hodges enjoys the scene after another
Dodger victory.

There was no joy in our clubhouse this day. A dejected Ralph Branca lies on the clubhouse steps shortly after pitching that never-to-be-forgotten ball to Bobby Thomson in the 1951 playoffs with the N.Y. Giants. Cookie Lavagetto sits beside Ralph, sharing his grief.
(*Below*) Six members of the 1951 Dodgers get together at the Polo Grounds in 1962 for a reenactment of Bobby Thomson's "Miracle of Coogan's Bluff" home run. Campy is in street clothes and behind him are (from left to right) Gil Hodges, me, Jackie Robinson, manager Charlie Dressen and Carl Erskine, all holding a memento of an event we'd rather forget.

Barney Stein

Herb Scharfman

New York was blessed with two other future Hall of Fame center fielders during my Ebbets Field days: New York Giant Willie Mays (*above*), and New York Yankee Mickey Mantle (*below*).

Here's Ebbets Field before the first game of the 1952 World Series. The bus carrying the New York Yankees has just arrived. (*Below*) That was the day I proved to myself I could deliver under pressure. My two-run homer off Allie Reynolds enabled us to defeat the Yankees, 4-2. Celebrating with me in the front row are manager Charlie Dressen and Jackie Robinson. Behind us are Joe Black, the winning pitcher, and Pee Wee Reese. Jackie and Pee Wee homered, too.

Barney Stein

Under a full moon and the Ebbets Field lights, I wait for a pitch against the Philadelphia Phillies. This is one of my favorite pictures.

(*Left*) We didn't know much about our new manager, Walter Alston, when he and I posed for photographers at the start of the 1954 season. (*Below*) I took pride in my fielding, too. Here I'm about to collide with the center field wall in Ebbets Field after catching a shot by Willie Jones of the Phillies. As always, Carl Furillo moves over from right field in case he's needed.

The front page of the *New York Daily News* tells it all the morning after the Dodgers won the World Series over the Yankees for the first time.

(*Above*) Don Newcombe and I whoop it up in the dressing room at Yankee Stadium after we defeated the Yankees in the 1955 World Series.
(*Below*) I won the Sid Mercer player-of-the-year award of the New York chapter of the Baseball Writers of America in 1955. National League president Warren Giles, Walter Alston and comedian Phil Silvers shared the happy moment.

On the home front, Bev and Dawna look out from the trailer Bev towed from California to New York to join me for another baseball season in Brooklyn.
(*Below*) Bev and I enjoy the beauty of Hawaii with Betty and Carl Erskine during a Dodger barnstorming trip after the 1954 season.

(*Above*) Gil Hodges and I look lost in our cavernous new home, the Los Angeles Coliseum, after the Dodgers moved from Brooklyn for the 1958 season. (*Below*) This home run was my eleventh in World Series competition, still the National League record. It came off another future Hall of Famer, Early Wynn, in the sixth game of the 1959 World Series against the White Sox in Chicago. The catcher is Sherm Lollar.

Herb Scharfman

The Snider ball players, Kurt (in front), Kevin and me, get together at the Polo Grounds in 1963 before a fathers-sons game.

Award-winning memories. August 26, 1960 was Duke Snider night at the Los Angeles Coliseum. Kevin, Pamela and Kurt seem apprehensive about their gas-powered autos, and so do I. But Bev was enjoying every moment of the ceremony at home plate. (*Below*) The Dodgers retired my number 4 on July 6, 1980, and I was proud when my fellow center fielders from New York joined me. Mickey Mantle couldn't make it, but Joe DiMaggio, Willie Mays and I got a standing ovation. In my opinion, Joe was the best of us all.

Associated Press Photo

EDWIN DONALD SNIDER
"DUKE"
BROOKLYN N.L., LOS ANGELES N.L.,
NEW YORK N.L., SAN FRANCISCO N.L.,
1947 - 1964
HIT 407 CAREER HOME RUNS AND TIED N.L.
RECORD WITH 40 OR MORE ROUND-TRIPPERS
FIVE YEARS IN A ROW, 1953-1957. BATTED .300
OR BETTER SEVEN TIMES IN COMPILING .295
LIFETIME AVERAGE. TOPPED LEAGUE IN SLUGG-
ING PCT. TWICE AND TOTAL BASES THREE TIMES
FIRST TO HIT FOUR HOMERS IN A WORLD SERIES
TWICE -- IN 1952 AND 1955. SET N.L.
RECORD FOR SERIES HOMERS (11).

National Baseball Library, Cooperstown, N.Y.

The ultimate honor for any athlete—enshrinement in his sport's hall of fame. Commissioner of Baseball Bowie Kuhn joins me in posing for photographers at Cooperstown, N.Y. in August 1980.

National Baseball Library, Cooperstown, N.Y.

9

Close But...

Jocko Conlon was one of the characters of those years, and an umpire to be reckoned with. He was always in charge of the game, and if you didn't believe it, Jocko would be only too happy to prove it. He threw me out of a few games, which was nothing to be ashamed of because he threw a lot of others out too.

He once even threw me out of an exhibition game. We were playing in Atlanta and there was a large overflow crowd of fans who had come out to see Jackie Robinson. We moved players around because it was only an exhibition game, and I was playing left field when a fly ball was hit down the line. I drifted over into foul territory, the fans in the standing-room-only area gave ground, and I made the catch.

Jocko was the third-base umpire and he ran down the line to see the play as well as he could and ruled the ball was out of play. We exchanged differences of opinion and when I yelled, "You don't even know the ground rules!" he gave me the heave-ho.

But I managed to put one over on him once in Chicago. I was getting on him from our bench and after he'd heard enough, he started staring in, looking for the culprit in case he decided to throw him out. I was waving a towel and continuing my verbal abuse when he began walking toward our dugout, squinting in to see who was waving that towel and staying on his case.

When he started coming our way, I told Johnny Podres, who was sitting next to me, to switch places with me, and take the towel. Johnny had pitched the day before and wasn't going to get into this game anyhow.

Jocko got close, looked in, and said, "The guy on the end of the bench with the towel can leave for the afternoon."

Podres stands right up, says, "Thank you very much, Jocko," and leaves. I got to stay in the game, and Podres got the day off.

Conlon topped himself long after we both had retired, and we weren't even on a baseball field. We were in a restaurant. He and I were to speak at the banquet of a junior college baseball tournament in Grand Junction, Colorado, a few years ago and we were having a drink in a restaurant/bar. After a while, Jocko's voice started getting louder and some four-letter words began coming out. Eventually a nice young couple seated near us complained and asked politely if we could hold it down. That worked for a while, but then Jocko got loud again, and the four-letter words came back.

The same thing happened only with a surprise ending. The couple complained again, but Jocko, instead of promising to keep it down, called the waiter over and asked for the couple's check.

When he got it, he paid their bill, then went over to their table and said, "I've just paid your check because you two are *outta* here!"

The nice young couple got up and left, the first time an umpire ever threw anybody out of a restaurant.

Augie Donatelli was another colorful National League umpire in the 1950s. He umpired in the International League when I played there, a hustling, hardworking umpire. He tried his best, but the players always had a problem with him when he was the home-plate umpire. He worked behind the plate on one knee and maintained a stationary position. As a result he had to guess on the outside strike, and that used to give hitters fits. But there was never anything we could do but argue. In business the customer is always right. In baseball the umpire is always right, even when he's wrong.

Pee Wee and I had a run-in with Donatelli in Chicago on a ball hit by Randy Jackson, who later became our third baseman. He was a good-looking son of a gun and his first name was Ransom, so the players around the National League called him "Handsome Ransom." On this particular afternoon, he hit a long fly ball with the bases loaded. I went back on it, all the way to the ivy that covered Wrigley Field's brick outfield wall. I went up to make the catch and a fan leaned over and touched it. It fell to the ground and I picked it up and threw into Reese. Donatelli was the third-base umpire and he ruled it a home run, a grand slam for Handsome Ransom.

Pee Wee started arguing immediately, and I dashed in to make the same argument because it was a clear case of fan interference. Jackson should have been held to a ground rule double; instead, Donatelli was giving the Cubs four runs. But our biggest beef with Donatelli wasn't the call he made. We were arguing about his position on the play, which frequently is what players and managers complain about when they're arguing. It's the umpire's responsibility to get himself into the best possible position to see the play so he can make the correct call.

Our complaint in this case was that Donatelli, instead of running into the outfield and getting as close to the play as possible, stayed around the edge of the infield and made the call on a ball that landed 200 feet away from him.

Pee Wee made the point more emphatically than Donatelli thought he should, including calling Augie an S.O.B., and Donatelli gave him the thumb. Then I started jawing away, calling Donatelli the same thing, and got thrown out too.

Pee Wee was still in the thick of the argument even though he had already been ejected and he still had the ball in his glove. "You made that call right here, dammit!" he yelled. Then he pointed to the outfield grass just behind third base and slammed the ball hard into the turf at the spot.

Donatelli was so furious he threw Pee Wee out—again. Pee Wee said, "You've already thrown me out once!" Then we both left for the clubhouse.

I signed my contract for 1953 on January 20, the same day Eisenhower was sworn in as President after beating Adlai Stevenson. It was for $23,000. Maybe we hadn't won a World Series yet, but at least the pay was getting better. Buzzie Bavasi was being fair with me, the way he always was when we were at Montreal and in all my years when we were with the Dodgers.

Buzzie, in fact, was so fair that Pee Wee and I had unlimited confidence in him, so much that one year we both signed blank contracts. We both told Buzzie we'd always found him fair and reasonable and that we knew he'd give us what he thought we deserved. So we signed our contracts at the start of spring training without knowing exactly how much we were getting paid for the season, and we didn't know until after the season started and we got our first pay checks.

One year Gil decided to hold out for $25,000, which would have been a raise of a whole $2,000. Buzzie remembers that he thought Gil deserved more like $27,000, but he couldn't offer a player more than the guy was asking or the word would get around and Buzzie would never have any leverage in his contract negotiations. He offered to write a number on five slips of paper starting with Gil's salary of $23,000 from the previous season and up to $27,000 and put them in a hat. The worst Gil could do was play for the same salary as the year before, so he took the offer. He might even get twice the raise he asked for.

He drew one of the slips of paper from the hat and got the top figure—$27,000. That was his salary for the new year. It was a rare story of an athlete actually getting more than the raise he had asked for. If Gil had seen those other four slips of paper he would have been in for a surprise. They all said $27,000. Gil never learned the true story.

That's the way things were in the '50s. It's hard to imagine any player doing that now. Today everybody is allowed to see how much everybody else is making; they have agents and lawyers and arbitrators and what have you. The players are making huge sums of money and more power to them. They are the entertainment, the ones the fans pay to see and the sponsors pay to televise, so they're entitled to all they can get. Still, things were simpler in the '50s and I think we had more fun than the players today. Sandy Koufax said it best: "Baseball hasn't changed. Only the money has."

We were a set ball club in 1953, something you always strive for, a team that appears to have no weaknesses. Some people say that those Dodger teams of the early and mid-1950s were the greatest ever, better than the 1927 Yankees and any other team you could name, and when you look at our lineup for 1953, you can see the validity in that argument.

We had Hodges, Robinson, Campanella, Reese, Gilliam, Furillo, Cox, and me in the batting order. Our pitchers were

Erskine, Russ Meyer, Billy Loes, Preach, Podres, Labine, and Black. No wonder we won the pennant by 13 games over the new Milwaukee Braves, who had just moved from Boston to America's heartland. The hated Giants were barely visible, 35 games behind us.

This was the team Roger Kahn covered for the *New York Herald-Tribune* in his second and last season with us, the team he wrote about 20 years later in *The Boys of Summer*. Most of us felt Roger, who was just a kid in his early 20s when he covered us, did an accurate job of portraying the Brooklyn Dodgers of 1952 and 1953. However, we didn't feel the same way about his description of us as individuals in later life.

He seemed to grope for the sad side, for pathetic tales of what happened to those boys when they were forced out into the cruel world of reality when their playing days were over.

In my case he wrote about my bowling lanes and my ranch, both of them in the north county of San Diego, where Bev and I moved in 1956. The bowling lanes did not succeed because soon after we opened for business, the Viet Nam war erupted into full fury, and the Marines from Camp Pendleton and the sailors from the Naval Ammunition Weapons Depot, whom our bowling lanes were dependent on, were shipped out. Half of our business was gone. I owned a ranch for several years with one of my Montreal teammates, Cliff Dapper, but I sold it when I found it was taking more time than I had because I was gone seven and a half months a year.

Kahn, however, made them both sound like financial failures, and to a degree the bowling lanes were, although by the time the accountants worked their magic with capital gains and losses, I just about broke even. The ranch was no failure at all. It was a success; I just was never there.

He quoted Bev and me as saying things that simply were not true. An example was describing us as steady churchgoers, which we are, and mentioning that Bev sang in the choir. Bev has never sung in anybody's choir. She laughs about that statement and says, "If Roger had ever heard me sing, he never would have put that in his book."

Carl Erskine was another example. I know Carl a whole lot better than Roger Kahn ever could. We lived together as roommates for ten years, we were neighbors over that same period in Bay Ridge, and the four of us have stayed in touch over the years. We go out of our way to make sure we visit each other at least a couple of times a year, and the half-continent between California and Indiana has never kept us apart.

In *The Boys of Summer*, Roger made it sound as if the Erskines have been wallowing in self-pity for years since their son, Jimmy, was born. They don't have that attitude at all. They are Christians, and their attitude toward having a son with Down's syndrome is that God blessed them with a special son and an opportunity to serve Him through Jimmy. That's a far cry from the impression Kahn gives in his book.

You realize how strong the Dodgers were in 1953 when you look back at what some of the guys did. We were playing with the Branch Rickey philosophy of putting the team first, knowing that individual success would follow, and it certainly did in 1953. Furillo won the National League batting championship with .344, eight points better than mine and up 97 points from the year before. Combine this with his averages in earlier years ranging from .284 to .322, and you can see why Skoonj was not fond of Leo Durocher for trying to platoon him.

I had my first 40-homer year, the first of five straight seasons when I hit 40 or more. Somebody figured out that I hit more home runs in the decade of the 1950s than anyone else in major league baseball—306—and in '53, when I hit 42, the writers started saying I was the heir apparent to Ralph Kiner's home-run crown in the National League. It was pretty heady stuff and I tried not to think about it too much. I didn't want to make my old mistake of putting too much pressure on myself.

I didn't lead the league in homers that year—Eddie Mathews did with 47—but I was pleased to make another contribution to the team by leading the league in runs scored with 132. That's when you know you're helping your team to win. Campy won the Most Valuable Player Award, for the second time in three seasons, with a sensational year. In addition to being the best catcher in the league, he hit 41 home runs, had a .312 average, scored 103 runs, and led the league in runs batted in with 142, 16 more than I had. Gil Hodges had a banner year too, with a .302 average, 31 home runs, 101 runs scored, and 122 driven in, after his miserable start and his dismal World Series the fall before.

Jackie was right up there with a .329 average, 109 runs scored, and almost 100 RBIs—95. Pee Wee scored over 100 runs too—108—showing that he was still an excellent leadoff man, and Junior Gilliam, our rookie second baseman, contributed by scoring 125 runs.

That's a lineup with batting averages of .302, .312, .329, .336, and Skoonj's league-leading .344, with Gil, Campy, and me in the middle of the batting order hitting 31, 41, and 42 home runs. The three of us had 390 RBIs among us, and six of us scored over 100 runs each for a total of 670 runs. Add that to a pitching staff which included a 20-game winner, Carl Erskine, and you can understand why we won the National League pennant going away with 105 wins, more than any other team in baseball and six more wins than the Yankees in the American League.

We wrapped things up early that year with such a powerful team, and we followed our usual practice of relaxing, having some fun, and then getting serious in time to go into the World Series. We followed this habit every pennant-winning season. Any member of the Brooklyn Dodgers in those days would have better career statistics today if he had stayed serious and played bear-down ball for the rest of the 154-game schedule after winning the pennant. But we knew we had won, we knew our individual numbers were great, so why worry about making them even greater? Relax, have a good time and that way you'll be re-charged and ready for the Series.

We clinched the '53 pennant early, but I had a 26-game hitting streak going. We came to the park for the game the next day with some admirable hangovers. But there was that hitting streak that I wanted to keep alive, and so did my teammates. Even our opponents that day, the Cubs, were being nice about it. Johnny Klippstein, a slender six-footer who spent 18 years in the major leagues, was in on some special arrangements to accommodate both my hitting streak and my hangover.

Johnny was going to groove one to me so I could get a hit, then he was going to pick me off base with some help from me, and I could go back and sit down. Baserunning was out of the question.

He kept throwing me fat pitches all day long, but my timing was off, for obvious reasons, and I couldn't do a thing against him. I wasn't doing any better in the field. I had to dive at the last minute to catch a routine fly ball. I almost got killed by a line drive. Finally, on my fourth time up, with my hitting streak in danger of ending, Klippstein hollers in to me from the mound, "Bunt one."

I popped it up. I went 0-for-4 and my hitting streak was snapped—with the fix on during the whole game.

There was one point while we were enjoying our latest pennant when I got upset. I always used to hit well on my birthday, September 19, but this time Dressen benched me. Late in the game he had to use me as a pinch hitter—and I hit a home run.

We may have been an overpowering team, but we didn't overpower the Yankees. They beat us in the World Series again, four games to two, even though we got some good hitting and some outstanding pitching by Erskine. Carl set a Series record by striking out 14 batters in one game to give us our first series win after the Yankees won the first two games. The next day I drove in

137

four runs with two doubles and a homer, Billy Loes and Clem Labine held the Yankees in check and we tied the series with a 7-3 win. But the Yanks won the next two games and we were gone again.

You wouldn't have expected Erskine to set any records in that World Series after his first game. He started the opening game in Yankee Stadium against Allie Reynolds and was roughed up for four runs in the first inning, three of them on a bases-loaded triple by Billy Martin. He pitched only that one inning. We tied the score in the sixth, but Joe Collins homered in the seventh to break the tie and we eventually lost, 9-5. Mantle homered with a man on in the eighth inning of the second game to break a 2-2 tie and give the Yankees a 4-2 win even though Preacher Roe held them to five hits.

Suddenly we're swimming upstream, down two games to none against an outstanding Yankee team. We had to do something fast, and Dressen did. The same manager who used to tell us to hang close until the seventh inning and he'd think of something thought of something before the game started. He went to Carl, who was scheduled to start the fourth game, and the seventh if there was one, and told him he was our starter in the third game instead. His reasoning was that Carl had worked only one inning in the first game, so he might be strong enough to start again with only one day's rest.

Dressen's gamble produced one of the best-pitched games in the history of the World Series. Our pitching opponent was Vic Raschi again. Both pitchers went the distance. Erskine's day got off to a promising start when he struck out leadoff batter Gil McDougald. He spent the rest of that October afternoon defying the old baseball superstition that it's bad luck for a starting pitcher to strike out the first batter he faces.

Carl gave up only one hard-hit ball all day, a single by Gene Woodling. From my spot in center field it looked as if the Yankee hitters were swinging at imaginary baseballs. By the time the ninth inning rolled around, Carl was nearing the World Series record for strikeouts in one game, even though we didn't know it. Casey Stengel sent up Don Bollweg to pinch hit. Carl had pitched against him in the minors and remembered he liked to hit the low pitch, so Carl got him on three fastballs in the upper half of the strike zone.

The crowd was going crazy, and when those 34,000-plus Dodger Faithful who were squeezed into old Ebbets Field heard the announcement that Carl had just tied the World Series record of 13 strikeouts, they got even louder. Carl never heard the announcement, because of the noise and his own concentration. He couldn't afford to be thinking about a record for himself anyhow. We were winning, but only by one run, the homer by Roy Campanella that put us ahead, 3-2—and pleased the folks getting ready to air the first broadcast of Ed Murrow's "Person to Person." But one mistake on Carl's part and we could be tied or even behind.

Now the hitter was Johnny Mize, a Hall of Famer today, a lifetime .312 hitter with 359 home runs. He'd homered against us three times the year before. A homer here and we'd be right back in the soup. It was pressure time, the 6-2 slugger against the 5-10 pitcher. The Yankee players told Carl later that Mize had been getting on them all day about swinging at bad pitches, a tribute to Carl's curveball. They were getting sick of hearing it from him. Now it was Mize's turn to show them how to hit this guy.

After throwing nothing but fastballs to Bollweg, Carl started Mize with a curve for strike one, called. His second pitch was a fastball which Mize ripped back to the screen behind home plate. Strike two. We could see Mize was upset at himself. That was the one he wanted, the fastball, and he couldn't handle it. He knew he might have missed his best chance with that swing. The next pitch was another curve. Mize was fooled completely. He took a weak swing, almost waving at the pitch with his bat instead of swinging at it. It was one of those pitches where the hitter gets so tied up he embarrasses himself with his swing. It's happened to all of us, and it happened to Mize that day. After criticizing his teammates, Johnny Mize took that awful swing at a curveball he couldn't hit—and put himself in the record book as the hitter who was the record strikeout, the 14th.

There is a P.S. to the story, which the Yankees also told Carl later. Stengel sent Irv Noren up as another pinch hitter and Carl walked him. Now things were stickier than ever. A home run here and we're on the verge of being only a game away from the end of our season.

The hitter was Joe Collins, who had already hit that go-ahead homer in the first game. Carl had owned Collins so far in this game, and Mickey Mantle too. He'd struck both of them out four times. Now Carl was fighting not only the pressure but the law of averages too. Collins was overdue to get a hit, maybe even bust one to win the game for New York. Carl says he stood there that day, thinking to himself, "Nothing too good, nothing he can pull. Right field is only 296 feet."

Collins, it turned out, was doing some sweating of his own. We heard from the Yankee players later that as he left the dugout to take his place in the on-deck circle while Noren was at bat, his teammates were giving Collins a sharp needle because he could become the first man in World Series history to strike out five times in one game. When Noren got on, the other Yankee players were sticking it to Collins even more.

He heard his teammates telling him, "Okay, Joe. You're going into the book." Another one hollered, "You're going to be an asterisk."

With Erskine pleading to himself, "Please, no home run," and Collins pleading to himself, "Please, no strikeout," Carl came over the top with a curveball. Collins hit a weak dribbler back to the mound, and Carl threw to Gil Hodges for the out to end the game and his day of history.

Something nice happened in that Series. Gil Hodges, after a dismal Series the year before, led our team in hitting with a .364

average. Most of us hit well. Furillo had a .333 average, Jackie and I both hit .320, and Billy Cox hit .304.

Billy Martin offset all of that singlehandedly for the Yankees with 12 hits and a .500 average. After his Series-saving catch of Jackie's pop-up the year before, he was back winning it for the Yankees again, this time with his bat.

There was some talk that the Yankees held a jinx over us. We felt we were just as good, but we still hadn't proven it. We weren't any less confident, though. We were sure there were some more World Series in our future, and our day would come.

Preacher Roe showed us that our attitude was justified—that some things might take forever, but sooner or later they happen. He proved the point by hitting a home run during the '53 season, the only one he ever hit in 620 times at bat in his career. After Preach hit the ball he didn't seem to know what to do. When he finally started trotting toward first, Jake Pitler, our first base coach, started needling him. "How should I know where to go?" Preach yelled as he rounded the bag. "I never hit one of these things before."

10

A Popular Dynasty

Dissension at the management level might have cost us the pennant in 1954, which would have been our third straight pennant and our fourth in seven years. But the Yankees didn't win in their league either. They ran into the Cleveland Indians and their record number of wins in one season, 111, so both of us finished second. It's a disappointment to win 97 games and still not win the pennant, but the Yankees must have been even more disappointed. They won 103 and still didn't make it into the World Series.

Charlie Dressen, with two pennants and a tie in his only three years as our skipper, chose this season to demand a multiyear contract, something the Dodgers never gave their manager. He argued his case with Buzzie Bavasi, and when Buzzie said flatly the demands were against the club policy set by Walter O'Malley, Dressen went right to Mr. O'Malley, armed with a letter from Mrs. Dressen arguing in her husband's behalf. It didn't work. Charlie lost his job, and Walter Alston signed a contract to manage the Dodgers. It was a one-year contract, the first of 23 which Alston would sign as manager. The club's policy didn't change—just the name of the manager.

Alston was a loyal and capable manager in Brooklyn's farm system, but relatively unknown to baseball fans. When O'Malley named him to be our manager, the *New York Daily News* headlined the story:

ALSTON (WHO HE?)
TO MANAGE DODGERS

Maybe the *Daily News* hadn't heard of Alston, but Buzzie had. The two had worked together at Nashua, New Hampshire, and in Montreal, and Buzzie was confident that Alston could keep the Dodgers strong contenders even though he had no experience as a major-league manager. When he talked O'Malley into agreeing with him, it would be a happy day for the Dodger fans, although they may not have known it then. Walt won seven pennants for the Dodgers, ranked fifth in total wins, fifth in World Series wins, and is in the Hall of Fame.

It was remarkable that we won 97 games that year because it was a transition year for all of us, with the players getting to know Alston and vice versa. He wasn't really able to take full control until the next season, when everyone was comfortable with each other.

Even though the Giants beat us and went on to sweep the Indians in the Series, despite that record number of wins by Cleveland, I didn't have any trouble keeping my enthusiasm up. I managed to do that by leading the National League in hitting most of the year. When the last morning of the 1954 season dawned, there was a three-way tie for the batting championship among Willie Mays, his Giants' teammate Don Mueller, and me. I hit a fly ball to the center-field fence and a line drive to short, both balls were caught, and I finished up 0-for-3. Mueller went 2-for-5, but Willie topped him with 3-for-5, so Mays won the championship with a .345 average, Mueller was runner-up with .342, and I finished third at .341.

I had complete confidence as a hitter now, and I was finally learning to live with those strikeouts, even though I had 96 that year. In fact I managed to win the strikeout championship, if that's what you want to call it. But by learning to shrug them off, following Pee Wee's advice, I was able to rise above those K's and finish among the leaders in nine of the 12 offensive categories. My hitting accomplishments included 40 home runs, 130 runs batted in, 120 runs scored, and 199 hits.

Willie and I put on an exciting duel that year. Mueller was an outstanding hitter, but he was basically a singles and doubles hitter. Willie and I were going at each other in every category. He was a leader in seven offensive departments. He led the league in hitting, slugging average, and triples. I led it in total bases and tied Stan Musial for the most runs scored. Willie and The Duke were having some fun out there.

People used to compare us, along with Mickey Mantle, during all our years in baseball. The Yankees were always publicizing Mickey Mantle and getting a lot of ink for him, but others were saying Mantle wasn't the best all-around center fielder in baseball, and maybe not even the best one in New York. All three of us enjoyed successful careers playing center field in New York in the 1950s, and all three of us made the Hall of Fame. When you add Joe DiMaggio to that list, that's quite a lineup of New York center fielders, and the truth is that DiMaggio, in my opinion, was better than the rest of us. He may have been the best of all time.

Willie, Mickey, and I weren't the only ones having fun. It was a fine time for all of baseball, the fans, the players, the media, everybody. We had some great pennant races in both leagues, some World Series games which are now considered classics, and that new thing called television was bringing all of it right into America's living room—and that's why Terry Cashman's song was a smash hit a few years ago: "Talkin' Baseball—Willie, Mickey, and The Duke."

The comparison of Willie, Mickey, and me went on for years. People used to ask if it bothered us, and I always told them, "No, it seems to bother the media more than it bothers us." We used to joke about it. We knew we were creating good box office for our teams, and in every city where we played. All of us were successful, everybody was making money, so why should we mind? I'd run into Willie and he'd say, "Hey, Duke, I got twelve points on you," and I'd say, "Yeah, but I'm leading you by fifteen RBIs."

The "best center fielder" argument reached some kind of a peak in the mid-1950s when two National League fans got into a fistfight over who was better, Willie or me. The cops were called to keep the two from killing themselves. They found out the guys were father and son.

I had some fun playing defense that year too. That was the year I made my best catch ever. I climbed the wall in Philadelphia on Memorial Day, dug my spikes into the wooden fencing, leaped, and took an extra-base hit—which would have been the game-winning hit—away from Puddin' Head Jones to end the game and save a 5-4 win for Clem Labine in the 12th inning. Labine was so excited and so happy that I was able to save his win for him that he got out there only a couple of seconds after the ball did.

Richie Ashburn even to this day tells me that I trapped the ball off the wall. My answer is always the same: "Richie, if I had, that would have made it an even better catch."

Dave Anderson of the *Brooklyn Eagle* wrote the next day, "To a man the Dodgers insist that Duke Snider's pogo-stick catch of Willie Jones's liner high against the left-center-field wall yesterday in Philadelphia was the greatest, absolutely the greatest, in baseball history."

That's a strong statement and it makes you almost giddy with pride, but Jake Pitler was a reliable source on the subject. He told the writers, "In forty years of baseball, I never saw a catch like Snider made." He said he remembered one other that compared to it—back in 1909. An outfielder for the Giants named Red Murray made a catch to prevent a home run off one of the greatest pitchers of all time, Christy Mathewson.

When they start comparing your defensive plays to some made back in '09, you have reason to feel you're doing all right.

The fun even included my third straight All-Star Game. I got three hits and drove in two runs. Everything was coming up roses, and not even another media controversy about me could dim my enthusiasm. A writer named Arthur Mann wrote a feature story in the *Saturday Evening Post* titled:

THE DODGERS' PROBLEM CHILD

In the article he quoted me as saying the occasional controversies about me were unfair. The article said, " 'It's really not my fault,' pleaded Duke Snider when he was ordered out of a training camp for not hustling. 'My parents are to blame. I'm an only child.' "

There were at least three things wrong with that sentence:

1. I never plead with writers about anything.
2. I was never kicked out of any training camp.
3. I've never blamed my parents for *anything*!

Even though we didn't win the pennant, we were still loaded with talent, as our total of 97 wins showed. From 1946 through 1956, the Dodgers and the Yankees dominated their leagues. Over that span, with the reputation the Yankees had as the all-powerful dynasty, they won only 20 more games than we did, 1,061 to 1,041, a difference of less than two wins a year. They had ten years in that 11-season stretch when they won at least 90 games, and we had nine.

In the National League itself, there was no contest—it was the Dodgers all the way. From that first postwar season in 1946 through 1956, four other teams won pennants—the Boston Braves, the Phillies, and the Cardinals each won one, and the Giants won two. We won the other six. Despite our heated crosstown rivalry and all the Willie-Duke talk, the Giants' record during the same period just wasn't in the same class with ours. When it came to naming the two best teams in baseball in the first postwar decade, there was no question. But if you had to pick between the two—the Dodgers and the Yankees—the record book says it's a tossup.

With the talent to dominate a league like that, a team doesn't always have room on the major-league roster for all its good players. They have to be "hidden" on minor-league teams with the hope the scouts for the other teams don't see how much talent is out there. That's what the Dodgers did in the case of one talent-rich kid we had in our minor league system.

He was an outfielder, but no rookie was going to crack our outfield of the 1950s, so Buzzie Bavasi tried to hide him on our Montreal roster. He was a "bonus boy," a designation in those days for any kid who received a bonus of more than $4,000 to sign with your team. If an organization shelled out more than that, they had to keep the kid on the major-league team for at least a year, or risk losing him in the player draft.

The Dodgers signed this kid for a bonus of $10,000 and then stashed him away in Montreal until a vacancy might open in the Brooklyn outfield. A few years ago, Buzzie told me he used every trick he could think of to fool the other teams about the kid's ability. They didn't play him against left-handers because the kid was a right-handed hitter and they didn't want him to fatten up his average against left-handers. So they played him only against the very best right-handers. They benched him once after he hit three triples in one game. And they got what they wanted. The kid hit only .257, hardly a performance to turn the heads of scouts from the other teams. Maybe the kid would remain safe under the Dodger version of house arrest.

Branch Rickey remembered the kid, though, and nobody ever fooled Mr. Rickey, especially the people who worked for him in the Brooklyn organization before he became the head of the Pittsburgh Pirates. The Pirates, under Rickey, drafted this minor-leaguer with only a .257 batting average because he was not protected on the Brooklyn roster, and the Dodgers lost the kid.

That's how the Dodgers just missed an outfield of Carl Furillo, Duke Snider, and Roberto Clemente.

The Reeses, Erskines, Walkers, and Sniders were neighbors in Bay Ridge all through the '50s, until the Dodgers moved west for the 1958 season. We were close teammates on the field and close friends off the field. Together we saw the movies of the day like *From Here to Eternity* with Frank Sinatra's comeback to prominence, and *Three Coins in the Fountain,* and the magical new form of movie entertainment called Cinemascope. We saw the wide screen feature called *Cinerama,* plus the new spooky technique called 3-D, where we sat wearing cardboard glasses and watched a bunch of actors throw things at each other—only we were the ones who were doing the ducking.

The eight of us would take the subway into Manhattan on Saturday night, without worrying about being mugged by a hood or being shot by a vigilante. You could still see the color of the subway cars because they weren't covered with graffiti, and the trip cost a dime.

We didn't lead any whirlwind social life because we had to take care of ourselves and make sure we got enough rest, but we made sure we got to enjoy a special Saturday evening with our wives from time to time—dinner in New York and a Broadway show was our idea of a Saturday night out. We had some great shows on Broadway to choose from in those years—shows people still pay to see on the stage, like *Mister Roberts, Call Me Madam,* and *South Pacific* in our early years together, and then productions like *Damn Yankees, Pajama Game,* and *The King and I.*

Everyone was singing the advice the manager of the Washington Senators gave his team in *Damn Yankees*—"You Gotta Have Heart." Even the kids had a favorite song:

"DAY-VEE! DAY-VEE CROCKETT! KING OF THE WILD FRONTIER."

We were watching more TV too, because there was more TV to watch. Sitting in front of our ten-inch black-and-white sets, we watched Sid Caesar's "Your Show of Shows," Jackie Gleason and Art Carney in "The Honeymooners," Ed Sullivan's "Toast of the Town," the Friday night fights, Bishop Fulton Sheen, plus, of course, "Mr. Television" himself, Milton Berle—who would come into my life later.

We enjoyed all of these things together, the Erskine Family, the Reese Family, the Walker Family, the Snider Family, all of us part of that larger group, the Dodger Family. That's what made us unique, and there's no question in my mind it's also what made us such dominating winners. We were not just good—we were also united like a family and nothing could separate us. We were a popular part of life in the United States in the mid-1950s, and I think the genuine feeling of each of us for our 24 teammates was something that fans all across America could sense, especially at World Series time.

At the end of the '54 season, some of us Dodgers went on a "barnstorming" tour of American cities. A team of National League All-Stars played one from the American League in a promotion staged by two investors, one of whom was Bobby Riggs. Ted Kluszewski, the 225-pound first baseman for the Cincinnati Reds, managed to make the tour something for the pitchers to remember.

Klu was coming off the best season he had in his 15 years in the major leagues. He'd led the National League that year with 49 home runs and 141 RBIs. He had forearms as thick as elephant legs and he had to cut out the sleeves of his Reds shirt to get his arms into his uniform. With all that weight and strength, when he hit a baseball it came off his bat like a rocket.

He was so strong he even hurt you when he tagged you at first base on a throw over from the pitcher. He'd smack that ball and glove on your shin bone and you'd feel it. The runners, including me, used to say, "Ouch! Hey, Klu—not on the shin bone. That hurts."

He'd tell us, "Well, don't take such a big lead and I won't tag you there."

At the beginning of our postseason tour, Klu met with the American League pitchers out of his concern for their personal safety. He used to hit some wicked shots up the middle and all the National League pitchers knew how to pitch him so the ball would be hit to the left or right side. Klu wanted to make sure the American League pitchers knew to do the same thing, because he was always concerned that he might hurt a pitcher some day with one of his smashes.

The first game of our barnstorming tour was in Montreal, and Klu met with the American League pitchers before that game and told them that he had broken the cheekbone of Bubba Church, one of the Phillies' pitchers, that year, and he didn't want that to happen to these guys. He told them the secret, as employed in the National League. "Don't pitch me low and away. That's the pitch I hit up the middle."

The American League stars had a pitcher named Ned Garver, who was known to have independent views on a variety of subjects, including this one. He told Kluszewski, "I'll pitch you anyway I want."

A few games later we're in Cincinnati, Klu's town, and Garver gave him that pitch. Klu smoked one right through the middle that nicked the button on top of Garver's cap as it whistled into center field. After the game he was thoughtful enough, and concerned enough, to go over to Garver and say, "Ned, I nicked you tonight, and I don't want to hurt you accidentally, so please don't throw me that low and outside pitch because that's where I hit it."

Garver wasn't going to back down. He said again to this muscular giant, "I'll pitch you any way I want." Nobody was going to tell old Ned Garver anything.

We were in New Orleans for our last game of the tour. It was coming to an early and unscheduled completion because the promoters had already lost $70,000 and Riggs and his partner wanted to get out while they still had their shirts on their backs. Again, Garver was going to show Klu who's boss, so he came in with another pitch low and away. This time, instead of the ball hitting Garver's cap, it hit his cup.

The ball rebounded with such force that it rolled toward the third-base line. Garver went over, as well as he could, bent over, picked the ball up, and threw to first. Then he passed out on the baseline.

They carried him off on a stretcher. Nobody remembered if Kluszewski had been safe or out on the throw because nobody cared. Some of us left the field and headed into the dressing room to see if Garver was going to live or die.

They cracked the smelling salts and waved the container back and forth under Garver's nose and he finally started to come around. There, bent over him in worry, was the guy who had hit the ball.

Garver blinked a couple of times, tried to focus his eyes, finally looked at the giant hovering over him, and said meekly, "You made a believer out of me, Klu."

After the season, and the barnstorming by some of us, the Brooklyn Dodgers went home and waited for 1955, hoping to improve over our 1954 season, not knowing that next year would be Next Year.

My Boyhood Dream

If there ever was a year that had everything, for the Brooklyn Dodgers it was 1955. Here's what happened that year:

We won our first ten games and 22 of our first 24.

We won our third pennant in four years and our fifth in nine seasons, clinching it at the earliest date in National League history.

We led the league in 11 departments.

Roy Campanella was voted the National League's Most Valuable Player, for the third time in five seasons.

I was named the *Sporting News* Player of the Year.

I had one of my best years, and one of my worst slumps.

I got myself into the worst controversy of my career by blasting the Brooklyn fans, saying they didn't deserve the pennant.

Pee Wee Reese was honored at Ebbets Field in one of the most touching salutes to a ballplayer I've ever seen.

We finally won our first World Series and every part of my boyhood dream came true: We not only won it, but we did it by beating the Yankees, and in Yankee Stadium too.

Realistically, we clinched the pennant in April with that quick jump out of the starting gate. When our lopsided record stretched out to 22 wins and only two losses, it was all over. Nobody was going to catch a team like the Dodgers after we got a jump like that. By the time the season ended, we led the league in runs scored, total bases, doubles, homers, runs batted in, team batting average, slugging average, fewest runs allowed, lowest team earned run average, fewest earned runs, and most strikeouts by our pitchers. We made everything official on September 8. The second place team, Milwaukee, was 13 and a half games behind us. Our friends, the Giants, after beating us out for the pennant by five games in 1954, finished 18 and a half games behind us in 1955.

At the end of the season I had a .309 average. It had been .320, but a late-season slump and our usual relaxing after we wrapped up the league championship dropped my average. I was still able to hit above .300 for the fifth time, the fourth year in a row. After we wrapped things up, I didn't even stay with the team. Alston let me fly home to spend a few days with Bev because she was expecting our third child, Kurt, any day.

I hit 42 home runs—topping 40 for the third straight year—including three in one game for the second time, and I led the league in runs scored with 120 and in runs batted in with 136.

My home runs were causing even more of a stir. The writers were saying I was a serious threat to break Ralph Kiner's record of hitting 40 or more home runs for five straight years, and when August came and I was ahead of Babe Ruth's pace in 1927, the year he hit 60 homers, the talk grew louder. I was aware of it all.

In my case, I had 38 homers early in August and was seven games ahead of Ruth. With 12 home runs the rest of August and 11 in September, or any combination totaling 23, I would break what was the most treasured of all baseball records. Hitting 23 homers in almost two months is well within the capacity of many home-run hitters, who tend to hit in streaks anyhow.

Fate stepped in during a game against the Cubs in Chicago and kept the Babe's record safe for six more years. Johnny Klippstein hit me on my left knee with a curveball. I rested the knee for a few days, but when I came back I hit only four more homers.

I was turning a lot of heads with my bat. I hit a 470-foot homer into the right-field seats in the Polo Grounds, to the same spot I reached on a grand slam against Ruben Gomez two years earlier. I hit a line drive to center field in Ebbets Field against Sheldon Jones that was still going up when it landed in the upper deck.

I was getting all the "ink"—the athlete's word for publicity—that you could imagine, but not all of it was good. Bev still has a scrapbook for each of my seasons, and the book for 1955 shows some contrasts. On the good side, Joe Sheehan of the *New York Times* wrote, "Snider goes about his business quietly, making the hard chores seem easy. Mickey and Willie have a long way to go before they can put on the record that they measure up to Snider."

Milton Gross said in the *New York Post*, "There is scarcely anything Snider cannot do better on the ball field than any other man in the game today." Just before World Series time, Gross raised the old business about the pressures I put on myself: "Here is a great player who wants to be among the great greats and wonders if he'll ever make it."

Sports Illustrated, a new magazine in those days, joined the continuing debate in the National League about Willie Mays and me. The headline said:

DUKE OR WILLIE?
A VOTE FOR SNIDER

SI said I was considered "the most dangerous hitter in the National League." The story in Bev's scrapbook says, "Snider reminds one of the careful, easy loping grace of Joe DiMaggio," and that aside from Ted Williams, I had the best hitting form in baseball. *SI* also mentioned what I liked to hear about the most, my team attitude: "Like Musial, he has developed more and more as a team player." Being compared to Joe DiMaggio, Ted Williams, and Stan Musial in the same article in *Sports Illustrated* would do wonders for any player's confidence, even a player like me who sometimes thinks too much.

That was the good ink. The bad ink came in a tidal wave when I suffered an attack of foot-in-mouth disease. This time it was a severe case. It was late in the season and we were cooling off a bit after setting a consistent pace all year. Our low point came when we lost a twilight-night doubleheader to the Reds in Ebbets Field, 8-5 and 6-5. I went 0-for-9 and left half the population of Brooklyn on base. By the end of the long, unbearable evening, the fans were booing me right out of the ball park.

I had given them plenty of material to work with. On the Fourth of July, which was then the traditional halfway mark in the major league season, I was hitting .331. Over the next 27 games I hit .196 and my average dropped to .299. I didn't hit a home run in 16 games. Alston was great about my slump, though, and came to my defense by saying, "How can you be critical of a man who virtually carried the club during the first half of the season?"

In the clubhouse after our doubleheader loss, with the usual gang of reporters around and my self-inflicted frustrations at their peak, I really let fire: "You guys want something to write about? I'll give you something. The Brooklyn fans are the worst in the league. I said it, and it goes. They don't deserve a pennant."

One headline the next morning told the story:

**BORO FANS DON'T
RATE PENNANT,
SNIDER SAYS**

The next day I told one of the reporters, "It's not only the booing. Some of the things I hear said in the center-field stands are not clean. Thursday night I was hit on the shoulder by a can opener. I was fed up and really mad after we lost the two to the Reds. I had left men on. I was booed, and some of the things yelled at me were unjust. I was perturbed and said that Brooklyn fans were the most critical in the league, that there were good fans too, but not enough of them."

Alston tried hard to defend me when the reporters went to him for his reaction to my comments. "They'll probably boo a little more, but they also cheer a little harder. They reserve the right to boo their own players, but let someone say something critical about a Dodger player and they'll be the first to stand up and fight for him."

I wasn't the only one feeling the frustrations of losing that night. Alston himself let out a blast, and against his own players. He walked past Reese, Robinson, Campanella, and Hodges in the dressing room after the second game while they were joking with reporters. Walt, the mildest of men, got hot in a hurry and told them, "I wish to hell *I* could find something to laugh about."

To the reporters later he said, "What could be so funny about losing a doubleheader? I don't believe in hanging your head after a defeat, but I don't think that was the time for joking."

Dick Young carried some of my later comments in his story the next day in the Daily News. His story started: "Duke Snider said it—and he's sorry. Well, a little bit, anyway."

He carried some more comments by me, which may or may not have eased the situation. "I didn't mean all the fans. I'm sorry, in a way, that I popped off. I guess I shouldn't have said what I did. There are quite a few good fans in Brooklyn. Maybe not as many good ones as bad ones, though. It would be different if I were dogging it. Everyone knows I'm trying."

Besides, I didn't know what the fans had to complain about. We were still leading the league by 11 games.

In our car pool going home after the two losses to the Reds, Pee

Wee tried to calm me down and also prepare me for what might be in store for me at the next game. "Well, Duke," he started, "you really did it this time. You wouldn't listen to me in there and now you've really put yourself in the soup."

The captain was right, of course. I shouldn't have said what I did, and I should have been smart enough to stop when Pee Wee tried to interrupt me while I was talking to the reporters. He jumped in when he saw me starting to paint myself into a corner and said to the reporters, "Wait, guys. Duke doesn't really mean that. Do you, Duke?"

And I, of course, said, "The hell I don't. I mean every word of it." Then I continued teeing off on the fans, without any further interruptions from Pee Wee.

So now we're driving home and Pee Wee is telling me how much trouble I'm in because of my mouth and my refusal to listen to him in the clubhouse. He told me he was going to stick with me the next night right up to game time in case there was a lynching party. He also told me something else: We were going to stay in that dressing room until the game started. No batting practice, no nothing. He didn't want me out on that field any sooner than necessary.

The next afternoon Bev said, "I'm coming to the game tonight."

I said, "No, you're not. Those fans are ready to tar and feather me."

She was insistent, and Bev doesn't scare easily. "I don't care," she said. "I'm coming anyhow."

When we got to Ebbets Field, Pee Wee became my self-appointed baby-sitter. He wouldn't let me leave, even though I wanted to take batting practice. We stayed in our bomb shelter right up to game time. Then we gritted our teeth, threw our shoulders back, and marched out onto the field toward whatever fate awaited me.

There were 12,840 fans in the stands, ready to let me have it. To make matters worse, the Reds were starting a left-hander. Pee Wee said he didn't like my chances. Neither did I.

The first time I came up, with enough boos and insults to last the whole game—wouldn't you know it?—I struck out. My second time up, some of my loyal supporters tried to drown out the boo-birds, but there was about a 75-25 margin against me. I got a single to the outfield. My third time up, after that hit, the boos and the cheers were about 50-50. I got another hit. My fourth time up, the crowd response was about 75-25 in my favor. I got my third straight hit. When I reached first base, I got a standing ovation.

The fans. God bless 'em.

I picked up some strong support from Don Newcombe earlier that season. I took an extra-base hit away from Monte Irvin that drew some nice comments in the press, and Dick Young quoted Newk as hollering in our dressing room after the game, "To hell with Mays. Our boy is the bestest." Another vote had been cast in the National League's unending Mays-Snider debate.

Not all of the publicity was in the stories about the Dodgers. A lot of ads and commercials were beginning to come in. The advertising money which ball players love New York for was starting to come my way. Some of it gets ridiculous, but it's part of your profession and one of the ways you make a living, so you take advantage of it, subject to certain limits and preferences where things like good taste are concerned.

Ad agencies were hiring me for newspaper and magazine ads and TV commercials for the wildest range of things you can imagine—dancing lessons (I could use them, according to Bev), underwear (I had enough, thank you), cigarettes, and shaving cream. Some of the wording in the ads was enough to break you up. Imagine picking up a magazine and seeing a picture of yourself and a message which says:

DUKE SNIDER WEARS
NEW MAYO SPRUCE UNDERWEAR

"On and off the diamond I like to feel free. Mayo Spruce underwear is all action—doesn't bind or bunch. Comfortable? And *how*! See for yourself—spruce up today!"

The one for Arthur Murray dance lessons was even worse:

"A few innings on the party sidelines and I got so fed up seeing others have all the fun dancing. So I hied myself off to Arthur Murray's. Now I wish I'd done it years ago. Lessons at Arthur Murray's are such fun and so easy. In almost no time at all I was dancing the latest steps . . . felt as much at home on a ballroom floor as on the field."

The ad offered a half-hour trial lesson for one dollar, at studios on Fifth Avenue in Manhattan and on Smith Street in Brooklyn. Then there was the ad for Lucky Strike cigarettes:

"Believe me, Luckies taste better! I've smoked enough different cigarettes to know what's what, and believe me, Luckies taste better than all the rest."

I never smoked and actually didn't know how to hold a cigarette. I felt uneasy making that commercial.

Carl and Betty Erskine and I posed for an ad for pediatric crib mattresses on sale at Gimbel's for $18.98. With the logic that only agency writers can apply, the ad said the mattresses were "recommended for children by leading athletes."

I made a TV commercial for Gillette razors. The producers told me to be sure to shave before showing up for the filming, and make sure I shaved extra close. Then we film the commercial—with no blade in my razor. I made a TV commercial for Ovaltine breakfast drink, but only after they put some chocolate milk in it so I could stand the taste of the stuff. Later the government got tough and said techniques like these could not be used because they were false advertising.

One of the most memorable occasions in that whole year, in addition to winning the Series against the Yankees, came on the night when the people of Brooklyn honored Pee Wee for his 36th birthday. They gave him 50 gifts, including savings bonds, two freezers—one with 200 pounds of hot dogs, shrimp, lobster, and roast beef—a TV console, two sets of golf clubs, movie equipment, a hunting coat, and 100 pounds of coffee. Vin Scully and Happy Felton were the emcees. The ceremonies took 50 minutes. Vin and Happy read messages from Vice President Nixon, Governor Averell Harriman, former Vice President Alben Barkley from Pee Wee's home state of Kentucky, and General Douglas MacArthur.

The high point came when they drove a lineup of new cars onto the field—a Chrysler, Buick, DeSoto, Pontiac, Chevrolet, Ford, and Plymouth. Pee Wee's 11-year-old daughter, Barbara, reached into a goldfish bowl and pulled out a set of keys and Pee Wee got to keep whichever car the keys fit. It was the Chevy. Campy said the next day the fix should have been on. He thought they should have made sure the keys fit one of the expensive jobs, like the Chrysler or Buick.

While the ground crew was dragging the infield smooth in the fifth inning, two huge cakes were wheeled onto the grass, the lights were dimmed, and 33,000 fans in the stands held lighted matches and sang "Happy Birthday." I got goose bumps and chills. Pee Wee had tears in his eyes.

It was a season packed with events, successes, and controversies. The more we won, the busier we were with interviews, commercials, personal appearances, and the rest of the workload that goes with winning. I was so busy on one trip that I wrote a letter to Bev and absentmindedly signed it, "Yours truly, Duke Snider."

Once again it was time for the World Series, and once again it was the Dodgers versus the Yankees. There may be matchups in sports which eventually become boring because the same two teams seem to be playing each other all the time, but that never seemed to be the case with the Dodgers going against the Yankees in October. The country loved it, and we did too.

Skoonj and I hit home runs off Whitey Ford in the first game, but Joe Collins hit two, including a two-run shot in the sixth which put the Yanks ahead, 6-3. Jackie stole home in the eighth on a play which people still argue about, but it got us only within one run of a tie. Collins had hit his second home run, and so had a rookie outfielder-catcher, Elston Howard, who was the Yankees' first black player—eight years after Jackie Robinson broke the color line. Those blows by Collins and Howard were enough to win the opener for New York, 6-5.

In the second game, it was more of the same. Tommy Byrne took charge of things. As the Yankees' starting pitcher, he held us to five hits. As a hitter, he capped a four-run rally in the fourth inning with a single which scored two runs. It was the only inning in which the Yankees scored, and Byrne became the first left-hander to beat us in a complete game that year. It happened on September 29, 156 games after the start of the season.

Some of the fans and reporters were giving up on us. Already the Brooklyn players were hearing that familiar chant, "Wait till next year." We had a different attitude. We were confident we could win it. The Yankees never really clobbered us in those previous World Series. We felt we were at least their equal, and in our more candid moments we thought we were probably better.

The next three games did nothing to change our assessment of ourselves or of the Yankees. We won all three games in Ebbets Field, by scores of 8-3, 8-5, and 5-3. We beat Bob Turley on six runs in the first four innings, Don Larsen on three runs in the fourth, and Bob Grim on a two-run home run by Sandy Amoros in the second inning, followed by two home runs from me. There were 17 home runs in that World Series, and the Dodgers hit nine of them.

We were happy for Sandy Amoros. He worked hard to make the grade as a major-leaguer. Sandy was a Cuban, and when he came to the United States from his home in Havana for spring training with us in 1952, he couldn't speak a word of English. He also had a lousy sense of direction. He had no idea of where Vero Beach was, on the East Coast of Florida, about 125 miles north of Miami. He was a no-show for two days and the Dodger management didn't know what to think. Then they found him wandering around Tampa, on the other side of the state. In a restaurant, the only thing English he could say was, "Apple pie a la mode." He lived on it—breakfast, lunch, and dinner.

Sandy made it up to the Dodgers in '52 for only 20 games and then was farmed out to the minors again, but he came back in '54, and now in '55 he was a World Series hero with a home run helping us to win a game. And Sandy's brightest moment in the sun was yet to come.

In the sixth game, back in Yankee Stadium, Alston decided on one of our kids, Karl Spooner, a 24-year-old left-hander, as our starting pitcher. Karl had come up from our farm system late in '54, and some people claimed we might have overtaken the Giants and won the pennant in '54 if we had called up "Spooner sooner."

Karl pitched in the major leagues for only those two seasons, 1954 and '55, and won a total of only ten games, two his first season and eight in '55. On that October afternoon in 1955, Karl suffered a disaster. He got only one man out. The Yankees knocked him out of the game with five runs in the first inning, including two walks, singles by Yogi Berra and Hank Bauer, and

163

a two-run homer by Moose Skowron. The results were twofold: an easy 5-1 win for New York, and the need for a seventh game the next day, in Yankee Stadium.

That sixth game produced another setback for me. I stepped on a sprinkler head in the Yankee Stadium outfield, the same thing Mantle did in 1951, and twisted my bad knee. I heard something pop, and had to come out of the game early.

Every athlete dreads a knee injury, and here I was with my second in the same season. The knee obviously was going to keep causing me trouble. I could still play on it, but for how long? And how well? And how long before the question of surgery would come up? A knee injury wasn't going to stop me from playing in that seventh game, but that whole scary problem lurked in the back of my mind.

On the morning of the seventh and final game, we were getting onto our team bus at Ebbets Field for the ride over to Yankee Stadium. Johnny Podres was going to be our starting pitcher that day. Most of us were already on board when he arrived. He hopped up the steps, started down the aisle, and told us with all the confidence in the world, "Just get me one run today. That's all I'll need. Just one."

That's the attitude you like to hear from your pitcher, and Podres wasn't whistling in the dark. He said it three or four times on the ride over to Yankee Stadium. It got so we made a joke out of it. Every once in a while somebody would yell, "Hey, Johnny! How many runs did you say you'll need?"

Johnny wouldn't hesitate. "Just one. That's all it'll take." We were kidding him, but he wasn't kidding us.

We got him two and won, 2-0, with both runs driven in by Gil Hodges. That was only right, because of Gil's awful World Series in 1952 when he went 0-for-21.

There were other nice ironies in that game. I didn't hit any homers or drive in any runs, but contributed with a sacrifice bunt in the sixth inning. Burt Shotton would have been pleased, I'm sure. The bunt put our second run in scoring position, the run that meant the Yankees couldn't play for one run and use the bunt themselves, the higher-percentage strategy. Instead they had to swing away and hope to get two runs. The way Podres was pitching, that wasn't going to happen.

Amoros got his big moment in the sixth inning, right after Alston sent him into the game for defensive purposes. He made an excellent running catch of Yogi Berra's fly ball down the left-field line near the stands, put on the brakes, wheeled, and threw to Pee Wee, who relayed the ball to Hodges and got Gil McDougald as he tried to get back to first base. Instead of a run and a threat for more, it was a double play.

There were two notes of irony on that one play. Not only had Sandy just come into the game that inning, he was a left-handed thrower. With his glove on his right hand, he was able to reach up near the stands and make the catch. A right-handed thrower with his glove on his left hand would have had to reach across his body to make that play, and he never would have been able to do it. Maybe fate was smiling on us.

Gil's two RBIs weren't the only note of irony involving him either. He got to make the last putout of the Series, on Elston Howard's ground ball to Pee Wee. Hitting it to Pee Wee was perfect. He was on the '41 team that had suffered when Mickey Owen missed the third strike, and he was on our '51 team when Bobby Thomson did us in. He was the only man in baseball to play in five World Series, all for the same team, and lose all five Series, all to the same opponent.

The town went crazy. Our bus route back to Ebbets Field was lined with fans on every sidewalk who somehow found out the route we were taking back to Brooklyn. Kids were celebrating by playing ball in the streets, as kids often do in those blissful moments of their youth, imagining themselves to be the heroes they thrilled to minutes before. Fans waved to us from telephone poles where effigies had hung four years before.

The Flatbush Faithful thronged to Ebbets Field and mobbed us when our bus rolled up. No more "wait till next year." This *was*

Next Year. We were the top story in all the papers and on the evening news. Steve Allen had started the "Tonight Show" only the year before, and he opened the show that night with his own brand new song, "Johnny Podres Wears a Halo 'Round His Head."

We weren't surprised at Johnny's confidence. He always felt he was going to win, the only way any pitcher should ever feel. The next morning, my roommate, Carl Erskine, and I were on the "Today Show" with Johnny. The host, Jack Lescoulie, was congratulating Podres on his superb performance. Johnny, in a polite, but completely serious way, said, "I'd go out there right now and do it again if I had to."

It was the World Series of my dreams. The homer I hit off Ford in the first game landed in the third deck of Yankee Stadium, the ball park in my fantasy. I finished with four World Series home runs, the first player ever to hit four homers in the Series twice.

Campy won his third Most Valuable Award, and I was second. That's how good the Dodgers were—two players on the same team finishing one-two in the MVP voting. Campy won by only five points, and goodness knows, if anyone was going to be the MVP instead of me, I'd want Campy to be the one. There was a controversy about the voting, however, and many of the fans and writers were upset, saying I should have won the award.

The reason for all the fuss was the ballot cast by a Philadelphia writer who was sick and in the hospital. On his list of ten candidates for the award, he put Campy down twice and didn't put me down at all. The argument was that the ballot was invalid and the Baseball Writers Association of America, which conducts the voting among its members, should have thrown the ballot out. No one knew if the writer did it accidentally or on purpose, but instead of voiding the ballot, the officials counted the writer's first-place vote for Campy and simply disregarded the fifth-place vote for him.

The vote for Campy was 226-221. When the voting was announced, Campy was gracious, as always. He told the writers, "I wish Duke had won this one." I was disappointed, but I was happy for Campy. Winning the MVP award three times put him in exclusive company. Only Musial, DiMaggio, Berra, Mantle, and Jimmie Foxx have won the award three times since it was begun in 1911.

It's always a letdown when people say you might win a prestigious award like the MVP and then you don't, especially when you miss out because of something like that. But at least we kept it in the Dodger family, and I had my *Sporting News* Award as the National League Player of the Year.

The New York writers also selected me as the league's Player of the Year and gave me their Sid Mercer Award. If I didn't win the Most Valuable Player Award from the writers' national association, at least I won the award of their New York chapter.

I won another award too. The Custom Tailors Guild of America voted me to its list of the ten best-dressed men in America. I was right up there with Vice President Nixon, Bob Hope, Frank Sinatra, Clark Gable, and Don Ameche. It was flattering, especially considering I didn't have that many clothes.

Carl and I headed west in a two-car caravan after our World Series triumph, and we looked like World Champions because each of us was driving a new Cadillac. Carl's was white, and mine was light blue. We should have had Pee Wee with us because we got stopped by a state trooper for speeding on the Pennsylvania Turnpike.

We thought we were going to beat the rap when the trooper recognized us and told us he was a Dodger fan. Our prospects changed in a hurry when he said, "I lost money on you guys again this year."

We said, "Whatta you mean? We *won* this year."

The trooper said, "Yeah, but I bet on you to win in '49 and in '52 and in '53. This year I bet on you to lose."

He let us off with a warning.

I came home to a hero's welcome, and this time I had the best of all worlds. They'd given me that nice salute in '49, but it was after that miserable World Series. There was another nice evening for me in '52 after my first good World Series, but we had just lost to the Yankees. This time we got it right. I'd had a good Series, and we'd won it all. The city fathers of Lynwood, the town where we were living at the time, declared November 7 "Duke Snider Day" and made me honorary mayor.

It was almost too much, but I was loving every minute of it. Life was becoming a piece of cake—and the frosting on the cake came in the birth of our second son, Kurt, who entered this world on September 19, my 29th birthday.

Nature has a way of reminding you that you're not completely in control of your own life and what happens in it. Three months after Kurt was born, Mom died of a heart attack on the morning of December 26. There was a special closeness between Mom and me, and she was always one of my biggest supporters. She even used to write to reporters if she thought they weren't treating me right. Every once in a while Dick Young would say, "I got another letter from your mom today."

She was overjoyed that now her son was a world champion. Little did we know it would be Mom's last hurrah. It was a sad ending to such a magnificent year.

Over Here,
Over There

The Brooklyn Dodgers won fans for themselves and baseball all over America with their first World Series championship. An item in Bev's scrapbook for 1955 shows how far and wide our popularity was spreading. It's a newspaper story about a three-year-old boy in Omaha, Nebraska, named Joey Chadek.

Someone contacted me about Joey and told me he liked the Dodgers. He had been hit by a car and dragged 16 feet while crossing the street near his home with his black cocker, spaniel, Poncho. He'd been hospitalized twice, and had lost 17 pounds. I got word about this during the off-season and wrote him a letter which is quoted in Bev's scrapbook:

I guess you will be a bit surprised to get this letter from me.

I meant to write you at Christmas time, but I was real busy. Now I have time to write my friends. You and I can be friends, can't we, Joey?

Are you being careful crossing streets now, Joey? How is Poncho these days? It sure is nice to learn you are a Dodger fan. We need lots of boys like you pulling for us. You keep on rooting for us. Also be sure and eat lots of good food and drink plenty of milk.

I guess that's all for now. You be a good boy.

> Your friend,
> Duke Snider

The article said Joey's mother told the newspaper, "Joey eats everything we give him now. We know he's getting well fast." She said he gained seven pounds right after he got my letter.

We learned you can make good things happen for others too, including a three-year-old boy in a city far away.

People were even writing songs and comedy routines about us. In addition to Steve Allen's "Johnny Podres Wears a Halo 'Round His Head," comedian Phil Foster recorded a routine about the Dodgers and their fans that became a hit record. The lyrics focused on my roomie, Carl Erskine. Foster played the role of a loyal bleacher fan in Ebbets Field who keeps hollering his support for his boy "Oisk" at a crucial spot in the ninth inning. But when Oisk walks the batter, Foster screams the ultimate insult: "Trade 'im to da Jynts!"

A fan named Bernie Friedman wrote a song about me, "The Dook of Flatbush," using the spelling that some writers used to imitate a Brooklyn accent. Erskine and I were roomies named "Oisk" and "Dook." Foster used to say, "That's spelled D-double O-K, Dook."

Bernie Friedman's song was a bouncy tune which went so far as to predict I'd be in the Hall of Fame some day. What he didn't know, and neither did I, was that the Hall of Fame would become an obsession with me after my playing days were over.

Two kid pitchers came up to us in the mid-1950s. The first was Sandy Koufax, the greatest pitcher I ever saw—period. And he might have been even greater if he had been as mean as the kid who came up the next year, 1956—Don Drysdale.

The Dodgers signed Sandy as a bonus player in '55 so they had to keep him on the roster of the parent club or risk losing him the same way they lost Clemente the year before, and Buzzie Bavasi was not about to let that happen twice. I hit against Sandy in batting practice that year and he was all over the cage, another wild fastballing left-hander. He was a Jewish kid from Brooklyn who already had plenty of fans when he joined us. He was strong—6-2 and 210 pounds—and as serious and quiet as he was conscientious. He had some of the same problems I had a few years before. He tried too hard and worried too much. He knew he was walking too many hitters, and those walks were eating away at him the way strikeouts used to eat away at me. He kept struggling to become consistent, but the fans didn't help much, especially after we moved to Los Angeles in 1958. The people in the Coliseum booed him unmercifully, but eventually, when he learned to relax and stop squeezing the ball, he turned those boos into standing ovations.

As big as Sandy was, Drysdale was bigger, 6-5. He and Sandy were born only seven months apart on opposite coasts. Drysdale was another California product, from Van Nuys. But the 3,000 miles between their birthplaces wasn't the only difference between them. Drysdale was a fierce competitor, a lot like Jackie Robinson. He didn't want to hear the word lose. And he was perfectly willing to move the hitter away from the plate with a well-aimed inside pitch. If the situation suggested it, he didn't mind hitting the batter.

Big D used to walk up to Mickey Mantle before a World Series game, pinch him around the ribs or on the hip, and say, "Well, Mick, where would you like one today?" Once Alston signaled from the bench to Drysdale to walk the next batter intentionally—Frank Robinson. Don went one better. He hit him with the first pitch. He said later, "I figured why waste three pitches?"

Between the two of them they pitched 26 years, and won 374 games. Sandy won the Cy Young Award as the National League's best pitcher three times and Don once, and they did all these things only for the Dodgers. Neither of them ever played for another major-league team.

Our strong team commitment shows up in the long list of men who spent their entire careers with the Dodgers. I spent 16 of my 18 years in the major leagues with them, and Koufax, Drysdale, Robinson, Reese, Furillo, Campanella, Gilliam, and Erskine—and many others before or since—spent their entire major-league careers with the Dodgers.

I got into more hot water in 1956 with an article in *Collier's* magazine written by Roger Kahn and me. Roger wrote it for both of us, after a conversation we had one night about the price you pay to be a major-league baseball player. I mentioned the long periods away from your family, the expense of maintaining two homes, and some of the other negatives, but I wasn't complaining about my life as a major-leaguer.

Kahn said we could both make some money if he wrote an article on the subject under a double byline. I said okay, as long as it didn't sound as if I were complaining. Kahn wrote the story, and I don't remember seeing it until it appeared in *Collier's* under a big headline that said:

I PLAY BASEBALL FOR MONEY, NOT FUN

That's a catchy headline, and the truth is, of course, all

professional athletes play their sport for money. That's why we're called professionals. But we also happen to enjoy our jobs, and I enjoyed mine as much as anyone. However, that's not the way the story came across—especially when Kahn wrote that I didn't care if I never played another game.

That one sentence caused me more controversy than anything ever attributed to me, even more than my blast at the Brooklyn fans the year before. The article was seen by the whole nation, and the response came from all over. I never said it, and I certainly never felt that way. Baseball has always been the great love of my life, next to my family. What the heck, we were the World Champions, and we were winning another pennant too. Baseball was plenty of fun in 1956, despite what Kahn wrote in that article.

Another article that appeared two months later kept the pot boiling. This time, instead of blasting the fans, I blasted my teammates—or at least some of them. We were struggling as a team, losing a lot of close games, when some criticisms of Walter Alston's managing started showing up in the papers, always attributed to unnamed players on the team. That's the part that really frosted me, so I let loose one morning in Cincinnati over breakfast with Dick Young of the *Daily News*.

Dick wrote an article for the next day's paper with a headline that said:

DUKE RAPS FLOCK SNIPERS
FOR CRITICISM OF ALSTON

The first paragraph read: "Duke Snider took a swing at teammates who make criticism of manager Walt Alston without the courage to have their names mentioned, and at the sportswriters who use the anonymous quotes." He said I made the comments "for the benefit of a dozen or more surrounding players and newsmen in the hotel dining room."

173

He was right. I fired one of my better shots. "If a fellow has something to say," I told Dick, "let him allow his name to be used in the papers. I'm getting a little sick of this 'unnamed player' business. Whenever I pop off, I always see my name in the papers. I'd like to see who some of these other guys are."

What started the latest flap was a story a few days before that Alston had chewed us out in a clubhouse meeting and said some of us were choking up under pressure. Certain "unnamed players" told reporters about the meeting.

Young talked to Pee Wee and Carl Erskine about my comments, and they told him the same thing. They both said the criticisms were unfair, and even more so when the players doing the criticizing would not let themselves be identified.

Reese said: "It's just not fair. How can guys blame Alston when most of us are hitting .240?" Besides, Alston's criticisms of us were not only justified, they were mild by comparison. "I've heard worse from Durocher and Dressen," Pee Wee said. "They put on some shows in the clubhouse that make Alston look like a lamb."

My roomie told Young, "I don't think it's right. I think Alston is taking a bum rap. Sure, he got mad and chewed us out, but what's that got to do with his managing? He's not losing the games; we are. We've been lousy. I've been lousy. My record is six-and-six right now, and I can't think of a thing Alston could have done to have changed it." And that was from a man whose arm hurt on every pitch he threw.

Carl predicted that the players' use of anonymity in criticizing their manager would pull most of the team together and the Dodgers would start winning again. That's exactly what happened. We regained our balance in time to beat out the Milwaukee Braves by one game and the Cincinnati Reds by two and win the National League pennant again, our sixth pennant in ten years. You didn't have to be a genius to figure out who our opponents would be in the World Series.

*   *   *

The book on losing close games wasn't closed, though. One more thing happened in Cincinnati. We had just dropped another close one, in 12 innings, and as we came off the field a fan ran up to me and started mouthing off about how I was choking under the pressure of the pennant race. He wasn't even supposed to be on the field in the first place—it's a violation of National League rules. But when he accused me of choking up, I gave him my opinion, complete with some choice profanity. He took offense to my response and took a swing at me. He missed—but I didn't. I still had my glove rolled in my left hand, and I hit him a pretty good one in the jaw. That did shut him up, but it wasn't the end of it. Carl Furillo said he would be glad to speak up for me if we ended up in court, and even the Cincinnati manager, Birdie Tebbetts, said he would, too.

I went into the clubhouse, threw a chair into the shower in a rage, and then saw two police officers walk into the room. They told me to go straight to the hotel, stay there until morning, and then appear in court for a 9 A.M. hearing.

When the fan stood up in front of the judge, I had to question my own actions of the night before. The guy was six feet, six inches tall. If I had noticed that, I never would have swung at him. The judge heard both sides of the story and then said, "Well, I don't think this is anything serious. Why don't you two gentlemen just shake hands and forget the whole thing?"

I said, "That's fine with me."

The fan wasn't satisfied. "What about my dental bridge?" he asked. "He broke my bridge."

The judge quickly said, "I'm no dentist. Case dismissed."

The fan at least got his day in court. That's more than another Cincinnati fan accomplished. A woman sued me for $70,000 after a foul ball broke her wrist. I hadn't hit the foul ball anyhow. It was Bobby Adams, a Cincinnati player. Some people will try anything.

*　　*　　*

The National League season ended on a sweet note. We had to beat the Pirates in the last game to win the pennant, and we didn't waste any time. Gilliam led off the first inning with a walk and Pee Wee moved him to third with a hit-and-run single. Two men on, nobody out, first inning, a good pitcher—Vernon Law—on the mound. But it didn't make any difference who the pitcher was. The Dodgers were not going to be beaten. I hit Law's first pitch into the center-field stands. Dodgers 3, Pirates 0, still no outs in the first inning. I hit another homer later in the game, off Ron Kline, my 43rd of the season, the fourth straight year I had hit 40 or more home runs. Branch Rickey was the head of the Pirates then. He saw his batting lessons of 1948 paying off for me, against his team. We won the game and the pennant, 8-6.

Despite all the ups and downs, we repeated as National League champions and I had another satisfying season. The strikeouts were still a problem. I struck out over 100 times—101—for the first time in my career. But the good news was I led the leagues in walks with 99, something Mr. Rickey must have been pleased about. My batting average dipped to .292, but I led the league in slugging average and home runs, finished second in home-run percentage and runs scored, third in doubles, fourth in runs batted in, and second in total bases behind Hank Aaron.

As satisfying as that season was for me, Don Newcombe must have felt more satisfaction than I did. He won more games than anyone else in the league—27—against only seven losses. He had the highest won-lost percentage in the league and was among the leaders in earned-run average, complete games, fewest hits per nine innings, shutouts, and fewest walks per nine innings. He topped it off by winning both the Cy Young Award as the best pitcher and the Most Valuable Player Award. Only six other pitchers have won both awards in the same season. It was a banner year for Big Newk, the one I called "Tiger," but 1956 wouldn't be finished for Don Newcombe, not even when the World Series ended.

Our pitchers not only helped us to another pennant, they did it with style. Carl Erskine and Sal Maglie, who had come over from the Indians in May, both pitched no-hitters, the only ones in the National League that year. Carl had the added pleasure of pitching his masterpiece—his second—against our rivals, the Giants, and Maglie pitched his against the Phillies.

Erskine's had a special taste of sweetness. Carl's arm was bothering him even more than usual. In Chicago near the end of a road trip, the Cubs' trainer and physician gave him his first two shots of procaine and cortisone in his right shoulder. When he came back to the Hilton, I told him Zimmer, Labine, and I were going bowling and we wanted him to come along.

"I can't," he said. "My arm's killing me."

I said, "Come on. You can't hurt that arm any worse than it is already."

So he came with us and everyone had a great time at the alleys, but Carl spent an excruciating next two days coping with the soreness caused by both his injury and the two shots. We returned to Brooklyn for a series against the Giants, and on our way to Ebbets Field, Carl picked up a copy of the morning paper, which is sometimes a mistake, especially if you're the starting pitcher.

When he turned to the sports page, he saw a story quoting the Giants' chief scout, Tom Sheehan, as saying the Dodgers were an over-the-hill ball club with injuries and the aging process catching up with some of our big guns. Then he reads Sheehan's evaluation about himself: "Erskine is supposed to be their best starter but he can't win with that garbage he's throwing up there." That really angered Carl, and what made it especially hard to take was that it was true.

Carl's arm and shoulder were so painful that he almost told Alston he couldn't pitch that day, which would have been a first for him, but he had never asked out of an assignment in his whole

177

career, and he wasn't about to sit it out after reading what Sheehan said.

Alston gave him a new ball to warm up with and Carl got loose, as much as he could. After warming up he told me he felt bad about the fans paying their hard-earned money to see him pitch. Then, for the first time in his career, he said a little silent prayer on the bench. He said later he asked God to take over and get him through the afternoon. He must have had a good connection—after six innings he was throwing a no-hitter—but Al Worthington, the Giants' pitcher, was almost as tough, and the game was a scoreless tie. After every inning, Carl was more amazed than the inning before. His arm hurt just as much, but he was getting people out, one inning at a time, one out at a time, one pitch at a time.

We didn't say anything on the bench because you're always afraid of jinxing a pitcher going for a no-hitter. But after the eighth inning some leather-lunged fan near our dugout bellowed out to Carl as he was coming off the field, "Hey, Oisk Baby! You got a no-hitter! Way to go, Oisk!"

Nothing could bother Carl that day. We had managed to take the lead, and as he sat on the bench while we hit in the bottom half of the eighth, Carl had this sensation. He just knew he was going to pitch a no-hitter. He told me later God seemed to be saying, "Well you asked for help. What did you expect?"

He was so sure that he would get his second no-hitter he started working out in his mind what he was going to say to the reporters after the game, but the ninth inning provided a scare.

Erskine had broken the webbing of his glove in the eighth inning, and he borrowed Don Bessent's glove for the ninth inning because Don used the same model. With one out, Whitey Lockman pulled a long drive down the right-field line and up against the screen just barely foul. On the next pitch he hit a comebacker, a low one-hopper back to the pitcher. Erskine was always an outstanding fielder, and he got his glove down fast, but when he brought the glove up, there was no baseball in it. The ball had been hit hard, but Carl had reacted so quickly he had pinned the ball to the ground with the back of his glove. He threw Lockman out. I never saw that again in my whole career. The ball was sitting there on the pitcher's mound just like an Easter egg. Two outs. One out away from his second no-hitter.

Then Alvin Dark did the same thing, another one-hopper. Carl turned to throw to first and Gil Hodges was giving him the take-it-slow sign as he hurried to the bag for Carl's throw. Carl meanwhile is standing on the mound and telling himself, "Don't throw it away. Step and throw. It's just step and throw."

After he stepped and threw, he was mobbed, as expected, but Carl had the quickness to notice something else as he walked off the mound. He saw Jackie Robinson, who was playing third base for us, go over to the box reserved for the Giants' owners. Tom Sheehan was sitting there, maybe reconsidering what he had said in the paper that morning about Carl.

Jackie had seen the article too, and there had been some discussion about it in the clubhouse before the game. Jackie went up to the short fence separating the box seats from the field and reached into his back pocket. He pulled out a copy of the article, with its reference to Erskine's "garbage." He had kept it on him all day during the game, ready for this moment.

He shoved it in front of Sheehan and said, "How do you like *that* garbage?"

It was a satisfying pennant. But our team was getting older, and we knew it. Jackie, Pee Wee, and Skoonj were all 34. Campy would turn 36 right after the World Series. Gil was 32. I was the lucky one. I turned 29 in September. I was able to play in the most games of my career—151—but I was paying a certain price. My knee bothered me most of the year, the aftermath of my injury when my spikes got snagged in Gene Baker's uniform years before. I was playing, and I got 542 at-bats, but I was hurting from time to time.

We had another victory party, this one at the Lexington Hotel in New York. There was a vast array of food and drinks, and when each player and his wife entered the room, the band played an appropriate song—"Back Home Again in Indiana" for Erskine, "California, Here I Come" for me, "My Old Kentucky Home" for Pee Wee, "The Pennsylvania Polka" for Furillo. When Maglie entered, the band struck up an Italian melody—it might have been "Arrivederci, Roma"—and Maglie swept his wife straight onto the dance floor.

We were having such a good time we called Buzzie at home and told him to join us. He did and he was delighted to share our fun. When he left, he announced to the crowd, "This party will be on the ball club."

Half the room hollered back, "It already is."

Before the World Series started, with the Yankees searching for revenge, I got my usual batch of good-luck messages. One was a telegram from my minister back in California.

ENLARGE YOUR ON-DECK CIRCLE TO INCLUDE YOUR PRAYING PARSON. YOUR PLAYING NEEDS MY PRAYING AND MY PRAYING NEEDS YOUR PLAYING. SO YOU KILL 'EM AND I'LL BURY 'EM.

REV. JIM ROBERTS

President Eisenhower helped us at the start of the season and at the end too. On Opening Day he gave us our 1955 championship rings. Then he returned to Ebbets Field in October with his Secretary of State, John Foster Dulles. It was a tense time for the world. Russia had invaded Hungary that year. Nasser had shut down the Suez Canal, and the world held its breath during "the Suez Crisis" hoping we weren't on the brink of another major war. Eisenhower had had his heart attack the year before, but had recovered and was running for a second term against Adlai Stevenson. He was winning our vote by bringing us good luck. We beat the Yankees in the first two games.

Maglie, our new friend, went the distance in the first game and we beat Whitey Ford. Gil hit two homers, including a three-run shot that broke a 2-2 tie, and Jackie, who would be playing in his last World Series, hit one too. The second game was an endurance contest which we won, 13-8. It lasted three hours and 26 minutes, the longest nine inning game in Series history at that time. The Yankees scored a run in the first and five more in the second, but we came right back with six of our own in the bottom of the second and knocked Don Larsen out of the game but not out of the Series, as the whole world would discover three games later. I hit a three-run homer in that inning, and the Yankees eventually used seven pitchers, including three in the bottom of the second. We were on our way to a second straight year of beating the Yankees in the World Series—or so we thought.

Enos Slaughter hit a three-run shot to win the third game for the Yankees, and they won the fourth too, even though Carl pitched respectably for us. He had to leave after four innings, though, with New York winning, 3-1. Ed Roebuck gave up another run and Don Drysdale gave up two more and the Yanks won, 6-2, and evened the Series. Then we were hit by history.

In the fifth game, Don Larsen defeated us with his perfect game, 97 pitches, the only no-hitter in World Series history, and he went one better than that by not allowing anybody to reach base in any manner. No hits, no walks, no errors, no hit batters, no nothing. We had an idea about the no-hitter, but we didn't realize it was a perfect game until about the seventh inning when somebody on the bench said quietly, "Hey you know, we haven't even had a base runner."

We were as shocked as anyone else by the perfect game, but we were shocked even more that it was Larsen who did it. We found him very hittable in that second game, and we thought we would do the same in this game. He was never an overpowering pitcher, and he certainly didn't have an outstanding career. I'm not taking anything away from the man, but he wasn't even a .500 pitcher, and he was traded six times.

181

When he pitched the perfect game against us, he set clean living back a whole generation. Larsen was known to enjoy the bright lights and certain liquid refreshments, and he admitted to the press and the rest of the world after the game that he had not followed the conventional training rules the night before. He named about eight different drinks to reporters as his intake during his nocturnal travels, without specifying the number of each. Mickey Mantle has written that Larsen showed up at Yankee Stadium for the game with liquor on his breath and that "he came to the ball park that day feeling pretty good."

Whatever his night life, Larsen was invincible that day, using that no-windup delivery he popularized. Still, as with all great achievements, fate seemed to smile on Larsen on that October afternoon. We hit some pretty good shots off him. I hit one out of the ball park, foul by plenty, and I hit a line drive which Hank Bauer caught at his knees. Amoros hit one out that was foul by only three or four feet. Jackie hit a ground smash that bounced off Andy Carey's ankle and rolled to McDougald. Mantle made an excellent over-the-shoulder catch of a ball hit by Gil Hodges which went 430 feet to left center. Mantle hit a home run to help Larsen even more.

The final score was 2-0. The Dodgers gave Larsen all the credit in the world, and we still do. He was the greatest pitcher in the history of the sport that day. And let's give Sal Maglie some credit too. He pitched a five-hitter for us, only to lose to a guy who pitched a perfect game.

Babe Pinelli helped Larsen on the last out. He called Dale Mitchell out on a pitch low and away. It might not have made any difference, but it was a bad call. It was a historic call for more than one reason. Pinelli, after a long career, retired after that season. It was his last game behind the plate, and the last strike he ever called.

You'd think that would have drained all the life out of us, but it

182

says something about the Brooklyn Dodgers that we came back the next day and won a ten-inning game in Ebbets Field, 1-0. It also says something about Jackie Robinson, our aging star—he drove in the only run of the game with a single in the tenth inning. Bob Turley and Clem Labine fought each other in one of the best-pitched games in World Series history, the day after the only no-hitter in Series history. That's a whole lot of pitching in two days.

The Yankees ganged up on us in the seventh game to prevent us from defeating them in the World Series two years in a row. Johnny Kucks held us to three hits, Yogi Berra hit two home runs, and Bill Skowron hit a grand slam. The Yankees whipped us, 9-0. That's the forfeit score in baseball, so we wouldn't have lost by any more if we had just stayed home. I got two singles, two of our three hits. In the parking lot after the game, an attendant mouthed off to Newk, and Newk slugged him.

Newcombe, with all his success in winning 149 games in ten years, being a 20-game winner three times and being voted the Most Valuable Player and the best pitcher, never won a World Series game. He made five starts, two in 1949 and 1956 and one in 1955, but never won one. He got the "can't-win-the-big-one" label hung on him because of his Series record of no wins and four losses, and it was a bum rap. Newk won plenty of big ones for us. He won 20 games for us in 1951, and pitched eight outstanding innings in the final playoff game when Thomson hit his homer. If our team had hit better in September, if any one of us had won just one more game with his bat, there wouldn't have been a playoff with the Giants. That wasn't Newk's fault. In 1955 and 1956 he led the National League in won-lost percentage when he won a total of 47 games. Any time a pitcher is a 27-game winner, which Newk was in '56, and your team wins the pennant by only one game, you can bet he won a lot of "big ones." And it certainly wasn't his fault he didn't win the 1-0 game against Allie Reynolds in the first game of the '49 Series.

We simply did not hit in the '56 Series. Our team batting

average was .195, and you're not going to win anything with a team average that sounds more like the price of a pair of socks. Gil and I led the Dodgers, each with a .304 average, but the closest guys to us were Jackie with .250 and Skoonj at .240. Even with averages that puny, we extended the Series to the full seven games. That's how close the Dodgers and the Yankees were in those years.

Deep down, however, we knew we were getting old. Too many of the players who were the nucleus of our team for the previous ten years were showing aging signs at the same time. Athletes, like every other group of people, vary greatly where the aging process is concerned. Some grow older sooner and faster than others. As an athlete, a certain time comes in your career when you stop being the type of player you were. You don't know when it's going to happen, but sooner or later you stop being the dominating force you used to be. When that happens you're on the other side of the mountain. That's where we were as a team. Jackie was thinking about retiring. Campy was looking at his 36th birthday. Furillo's legs were beginning to bother him. My knee was hurting more often. Erskine's pitching pains were worse.

It had been a long and grueling year, and every day of it carried the added burden defending champions always feel. We played 30 exhibition games in spring training, 154 regular season games, seven World Series games, and the All-Star Game, nearly 200 games. It was time to go home and collapse for a while. Or was it?

Some of the major-league teams were making barnstorming tours in Japan. The Yankees had done it the year before, and Walter O'Malley wanted the Dodgers to take the same kind of tour in '56. Mr. O'Malley always anticipated the future. Two years later, he masterminded the move of the Dodgers and the Giants to California, the first time in history major-league baseball moved west of St. Louis. I suspect the same kind of vision prompted him to schedule our 1956 postseason tour of Japan. I'm sure he wanted all of us to have a good time, including himself, but I also think he was anticipating the possibility of international baseball, and he wanted to know as much about the Japanese potential for major-league baseball as he could, and before anyone else.

Several of us wanted to duck the trip. Pee Wee didn't want to go because he and Dottie were expecting a child. Furillo didn't want to go, and he didn't. Rube Walker didn't go. Gil didn't want to go, and neither did I. Newk didn't want to go; he didn't like flying anyway. As far as we were concerned, we had played enough baseball for one year. We were disappointed about losing the Series to the Yankees, especially after winning the first two games, and we didn't want any part of a baseball trip to Japan or the moon or anywhere else. Pee Wee and I took our case to Buzzie, but Mr. O'Malley wouldn't hear of it. We were going. We were the last two players to get our shots.

Newcombe's luck continued. He lost a game at Hickam Air Force Base in Hawaii on our way over, the first time a major-league team had ever lost there. Then we flew on to Japan, lost our opening game there, and achieved another first—the first American team to lose to a Japanese team.

Mr. O'Malley talked to the team before that first game in Japan. He said he wanted us to be goodwill ambassadors for our country and for our sport. He wanted us to behave well and to be nice to the Japanese people.

We won the second game, and then Newk got the assignment for the third game. He still had a bug in his craw about losing the seventh game of the World Series, and losing to the American GIs in Hawaii hadn't improved his state of mind any, so he told Alston before his start, "Skip, if I can't get these guys out, I'm not going to throw another pitch the rest of this trip."

The first seven Japanese players got base hits. Alston finally had to go to the mound, motioning for a relief pitcher from the bullpen on his way. When he got to the mound, Newcombe took his glove off, folded it lengthwise, jammed it in his back pocket, and said to Alston, "That's it, Skip. I ain't throwin' another pitch."

185

And he didn't. He was in uniform for every game but by the end of the trip, he looked like the Goodyear blimp. He had gained so much weight that we just had to stick him on the scales at the airport. In three weeks he had gained about 30 pounds.

Newcombe's frame of mind wasn't any worse than mine. I'd never wanted to go to Japan in the first place, and I made up my mind when I got there that I wasn't going to have a good time—and nobody could make me change my mind. I was rude and mean to a lot of people, including Bev.

Things reached a peak one night in Tokyo. I had promised to take Bev out to dinner with a few other couples, followed by a special evening on the town. During the meal I asked Bev about my bidding of a bridge hand that afternoon in a game among us players. I had gone set. She didn't agree with my play because she always played strictly by the book and in this hand I hadn't followed the book. We proceeded to debate my play until she finally got up and left.

She waited for me in the lobby, talking to Don Drysdale while I sat in the dining room with my mouth hanging open. When I came out to the lobby, Bev knew there would be no special evening. Back in the room, she started to throw some aspirin down in her anger, but then she picked up a bottle of V.O. liquor and let fire right into the bathroom, where I was brushing my teeth. POW! I'm sure you could hear the explosion all up and down the corridor. We reconciled only long enough to clean up the mess.

The next day some of the others were joking with Bev and me about hiding their booze. Bev couldn't understand what they were talking about, until I explained they were referring to the explosion that came from our room the night before. "The walls are paper-thin," I said. "Newcombe's room is next door, and he heard the whole thing."

As the trip continued, the players were on one schedule and family members were on another. The two groups met here and there, and when we did, Bev and I pretended we were happy, but we were still upset with each other. In Nagasaki, I got to our hotel first and wrote her a note apologizing for my actions. While I was in the shower, she came into the room and found my note. The air was finally cleared, and we were both able to enjoy the rest of the trip.

I'm glad Bev took home movies of the trip. That's how I got to see what I had missed.

After Newcombe's game gave us our second loss in the first three games of our trip, Mr. O'Malley spoke to the team in the clubhouse before the next game. It was a classic in getting your point across.

"Fellas," he said, "it occurs to me that some of you may have misunderstood my remarks before our first game over here. I want you to be goodwill ambassadors, yes, and I want you to be nice to the Japanese people when you're out in public, yes. But when you put your uniform on and its says Dodgers across your shirt and you go out onto that field, I want you to remember Pearl Harbor."

We played 20 games after that, and we never lost another one.

Mr. O'Malley had to pay a certain price for our improved performances. A group of us ran up a big bar bill one night, and Pee Wee signed O'Malley's name to the check. The next morning, as our team bus was leaving the hotel, the desk clerk came running out waving his arms in the air. He got on the bus and told Mr. O'Malley there was a late charge that had to be added to his bill.

O'Malley said he hadn't charged anything, but when he looked at the bill he knew what the answer was. "Well," he said, as he signed for several hundred more dollars, "it looks as if I certainly had a good time last night."

There was a tradition in Japan at that time which called for a player to take himself out of a game if he made a mistake. He had embarrassed his country and must leave the field. But the tradition applied to an extent that surprised us. Gino Cimoli hit a fierce line drive up the middle in one game and the ball hit the pitcher squarely in the head. The ball was hit so hard it bounced off the pitcher and rolled all the way into the right-field corner. Gino got a triple out of it.

The pitcher staggered around the middle of the infield wondering what happened—and then suddenly walked off the field, upholding the tradition. He had embarrassed his homeland. Another pitcher was ready. Because of the tradition, the Japanese team always had a couple of players warmed up and ready to enter the game.

Pee Wee thought the Japanese hitters would have trouble with slow stuff, so he suggested to Carl in one game that he go to his change-up. Carl did, and he almost got another no-hitter. He pitched a one-hitter and faced the minimum 27 batters.

By the day of the last game I was enjoying myself more, and I wanted to leave something for the Japanese youngsters. We were playing in Osaka, and in the ninth inning I took my cap off and put it near me in right field, where I was playing that day. I motioned to the fans in the stands that they could have it, but to wait. I wanted the game to end before they came charging onto the field for some souvenirs.

Then I took off my uniform shirt and put it a few feet away. Then I dropped my glove in a third spot. I put my shoes somewhere else. I kept leaving various items in different spots around right field. If the ball had been hit to me, I would have been defenseless. Immediately after the final out of the tour, the fans poured out of the right-field stands and gobbled everything up in a flash. The Duke Snider yard sale, all items free, was over in 15 seconds.

Two contrasting developments took place at this point in

Dodger history. On the day we won the 1956 pennant, Walter O'Malley told the fans of Brooklyn, "The time seems propitious to report that real progress is now being made to get a new stadium, worthy of our team, our community, and our fans." He had been expressing concern for several years about our aging but beloved Ebbets Field and the limited parking around it. He wanted a new stadium in Brooklyn, and was suggesting a domed stadium, many years before they built the Houston Astrodome.

However, less than a month later, while we were still touring Japan, the players began hearing rumors that the Dodgers might not get that stadium in Brooklyn, and Mr. O'Malley might move the team to Los Angeles, my hometown. I wasn't happy over that prospect. It would be convenient to play in southern California, but I much preferred to stay in Brooklyn. In our natural life Bev and I were born in Los Angeles, but in our baseball life, we were born in Brooklyn. That was our baseball home, and we didn't want to leave.

The second development came during the 1957 spring training camp at Vero Beach. Mr. O'Malley announced the Dodgers were buying the Los Angeles Angels, my boyhood team in the Pacific Coast League, and their ball park, Wrigley Field, for $3,250,000.

Suddenly all of us—fans, players, reporters, and everyone else— began waiting for the second shoe to drop.

"There Used To Be A Ball Park Right Here"

We knew as soon as we got to Vero Beach for spring training in 1957 that it was going to be a different kind of a year, and not necessarily better.

The first thing we noticed was the absence of Jackie Robinson. He'd retired shortly after the '56 season. The Dodgers had traded him to the Giants, which was like being traded from Macy's to Gimbel's, and Jackie decided to hang up his spikes. The feeling has always been that Jackie retired rather than play for our crosstown rivals, but Buzzie Bavasi still questions that. He's told me that Jackie came out with a story in *Look* magazine about his retirement a few days after announcing his decision. Knowing that magazines need more than a few days to publish a story, Buzzie suspects Jackie had made up his mind to retire before the Dodgers traded him and had sold the story to *Look* in advance.

But whatever Jackie's reasons were, he wasn't there any more. The Brooklyn Dodgers without Jackie Robinson were an engine without one of its biggest spark plugs. Our flaming competitor was gone, and the team that had won four pennants in the previous five years finished the 1957 season in third, 11 games behind the Milwaukee Braves and three games in back of the Cardinals.

Jackie was 38 years old when he retired. He was old for a rookie, 28, when Mr. Rickey brought him to the major leagues, and he defied Father Time enough to get in ten outstanding years as a Brooklyn Dodger. He left the game with a lifetime batting average of .311. His World Series stats tell you something: He ranks eighth in doubles, ninth in runs scored, and eighth in walks. More than any of those stats, however, one other stands out: In his ten years as a Dodger, the team won six pennants. The hero of my youth could win anywhere, on the junior college fields of southern California, where I first saw him, or on the baseball fields of the major-league stadiums, where I played with him for his entire career. He was elected to the Hall of Fame as soon as he was eligible in 1962. Nobody asked what color he was.

One of the few bright spots about 1957 was that Don Drysdale— Big D—came into his own as a successful major-league pitcher with 17 wins. Koufax was still struggling to find himself, but Don was among the leaders in wins, earned-run average, strikeouts, and shutouts. It's a good thing that he, Newk, Podres, and Clem Labine were pitching as well as they were. Podres led the league in earned-run average and shutouts, Labine had the most saves, and Newk had the fewest walks per nine innings.

The reason we didn't repeat as champions, in addition to Jackie's retirement, was that we didn't hit any better than we had in the World Series the year before. Fortunately, I tied Ralph Kiner's record of 40 or more home runs for five straight years. I'm told the only other player to do that besides Kiner is Babe Ruth. I finished third in homers, fourth in slugging average, and led the league in home-run percentage. But the strikeouts were more of a problem than ever, at least in number, with 104, more than any other hitter in the league. And my average dropped to .274 from .292 in 1956. As a team we had the lowest batting average of any of the four first-division teams and the lowest number of runs. Furillo was still a respected hitter. He finished with .306, and Gil hit .299, but two of our biggest bats—Pee Wee and Campy—hit only .224 and .242 in that order. We weren't the feared top-to-bottom scoring machine we had been. Third place was never acceptable to the Brooklyn Dodgers, but in 1957 it happened.

With Drysdale's arrival as a prominent pitcher, we picked up a bright new personality. He never backed away from anything on the field, and he never backed away from a good time off the field. He is so competitive in everything he does that he even got on me during the first fantasy camp the Dodgers ever held, a few years ago in Vero Beach.

These are the camps, usually a week long, where guys in their 40s and 50s get to live out the fantasy of their youth—to be a big-league baseball player. They go to spring training for a week, work out every day, play games, wear the team uniform, the works. In this first camp, Drysdale was managing a team, and I was umpiring the game by myself. In the first inning, Drysdale's team was jumping all over the other guys. The Drysdales had scored 11 runs when Double-D calls out to me from the third-base coach's box, "Hey, Dookie," and he starts laughing up his sleeve. His next hitter kept the laffer going with a triple to score two more runs. We weren't going to get that game over before Christmas at that rate.

I told the opposing pitcher to make the appeal at first base, where a member of the team in the field tags the bag and appeals to the umpire that the runner missed the bag. When the pitcher made the appeal, I called the runner out.

The runner, the guy who was so happy about his triple, was in shock. He said, "Duke, I tagged that bag. I stepped right on the middle of it."

I said, "You're supposed to tag the inside corner. The runner is out."

Drysdale knew what I was doing. Somebody had to end that inning or we'd be there forever. Besides, the other team wasn't having any fun, and a fantasy camp, just as the name implies, is supposed to be fun for everybody.

My little trick not only stopped Drysdale's team from scoring any more in the first inning, it stopped his guys from scoring any more period. The other team, behind 11-0 in the first inning, began chipping away at the deficit. By the middle innings a frightening thought began to occur to me: "You don't suppose. . . . Nah."

Well, it happened. The other team closed the gap, started another rally in the last inning, and then needed only a base hit to climax a fantastic comeback and beat Don's team. I was keeping my fingers crossed, and holding my breath. I thought, "If Drysdale's team loses this game after what I did to him in the first inning, he's going to kill me—and he's big enough and mad enough to do it."

You guessed it. The hitter sent what the ball players call a "flare," a little blooper, just behind first base and down the right-field line, the other team scores two runs and Drysdale's team loses, 12-11.

As we're coming off the field after a game that's supposed to be fun for everybody, Drysdale is seething. He walks past me and growls, "Too bad they don't have a line in the box score for 'losing umpire.'"

At dinner that night, Double-D went public. He told the crowd what I had done, and I apologized, explaining that I thought my decision in that first inning was in the best interest of all concerned. I'll say this, though: The guy who hit that triple sure learned how to hit the bag.

Drysdale sizzled after every defeat. Fantasy camp, training camp, National League season, World Series, All-Star games—it never made any difference. He could not tolerate losing, and he didn't want anyone on his team to tolerate it either. He made a unique suggestion once, a few years after I retired. He went to the cooler in the locker room after a game and noticed all the beer was still there, but the soft drinks were gone, just the opposite of what you'd find with the Dodgers of the 1940s and '50s.

He kicked the cooler and exploded, "That's another thing that's wrong with this ball club—we got too damn many milkshake drinkers! If you guys want to start winning, you better start drinking something with foam on top!"

He could handle his own in that department too. He drank some, so did I, and so did most of the rest. But we knew enough to be sensible about it.

His competitiveness showed up on a Saturday afternoon in San Francisco after Don had just beaten the Giants. He was so pumped up he had eight or so drinks—V.O. and water—with the same ice cubes. I told him he had made the Guinness Book of World Records.

Don Newcombe, who admits he developed serious alcohol problems in his later years as a player, once said that all but three or four guys on our team were heavy drinkers. That's wrong, and Campy, his old roomie, told him so. Carl didn't drink at all, and neither did Jackie. Some guys might overdo it once in a while, like the nights after we won a pennant, or in '55, when we won our first World Series. But to say that 20 players on the Dodgers were heavy drinkers is just not true.

Drysdale and I even had some fun after I left the Dodgers in the

195

spring of '63. We had appeared for seven weeks during the winter in a nightclub act with Milton Berle—Drysdale, Sandy, Willie Davis, Frank Howard, Maury Wills, and me. We did a 20-minute routine on stage at the Desert Inn in Las Vegas for five weeks, two shows a night. Then we played the Fountainbleau Hotel in Miami for two more weeks before starting spring training. We sang a parody of "Oklahoma!" poking fun at ourselves. Don sang a solo, Maury played the banjo, Willie did a little soft-shoe, and we did the whole routine in our Dodger uniforms.

We were always pulling stunts on Berle, because he was so good about taking a joke. We topped ourselves the night we loaded up his harmonica with Tabasco sauce. Berle grabbed it at the usual point in his act, stuck it in his mouth as he always did, and his eyes almost popped out of his head. He was a game guy, though. He finished the act, in the best tradition of show biz. The second it was over he dashed off stage yelling, "Quick! Get a doctor!" Then he saw us peeking around the corner and he yelled, "I'll get you Nazis!"

At the start of the '63 season, right after our nightclub act, I was sold to the Mets, so here I was hitting against Don in Dodger Stadium and Berle is there, in a box seat along the first-base line. While I was in the on-deck circle, Milton hollered at me, "The Nazi is going to get you!"

I said, "I'll probably hit one out of the park."

He said, "No way."

Well good ol' Don threw me a fat pitch, a real cookie, and I hit it out.

As I'm trotting to the dugout after my homer, Berle screams from the box seats, "Fix! Fix!"

My knee got worse during the 1957 season. I started only 139 games that year, the least of my career and 14 fewer than the year before, and the knee was the reason. Something had to be done.

Buzzie retained a respected surgeon, Dr. Daniel Levinthal of Beverly Hills, who performed the surgery a week before Christmas to repair the damage from three injuries. He didn't say I had an unlimited future, or that I would be as good as new, but he at least gave me a chance to play a few more years and to play in less pain than before.

The pain that hurt the most, though, was the heartache all of us felt when Red Patterson, the PR man for the Dodgers, announced on October 8 that the Dodgers were moving to Los Angeles. The City Council was giving Mr. O'Malley 300 acres of choice land called Chavez Ravine, in return for Wrigley Field's 10 acres. While they were building the new Dodger stadium, we would be playing our games in the Los Angeles Coliseum, a football stadium built to host the 1932 Summer Olympics. It may have been a good stadium for football and the Olympics, but for baseball it was a freak, as we were to discover on the first day of the 1958 season.

The gloom over our fate began to settle over us during the final weeks of the '57 season. It hadn't been made official yet, but it was an open secret that the Dodgers were moving to California. O'Malley had thought of everything. He convinced the Giants and their owner, Horace Stoneham, to move to California with him, eliminating the problem of excessive travel expenses for teams traveling to the West Coast to play in only one city. Stoneham's Giants would move to San Francisco.

As the word got around, the thought of leaving Brooklyn bothered us more and more. Bev and I had spent our first 11 summers there. Kevin, Pam, and Kurt had started their young lives there just as much as they had in California during the winters. Our roots there weren't as deep as they were in California, but they were just as strong.

The people of Brooklyn had become more than just neighbors. They were like family, and the thought of leaving them was a sad one. We'd be leaving so many terrific people who meant so much to us, people we'd known and grown to love as long as I had been a Brooklyn Dodger.

The thought of leaving these people made us heartsick. No more Bay Ridge? No more McKinneys or Steiners or Barwoods or Baumans for neighbors? No more living close to the Erskines, Reeses, and Walkers? No more taking the subway into New York on Saturday night? No cop telling me he hates baseball while he gives me a speeding ticket? No more Vinnie's Meat Market for club steak when I'm in a slump? And no more "Duke of Flatbush"?

Worst of all, there would be no more Ebbets Field. No more Hilda and her cowbell. No more Sym-Phony playing Dixieland music. No more Happy Felton and his Knothole Gang, or Tex Rickart announcing that "a little boy has been found lost" or telling the fans along the bleacher railing to remove their clothes. No more fans screaming at us as "dem Bums" and calling my roommate "Oisk" and me "Dook."

It was sad for everyone, and I think for Mr. O'Malley, too. He had his roots in Brooklyn, deeper than most of us, but I'm sure he felt he had no choice—"cherce," the fans would say. In his mind, the Brooklyn Dodgers had to move—somewhere—to survive, and so we moved.

I hit a home run onto Bedford Avenue on the Sunday afternoon of our last weekend in Ebbets Field. It would be the last home run anyone ever hit there. After the game, I told Walt Alston I didn't want to play the next two-game series against Pittsburgh, the last two major-league games that would ever be played in Brooklyn. I'd hit a home run, not knowing it would be the last by anyone, and I wanted to remember that as my last Ebbets Field experience. I was being torn away from my baseball home, and I wanted to remember her that way. Walt understood.

A few years later, when they sent the wrecker's iron ball crashing into Ebbets Field, one of our friends, Barney Stein, a photographer in New York, sent Bev and me pictures of the event.

I saw the wall I used to aim at, the wall which Skoonj and I stood in front of and leaped against, with the familiar signs of GEM razor blades and Esquire Boot Polish and the clock I cleared for my first World Series home run in 1952, the one that said, "Bulova—official timepiece of the Brooklyn Dodgers."

Only the wall wasn't standing. In each picture, and in the ones of the grandstand and the bleachers, Ebbets Field was tumbling down under the impact of that big iron ball. I had worried about curveballs and fastballs and knuckleballs in that ball park, but never had I ever been worried with thoughts about a *wrecker's* ball. The good people of Brooklyn had lost their team. Now they had lost their last link to their Dodgers and to our past.

At home in California, 3,000 miles from what used to be Ebbets Field, Bev and I looked at those pictures from Barney Stein and cried.

Frank Sinatra sang for millions of Americans—the people of New York who lost Ebbets Field and the Polo Grounds, the people in Washington who lost Griffith Stadium, the people in Philadelphia who lost Shibe Park, the people in St. Louis who lost Sportsman's Park, the people in Cincinnati who lost Crosley Field, the people in Pittsburgh who lost Forbes Field, the people in Boston who lost Braves Field, and people anywhere who ever lost a ball park—when he recorded a song by Joe Raposo, a song both sweet and sad:

> There used to be a ball park
> Where the field was warm and green
> And the people played their crazy game
> With a joy I've never seen,
> And the air was such a wonder
> From the hot dogs and the beer.

199

Yes, there used to be a ball park
Right here.

Now the children try to find it
And they can't believe their eyes,
'Cause the old team just isn't playing
And the new team hardly tries,
And the sky has got so cloudy
When it used to be so clear
And the summer went so quickly this year.
Yes, there used to be a ball park
Right here.

14

"You're Done, Man!"

Willie Mays ran up to me as we arrived at the Coliseum for our first home game as the Los Angeles Dodgers. The city had thrown a big welcoming parade for us and we were late getting to the stadium to open our home season after playing a series against our old New York pals, the Giants, who were now the San Francisco Giants. None of us had seen how the Coliseum had been remodeled for baseball. We didn't even know where home plate would be.

Willie intercepted me as the Dodgers walked down the runway which led from the dressing room to the field. His eyes were as big as baseballs. "Look where that right-field fence is, Duke," he said. "And look what they gave me—250 feet. They sure fixed you up good. You couldn't reach it with a cannon. You're done, man! They just took your bat away from you."

I looked out at the view that was causing Mays so much excitement and couldn't believe my eyes. My teammates couldn't either. We saw a "short porch" in left field, the closest outfield fence I'd ever seen, only 250 feet from home plate with a 35-foot green screen on top of it. Center field was 410 feet. Nothing unusual there. But right field was a story all its own. The fence was 402 feet down the line, compared to 296 feet in Ebbets Field. Some people used to say I was lucky to hit in Brooklyn because of that short distance, but I wasn't the only hitter in New York with a fence 296 feet away. That was the distance in Yankee Stadium too, and Mantle and Berra didn't have to clear a 40-foot wall. In the Polo Grounds, the distance was even shorter.

If there hadn't been a right-field wall 402 feet from home plate anywhere in the major leagues, there was now. It didn't take a genius to figure out that our left-handed hitters weren't going to get as many home runs as they used to, and Rube Walker's chances of succeeding Campy were doomed because he was a left-handed batter, too. What about the right-handed guys? Carl Furillo and Gil Hodges had to be smiling broad grins that day.

But things don't always turn out the way you think they will. Skoonj hit 18 home runs in the Coliseum in 1958, but he had hit more than that four times in Ebbets Field. Gil hit 22, but that was five under what he hit in Brooklyn the year before. In fact, neither of them hit as well for average either. Age may have had something to do with it, but overswinging toward that friendly fence had to be a factor too.

Don Drysdale was as shocked as Willie Mays when he saw our freak field. He knew he'd be pitching half of his games there, 15 or 20 starts, and to say he didn't like the prospect would be an understatement. "I gotta change my style of pitching," he said one day. "My knuckles are scraping that left-field wall every time I throw a pitch."

We were playing the Cubs in the Coliseum on a day when Don

was scheduled to pitch, but beforehand there was an exhibition game with the writers and broadcasters. Big D was watching the game and saw some of the media guys hitting home runs over that fence in left. A few minutes later some of the hitters Drysdale would face walked by, including Ernie Banks and Billy Williams, and he was struck by the thought: "What chance do I have of getting these guys out if even the *writers* are clearing that fence?"

The stats bear out Drysdale's concern. His earned run average jumped to 4.17 from 2.69 the year before. He won five fewer games and lost four more. But there was a plus for him—he hit more home runs himself, seven, compared to two the year before in Ebbets Field.

Wally Moon hit his "Moon shots" over that left-field wall after coming to us from the Cardinals the next year, but the Dodger who would have absolutely owned that left-field fence wasn't even there on that day in '58. Roy Campanella, our great catcher, three times Most Valuable Player, and always the world's best friend, was 3,000 miles away in a hospital, paralyzed from the neck down. Campy's car had skidded on the icy streets of Long Island one night in January. There was an accident, and now Campy was struggling just to make his body move, the same Gibraltar body that caught over a thousand games for the Brooklyn Dodgers and thousands more in the Negro League, the body that once caught every pitch of four games in one day, the body that hit 242 home runs in a Dodger uniform and hundreds more before that.

That left-field fence would have been his—Campy's fence. They used to call Bedford Avenue behind the right field wall in Brooklyn "Snider's Alley," and left field in Pittsburgh was "Kiner's Korner." Somebody would surely have come up with a name for that Coliseum screen if Campy had played there because he would have worn it out. He had years in Brooklyn when he hit 31, 32, 33, and 41 home runs. More than that, it was the *kind* of ball he hit that would have made him a home-run phenomenon in the Coliseum. He hit a ton of fly balls to left field over the years that went only around 300 feet. We used to kid him even about those homers and tell him they always seemed to just barely make it into the first or second row.

"Doesn't make any difference," he used to chirp in that squeaky voice of his, "long as they need a ticket to catch it."

Moving out of Brooklyn was hard enough, but having to do it without Roy was even harder. That short porch in left added to the pill's bitterness. If Campy had played just one season in the Coliseum, Roger Maris might have had to break Campy's home run record instead of Ruth's.

Campy did have one day of glory in the Coliseum, though. In 1959 we played the Yankees in an exhibition game that drew baseball's biggest crowd up until then—93,103 fans. Buzzie writes in his autobiography that the Dodgers contributed $50,000 from their share of $87,000 from the gate receipts to Roy.

Early in the '58 season, we made our first big swing East. One night in Philadelphia when we didn't have a game, Carl Erskine slipped away from the rest of us and made a spur-of-the-moment trip to New York. We hadn't been able to see Campy yet because we were either on the West Coast or playing in other cities, but Carl took matters into his own hands and hopped on the train to New York.

The hospital officials didn't want to let Carl in to see Roy, but when they called his room, Campy was so thrilled to hear that Erskine was there that they waved Carl in. He was the first Dodger to see Roy, and they talked for a few minutes. Then they both cried. Campy showed Carl a snow scene hanging on the wall, painted by a boy who had no hands. He painted with the brush between his teeth. Then Roy said, with great enthusiasm, that he had started a rehabilitation program. "Tomorrow," he said with excitement, "I'm going to lift five pounds."

Carl remembers that remark today, so many years later. "It struck me," he says, "that here was this bull of a man who was known for his strength and durability, and he's telling me how thrilled he is that he might be able to lift five pounds. That really hit me."

Erskine told Campy that he was scheduled to pitch the next day, and Campy was elated because he could get the Phillies' games on TV. He told Carl he'd be rooting for him, and to say hello to all the guys. Carl promised he would.

The next day, Carl couldn't get Campy off his mind. "I just kept thinking of him all day," he says. "I loved the guy so much that I decided, and this may sound corny, that I was going to win that game for Campy because I knew he was watching."

Carl made good on his private promise. He was going to be 32 years old that December, and his right arm was probably 150. Every pitch hurt worse than ever, but none of that made any difference that night. He pitched a two-hitter and beat the Phillies, and he didn't need any help from the bullpen. It was the last complete game Carl Erskine ever pitched.

There were 78,000 fans in the huge Coliseum when we played our first game there as the Los Angeles Dodgers after opening our season in San Francisco in a home-and-home series against the Giants. Carl spent a restless night before that opener. Alston told him after the series in San Francisco that he wanted Erskine to throw at Jim Davenport, the Giants' rookie third baseman and leadoff batter, who had swung a hot bat against us in San Francisco. "I want you to knock him down," Alston told Carl. "I know you don't like to do that, but I'm going to order you to do it." Alston was determined to cool Davenport off, and if it took a low-bridge pitch to do it, so be it.

"I was honored to be named the starting pitcher in the first game the Dodgers ever played in Los Angeles," Carl said later, "and I wanted that first pitch to be a strike. But the skipper is telling me I have to knock the first hitter down." Carl never liked to play the game that way, and when he says he spent a restless night before the game, you can believe him.

As a part of being such a clean and upright person, Carl never ducked responsibility. As much as his arm hurt him, he didn't ask to be taken out or be allowed to miss a turn. He was always right there, and he always did what he was told.

On the first pitch that anyone ever threw in the Los Angeles Coliseum, Carl knocked Davenport down into the dirt. On the next pitch, Davenport doubled off the wall. When Carl looked into the dugout, Alston could only shrug his shoulders as if to say, "What do I know?"

I got a certain amount of revenge for my roomie. I was hitting third in the batting order. We didn't get to take any batting practice before the game, but I singled to centerfield in the first inning, the first Dodger hit in the Coliseum. I hit the last home run in Ebbets Field and got the first Dodger hit in the new Dodger stadium. Those stats don't mean anything to anyone else, but they have a nice special meaning for me.

After complying with Alston's orders—and seeing them fail—against Davenport, Carl was equal to the history of the moment. He went the distance and beat the Giants.

Frank Howard lumbered into our lives that year. We named him "Hondo" after the John Wayne movie about a big cowboy hero by that name. The record book says he was six feet seven and weighed 255 pounds.

Hondo was as nice as he was strong, a gentle giant. He's the most polite, most sincere person you'll ever meet. He had a successful career in the major leagues over 16 seasons, mostly with us and the Washington Senators. And he wasn't just strong. He could hit for average too. He batted between .273 and .296 nine times. His power, however, was what he was famous for. He hit more than 20 home runs ten times, and in three straight seasons with the Senators he hit 44, 48, and 44 home runs. He finished his career with 382.

Howard was so strong that the ball simply exploded off his bat. Brooks Robinson says Frank Howard was the only hitter he ever really feared down at third base. He had good reason to, and I could vouch for that. I was a runner on third base one afternoon when Hondo sent a screaming line drive right down the line. It hit me on the right shoulder and right ear, and could have killed me if it had been two inches higher. As it was, the shot knocked me off the base path and into the third-base coach's box, and suddenly there I am, on my rear end, looking up at our coach Charlie Dressen. Now that's power.

Fortunately, Howard was a real pussycat to get along with. If he had been mean or short-tempered, the whole human race would have been an endangered species. On a day in Chicago, though, Pee Wee saw another side of Frank Howard.

The two were becoming good friends, and are to this day. Hondo had a pulled muscle, and Pee Wee was getting on him in a kidding way about how long it was taking Frank to recover from a simple little muscle pull. Alston decided to have some fun with both of them.

The skipper went to Hondo and said, "I don't know if I'd take much more of that from Pee Wee. I'd grab him and shake him the next time he says something to you about not being able to play."

Then he applied the zinger: "Don't let that little guy get on you like that."

Pee Wee was not much under six feet, but to Hondo, even six feet is little.

Then Alston, a schoolteacher in the off-season back in Ohio, went to the other student in this case and said to Pee Wee, "I wish Frank Howard would play more often so I could get more of a look at him." Then he let the rest of us in on the gag.

The next day Reese is in the dugout just before game time and Hondo is on the bench next to him. Pee Wee looks at him, and following Alston's suggestion, says, "Aren't you playing today either?"

Hondo, following Alston's other suggestion, yanks Pee Wee up in the air by his uniform shirt and growls, "What the hell business is it of yours?" When the rest of us almost fell off the bench in laughter, both guys knew they had been had.

Hondo was beside himself with apologies to Pee Wee, his face red with embarrassment. "I'm sure sorry, Mr. Reese," he said. He called all of us veterans "mister" and "sir," and he meant it. "I didn't mean to do that. They put me up to that, Mr. Reese. They sure did."

After 16 years in the bigs, Pee Wee had it figured out right away. He turned to Alston and said, "Walt, you wanta get me *killed?*"

Not long afterward, the veterans told Howard he didn't have to call us "mister" and "sir." "We're a team," we told him. "We're all on a first-name basis." Frank said, "Okay. I got it."

A few days later, Hondo tripled. Leo Durocher, who had rejoined us as our third-base coach, gave him the signal for the squeeze play. The play was put on by calling the runner by his last name, so Leo said, "Okay, Howard, be alert. Be alive, Howard."

Frank turned to Durocher and said, "Leo, we're all on a first-name basis on this team. Won't you call me Frank?"

Durocher said, "You big dummy! I just gave you the squeeze signal."

The third baseman heard it all. Durocher had to take the play off and we had to change our signal for the squeeze play.

Pee Wee's run-in with Hondo was the second time that Pee Wee was the victim of a practical joke in Chicago. We were there one year for a series against the Cubs and we had just checked into the Hilton when I turned to Carl with a brilliant suggestion. I said, "Why don't you call Pee Wee and tell him the hotel made a mistake and that he's in the wrong room?"

That was believable, because that hotel is so big it's easy for a slipup, and we'd had our share there. What made the gag even more believable is that when there was a snafu, it was Pee Wee who was usually the victim. In that polite, ever-the-gentleman manner, he would tell the hotel people not to worry, these things happen, and then he'd change rooms, or correct whatever the problem was.

Carl didn't want to do it, but I finally convinced him, so he picks up the phone and asks for Reese's room and when Pee Wee answers the phone, Carl says, "Mr. Reese, this is Mr. Cavanaugh, one of the assistant managers, and I'm afraid, sir, there's a problem. We seem to have put you and Mr. Walker in the wrong room." That was Rube Walker, our backup catcher and an old Brooklyn neighbor.

Fate was helping us. Carl didn't know it, but Pee Wee was getting ready to call the desk when the phone rang. The reason? Someone had left a bag in the room. So when "Mr. Cavanaugh" calls to say Pee Wee and Rube are in the wrong room, naturally they don't suspect a thing.

Then Carl says, "We'd appreciate it, sir, if you and Mr. Walker could bring your bags down to the lobby and—"

Pee Wee hollers, "I'm not going to bring my bags down to the lobby. You can come up and get them yourself. I'm sick and tired of your damn hotel and the way you people are always fouling things up!"

"Fine, sir. But if you could please go over to the B wing on the other side of the hotel, to Room 1211, you'll find everything in order." Carl had no idea of where 1211 was. He made it up on the spot, the same way he invented Cavanaugh.

Pee Wee and Rube innocently head all the way across the hotel to the B wing, but not before throwing their first room into upheaval by tearing the bed apart and pulling all the cushions out of the chairs as their parting shot. Then they get to the B wing, looking for 1211. They see 1212 They see 1210. But they don't see 1211. Carl didn't know it, but there wasn't any such room.

Now Pee Wee is really beside himself. He finds a house phone and calls down to the lobby and screams. "Lemme talk to Cavanaugh!"

"Who?"

"That Mr. Cavanaugh!"

"I'm sorry, sir. We don't have any Mr. Cavanaugh working here."

Pee Wee is at the explosion point. "Lissen, I've had it with your damn hotel!" Then he relates his conversation with Mr. Cavanaugh, and the clerk doesn't have any idea what the heck he's talking about, but between the two of them they finally wade through the confusion. Then Pee Wee and Rube have to walk all the way back across this huge hotel and move back into their original room, but not until they straightened up the mess they'd made.

Carl and I meet Pee Wee and Rube for dinner, as we usually did on the road, and they're telling us about this unbelievably bureaucratic mess they finally straightened out. Carl and I started laughing and the harder we laughed, the more suspicious Reese and Walker became.

Finally we had to own up to what we had done. Then we spent the rest of that trip to Chicago avoiding getting murdered.

The knee had been operated on, but it still plagued me. I dropped to another new low in number of games played, only 106, down 33 from the year before, and my at-bats dropped from 508 to 327. On the plus side, my strikeouts dropped from 104, tops in the league in '57, to only 49, but my homers went in the same direction, from 40 to 15, thanks to one bad knee and one distant wall. I didn't feel I had anything to apologize for. I hung in there as well as I could and raised my batting average from .274 to .312, the sixth time I hit over .300 in the major leagues. Any power hitter would feel proud about that.

The knee bothered me right from the start of the season, and in spring training I got a real scare on a drive back to Dodgertown in Vero Beach after a night at the races with Don Zimmer and Johnny Podres. It was a drizzly night and we wanted to get back on time, and I ended up taking a shortcut across a set of railroad tracks in the dark without knowing it and tossing all of us around.

Zimmer banged his head on the windshield and I hit my knee hard against the dashboard. What nobody believed was that we hadn't been drinking.

I got off to a lousy start, and by mid-May, Buzzie Bavasi had seen enough. He went back to one of his favorite tricks with me.

Every once in a while he would get on my case in the papers, criticizing me in public in the hope that it would get my adrenaline flowing again and I'd get so mad I'd explode out of my slump. It usually worked too.

He never fooled Bev, though. On two occasions, she even got Buzzie on the phone and asked whether he really meant what he said in the paper that day, or was this just another one of his efforts to get me untracked?

Buzzie didn't resent her calls and told her not to worry—he was just trying to get me started again.

Bev's scrapbook for 1958 has a clipping of one of those episodes. Buzzie told the reporters after a game, "I just can't understand it. Snider has all the talent in the world, but he doesn't seem to apply it to baseball. Maybe he ought to try something else."

I took the bait. I always did. "If he's got a beef," I told the reporters, "why doesn't he come to me about it instead of talking to you guys about it?"

When the writers asked Mr. O'Malley about his general manager's comments about me, Mr. O'Malley said, "I think Buzzie Bavasi is engaged in a bit of psychological warfare with Duke Snider. People have to be handled differently, whether you are raising a family, bossing an office, or directing a movie. Some are helped by sympathy, some by being let alone, some by needling. Bavasi and Snider have been together long enough to understand each other, so I'm not going to butt into it. I'm sure Duke's knee is bothering him a lot, not only in his running but in his stance, stride, and pivot at the plate." He was right about that. I couldn't round first base the right way until June.

Then he mentioned that I wasn't the only one off to a slow start. Hodges, Drysdale, and Newcombe were having troubles, and Pee Wee wasn't even starting. Don Zimmer had taken his place.

That night I came up as a pinch hitter in the 11th inning and got a double to knock the Braves out of first place.

The Coliseum was a source of both frustration and amusement in our first season there. One night in June, Don Zimmer and I were talking in the outfield during batting practice about the enormous size of the place. Then Zimmer got an idea. He asked me if I thought I could throw a ball out of the Coliseum. I told him yes, I thought so.

"I'll make a deal with you," he said. "Let's get some bets down with the guys and I'll give you half the action if you can throw the ball all the way out."

For a minute there, I thought I was back on board the USS *Sperry* in the Pacific.

It sounded good to me. What the heck, if I couldn't *hit* the ball out, I might as well *throw* it out.

Zimmer got the bets lined up, $400 worth, and I stepped up to make my first throw, from the outfield toward the top of the Coliseum. I let fly, and the ball hit the top concrete railing. It missed going all the way out by a foot. My second throw missed by a little more, maybe six feet. I told Zimmer, "Okay, this one is it." I raised my right arm and took my stride to uncork my third throw, but the ball slipped off my middle finger and my elbow popped.

Ed Roebuck—Sears to us—had been standing nearby with a fungo bat, the extra-long bat which coaches use to hit long fly balls to outfielders. He was one of the masters of the fungo, and while I was trying to heave the ball out of the stadium he was popping balls all the way out, trying to hit one over the Olympic torch.

The fans on their way into the park were dodging baseballs—Roebuck's fungo hits. Some of them came down toward the batting cage to see who the new monster hitter was who was hitting balls out of the Coliseum.

Walt chewed us out in a meeting later. Besides, he said, somebody could get hurt.

After the meeting I said, "You're right, Walt. I just hurt my elbow. I can't play tonight."

When Buzzie heard that, he blew a gasket. "Take that uniform off and go home. And it will cost you two hundred dollars for every game you miss."

I said, "Okay, I'll play tonight."

"No, you already said you can't play tonight. Take the uniform off and go home." I drove home with a throbbing elbow, took some pain pills, and went to sleep.

I could have lied and said I couldn't play because my knee hurt, which it did, but I told the truth so it cost me $200—and $200 more if I couldn't play the next day.

When I got to the ball park the next morning for an afternoon game, I told Alston, "Walt, it hurts when I throw, but for two hundred dollars a day I feel just fine. Put me in the lineup. I'm playing today."

"I'll put you in left field," he said.

I got two hits and threw out two runners, one at third and one at home, and the elbow was killing me.

I told Zimmer to keep the bet open because this was only June, my arm wasn't seriously hurt, and we'd do it on the last day of the season. He held onto the $400 in bets, and our teammates waited for the showdown at the Coliseum.

I spent the last week of the season making extra-long throws, getting ready for the challenge. When the last day came, I threw a ball out of there on my first try. I got $200 as my share from Zimmer, and we both ended the season happy.

I ran into Buzzie once during the winter. "Well," he said, "did you learn your lesson—that you can get hurt by fooling around?"

"Buzzie," I said, "I don't think I'll ever learn my lesson, but my arm feels a lot better."

He refunded my $200 fine.

213

15

On Top Again

Life in L.A. had two of the same fringe benefits as life in New York—commercials and TV appearances. In New York I managed to show up on the hit TV shows of the 1950s like "Masquerade Party," "Arthur Murray," the "Ed Sullivan Show" (when it was still called "Toast of the Town"), "Name That Tune," and "What's My Line?"

In Los Angeles I did guest shots on the "Dinah Shore Show," the "Bob Hope Show," and "Edgar Bergen and Charlie McCarthy," and had a part with Robert Young in "Father Knows Best." I even made an episode of "The Rifleman" with my old teammate and friend from Montreal and the Dodgers, Chuck Connors. I made a couple of movies too, the first when I was with Brooklyn and the second after the Dodgers moved to Los Angeles.

In the first, Willie Ramsdell and I appeared with William Bendix in *Kill the Umpire*. After our move to L.A., I also had a small part in *Geisha Boy* with Jerry Lewis. We filmed it at Wrigley Field in Los Angeles.

I made my appearance on the "Bob Hope Show" not long after the knee surgery. The writers made me the straight man. Bob asked me, "How's the knee, Duke?"

"Oh, I can't kick."

"Then you should play for the Rams."

Years later I ran into Bob and he did the same routine with me, right there on the spur of the moment. He remembered the script better than I did.

I ran into him on another occasion, in a restaurant, and sent our waitress over to his table to say I'd like to buy the members of his party a drink if they would tell her what they would like.

The waitress came back and said, "Mr. Hope asked me to thank you, but they're not having anything to drink. He said send over the money instead."

The commercials kept coming my way. The funniest two involved Clairol and Pittsburgh Plate Glass. I was getting gray fast, and when the people at Clairol saw my silver they also saw gold—an opportunity to sell their product with me as their spokesman. They flew me to New York to film a commercial showing how great their product was with a unique demonstration, at the expense of my own temporary embarrassment.

They had me color one side of my hair with a product named Great Day. The other side we left its natural silver color. I was a walking before-and-after look. After a couple of takes, wouldn't you know it? They decided to break for lunch. Well, where the heck was I going to go looking like a zebra? I ducked into the first hat store I saw and bought a straw hat. That worked fine, until we got to the restaurant. I couldn't very well keep my hat on all during lunch. I talked the waiter into seating us next to a wall, and I took a chair on the wall side of the table. The people in the restaurant saw only the silver side of me.

After we went back and finished the commercial, the Clairol people colored the other half too. For the next three years I had brown hair.

Pittsburgh Plate Glass once asked me to make a commercial with a popular TV announcer, Art Gilmore. PPG had just developed a new shatter-proof glass. The idea was for me to swing a bat against the glass to show that nothing could break it, not even the home-run hitter from the Dodgers.

The PPG people and the executives from their advertising agency met me at the studio for the big shooting. I put on my Dodger uniform, picked up my bat, and when Art Gilmore gave me my cue, I stepped up and took my best swing at this new breakproof glass. *BOOM!* It was the loudest explosion you ever heard and glass went flying in every direction. The director was cut and so was one of the cameramen. Friends of mine who saw a film of this on the Johnny Carson Show say the look on my face was as funny as the explosion.

The shocked execs got on the phone to Pittsburgh and reported the crisis. The big wheels at PPG's home office didn't want to believe what they were hearing. They said it was impossible for anybody to break that glass, including me. They had hit it with the heaviest hammers and even with a steel ball.

PPG put in a new piece of glass and we showed up again for a second try. An official from the Federal Trade Commission was present to make sure there weren't any tricks, but he didn't have to worry. We were playing it straight, except that I decided, without telling anyone, to take only a half swing. The people at PPG were being good to me, and I wanted to help them as much as possible. I even had a new bat to use. The old one had gotten pretty chewed up after the first attempt.

I stepped up to do my stuff and looked around. Everybody on

217

the set was behind something—a camera, a corner, a piece of furniture, anything offering protection. They looked like a bunch of people who just got word a tornado was approaching. Then I caught a glimpse of the director peeking around the corner. He was wearing a welder's mask. The sight broke me up. The director hollered, "Cut!"

Take three. I stepped up to the glass again. I kept my composure, took just a half-swing, and *BOOM*! It was the same thing all over again. In this case, three takes and you're out. The PPG people decided not to push their luck, the FTC man said they had to pay me even though they couldn't use the commercial, and I got my money.

The 1958 season wasn't any better for the Dodgers than 1957. In fact, it was worse. It was the only year we finished in the second division in my 16 seasons with the team. We finished a miserable seventh, ahead of only the Phillies. Seventh place was a strange neighborhood for the Dodgers. For years we were so successful, and now we were near the bottom of the National League.

Pee Wee's back was bothering him, and so were Furillo's legs, not to mention my knee. Gil's average dropped to .259, Erskine's arm was hurting more with each pitch, Jackie was retired, Campy was paralyzed, and Newk was gone—traded to Cincinnati for Steve Bilko and Johnny Klippstein after an off-year in '57 and a poor start in '58.

Only three years after standing at the top of baseball's mountain, we were far down on the other side.

Another change was closing in on me. I could see it coming, and there wasn't a thing anyone could do to stop it. Carl Erskine's days were numbered. Soon I would lose my roommate and close friend.

The right shoulder and arm were protesting too much. The years when he got by as much on his grit as on his exceptional ability were taking their toll. The man they called "Oisk" back in Brooklyn, who started from 26 to 37 games a year, started only

218

nine in 1958. The man who pitched 260 innings in 1954 pitched only 98 in 1958. He won four games for us in '58, and his fourth was the last game he ever won.

Soon he would be leaving. We both knew it. We were sort of an odd couple as roomies go, but we were a perfect match. We drew strength from each other because we genuinely liked and respected each other. He was always stable and I was sometimes moody. Carl was a fisherman and I enjoyed golf, but we both enjoyed movies and Broadway plays. We were from different parts of the country, but we were the same age and had kids the same ages. We always lived in the same neighborhood in Brooklyn, and the two families shared a house in Vero Beach during spring training every year. And we roomed together on the road—all of this closeness for more than ten years.

There never was a harsh word between us, and that's a remarkable record given the tensions of all the pennants and playoffs and World Series we were in. We didn't pal around together a whole lot on the road, but we always ate together and spent many a contented hour in our room watching TV or just reading and talking.

Any time I needed Carl, he was there. Any time he needed me, I was there. He always gave me his best, and I did the same for him. I'd wake up at 3 A.M. after Carl pitched a night game and there he'd be—sitting at the window just staring out.

I'd say, "You okay, Roomie?"

He was always so keyed up during the game, and so analytical after the game about what he had thrown in certain situations, that it always took him two nights before he could get a normal night's sleep. So we'd sit and rehash the game, and eventually we'd both go to sleep.

Carl did the same for me when the strikeouts got me down. He couldn't tell me what I was doing wrong, but he would always listen and console when I needed consoling.

I especially remember one night in Cincinnati. I hit a long home run that really popped Carl's eyes out, and got the crowd buzzing. On my next time up, I hit an easy ground ball, and when

I got halfway to first, and was out, I turned and headed for the dugout. I used to do that once in a while, but I never realized how bad it looked. In later years, when I started managing in the minor leagues and saw young players doing it, I corrected them in a hurry and thought, "Oh, boy, I'm really getting paid back for doing that same thing myself."

When I did it in Cincinnati after hitting that long home run, it made a deep impression on Carl, although I didn't know it at the time. But I found out soon enough. This time it was my turn to be awake in the middle of the night. I was lying in bed in the hotel room feeling bad about not running out that ground ball. I wondered what Carl thought about it. I decided to try to find out. I said softly, "Hey, Roomie—you asleep?"

"No."

Then I said, "I know what you're thinking about."

We talked about it right then and there, at four in the morning. He didn't chew me out. He didn't have to. I already had. Instead he told me how proud he had been when I hit that home run shot, only to have that pride shattered—and that's the word he used—when I failed to run out the ground ball. He told me how much talent I had, maybe enough to make the Hall of Fame some day. He accented the positive with me, he listened to my side of the story, and we talked it out, with understanding and genuine concern.

Carl told me not long ago that he spent many of his years in the major leagues in a state of anxiety. With nobody getting more than a one-year contract in those days, and saddled with an arm problem that the whole baseball world knew about, Carl was always anxious about the team's willingness to stick with him and his ailing right arm. If he had been less modest he never would have worried, because he would have realized that the Dodgers didn't regard his arm as a problem. They thought of it as one of the most talented arms in the major leagues, and everybody else thought the same way.

*   *   *

My new roommate, Ron Fairly, was a worthy successor to Carl. He was a native of Macon, Georgia, a baseball product of Southern Cal, a big-leaguer for 21 years, and a class guy. He's now a radio/TV announcer for the Giants.

I have a lot of great memories about my years of rooming with Ron, but one stands out—when the Dodgers came back to New York. We were there to play the new Mets, and it was our first trip back since leaving Brooklyn five years earlier. There was a full house at the Polo Grounds.

Ron intentionally waited in the dressing room until I finished dressing because he wanted to walk onto the field with me. We could hear the fans outside yelling, "We want Duke!" and as we came out of the dressing room onto the outfield, a roar erupted from the crowd. The fans were on their feet and really letting me hear them. I talked to some of the Met outfielders, and the standing ovation continued. As we walked to the visitors' dugout on the third-base line, it was still going on. Ron got goose bumps, and I did too.

When I took batting practice, the fans were hollering for me to hit one out of the Polo Grounds, just like old times. Carl Berringer was pitching, the best BP pitcher I ever saw because he threw nothing but strikes—except then. He couldn't get a ball over the plate to save his soul. They started to boo him, but he finally was able to throw a strike and I hit it out. The place went nuts all over again. It was the longest ovation of my career, even greater than the one I would receive the following April when I came back to New York as a Met.

Ron always tells the story of that first time back in New York, and I will always remember. How could anyone forget a moment like that?

After that 1958 misery, Buzzie Bavasi didn't fool around. We got off to a slow start in '59 and were in fifth place in early June. He wanted to get back up to the top of the mountain, and the moves and changes started coming thick and fast. We didn't just get some new blood—we got a major transfusion. Buzzie went out and obtained the talent we needed to win, making the moves that an experienced and successful general manager knows how to make, and at the end of 1959, after being so far down the other side of the mountain, we were on top again.

By the time Buzzie had finished calling kids up from the minors, recalling others like Frank Howard who had been sent down for more experience, and performing other forms of wheeling and dealing, the Dodgers had a whole new look—Maury Wills, Wally Moon, Chuck Essegian, Don Demeter, Ron Fairly, Frank Howard, Tommy Davis, Larry Sherry, and Roger Craig. We even had a new third-base coach—Pee Wee. Chuck Dressen was moved to the dugout to help Walt Alston. From one season to the next, we were a whole new ball club—and different from any we had ever known.

The new Dodger team couldn't overpower anyone the way the Brooklyn teams did for ten years. We weren't going to lead the league in home runs and runs scored and have the Cy Young and MVP winners in our lineup. Instead, we were going to finesse you to death.

There wasn't a Dodger anywhere in the top five in batting average, slugging average, home runs, total bases, runs batted in, hits, or runs scored. Those were the places where the Dodgers used to live. But Jim Gilliam, our third baseman, led the league in walks and was second in stolen bases. When Jim came to us as a rookie, he said, "I'm going to have fun leading off for this team because I love to run so much." We said, "Don't worry. We're going to run your tail off." By July he told us, "Man, you guys were right. I need a couple of days off." Drysdale led the National League pitchers in strikeouts with 242, and Koufax was third. Those two young arms were getting cranked up for the 1960s.

Branch Rickey would have loved the 1959 Dodgers because we worked so successfully as a team. Buzzie Bavasi says today that the 1955 Dodger team was his best, but the 1959 team was his favorite. His reason is that we won the pennant, and the World Series, in

1959 even though we did not have the most talented team. We just went out and worked together and wouldn't take no for an answer. We hung in against the Milwaukee Braves, who had won the pennant for two years in a row, met them in a playoff after we finished tied with them, won the playoff, and then beat the White Sox in the World Series.

One of the most positive developments of the season came during our stretch drive for the pennant. In early September we had an open date because the NFL Rams were playing an exhibition football game in the Coliseum. Bev and I threw a party at our ranch and invited everybody to come down and have a day of fun and games and forget the pressures of our pennant race.

It was just the tonic everyone needed. We laid out a spread of fish, turkey, and a roast pig with all the trimmings. Almost everybody was able to make it. There was swimming in the reservoir nearby, some rifle shooting, rides in our jeep, and basketball. It was a day in the country on the 60 acres we shared next to Camp Pendleton with our friends Cliff and Stanna Dapper.

After that refresher, we maintained our momentum against the Braves for the rest of the regular season and into the playoff.

Individually we didn't have the stickout performers we had in Brooklyn, but our success showed up in the team statistics. As a team, we led the league in stolen bases, fielding, strikeouts by our pitchers, and saves by our bullpen.

We had lost both Erskine and Reese to retirement. Furillo was playing part-time and I was moved to right field. Gilliam, Hodges, and I were the only starters left from the Brooklyn days. All the others were gone. Gil came back with an excellent season after dipping in '58. He raised his average 17 points to .276, hit 25 home runs—three more than the year before—drove in more runs, and led the league's first basemen in fielding. Not bad for a guy 35 years old.

I had my seventh .300 season with .308. I hit 23 home runs, eight more than in '58, and raised my RBIs from 58 back up to 88.

When we met the Braves in the three-game playoff there was no question about which team was more talented. We had our collection of kids blended in with veterans, but the Braves had some of the biggest stars of the late 1950s—Hank Aaron, Joe Adcock, Eddie Mathews, Del Crandall, Johnny Logan, and Wes Covington, plus a pitching staff of Warren Spahn, Lew Burdette, Bob Buhl, Juan Pizarro, Bob Rush, and Don McMahon.

We beat them in the first game in Milwaukee, and finished the job back in L.A. when we came from behind in the last of the ninth. We did it the nice way—Carl Furillo drove in Gil Hodges. Shades of Brooklyn.

In the World Series we finally got to play somebody besides the Yankees, but the White Sox might as well have been wearing Yankee uniforms, in that first game anyhow. They beat us, 11-0, with five runs batted in from Ted Kluszewski and Early Wynn pitching a shutout, Gerry Staley finishing up in the eighth and ninth.

The loss didn't upset us as much as you might expect. Going into the Series we were sure we were better than they were, and the result of the first game didn't change our opinion. We were loosey-goosey in the dressing room after the opener, with no tails dragging. We were anxious for the next day to dawn so we could go out and get our first win, which we did.

Johnny Podres was smelling the roses again, sensing another World Series championship. He gave up two runs to the Sox in the first inning and then slammed the door. Larry Sherry came in and gave up only one run in the last three innings. In the meantime, Charlie Neal hit two home runs and Chuck Essegian one for a 4-3 win. So much for the new hitters. Then the veterans came back to take one more moment in the sun, one final curtain call for the boys from Brooklyn—Furillo, Hodges, and Snider—Skoonj, Gil, and the Duke.

Skoonj came through with a pinch single in the seventh inning of the third game with the bases loaded to break a 0-0 tie and lead us to a 3-1 win over Dick Donovan. Don Drysdale got the first World Series victory of his career.

In the fourth game, Hodges hit a home run in the eighth to break a 4-4 tie and win it for us, 5-4. Sherry, who saved the win for us the day before, did it again with two more strong innings, only this time he got the win. The Series was four games old, we had three wins, and Sherry, the rookie, had a win and two saves.

We moved in for the kill in the fifth game, but we weren't able to finish them off. Sandy Koufax and Bob Shaw hooked up in a battle that ended in a 1-0 win for the White Sox, thanks to a game-saving catch by Jim Rivera in the seventh inning with his back to the plate on a long drive by Neal with two men on base. Al Lopez, Chicago's manager, had his managerial gears working overtime in this one. He used three pitchers in a 1-0 game, the only time that had been done until that time. It may still be. Bob Shaw, Billy Pierce, and Dick Donovan all pitched so the White Sox would have a tomorrow. It worked. We were disappointed more for our fans than for ourselves. We were still up, three games to two, and still confident—but the biggest crowd in World Series history, 92,706 in the Coliseum, went home without the World Series championship it had come to see.

I pinch-hit in that fifth game and grounded out. I got another cortisone shot after the game because I wanted to be in the next game's starting lineup and make a contribution.

I went to Alston and said, "Skip, I gotta play." Alston said immediately, "You're in there."

There was tension on our bench before the sixth game at Comiskey Park. We knew we should win the Series. The White Sox were a running team that year without much of a power offense. Their attack consisted mostly of Luis Aparacio and Nellie Fox getting on base and playing games like hit-and-run and double-steal. They were called "the Go-Go Sox" with good reason. But our pitchers and Johnny Roseboro, who had established himself firmly behind the plate as Campy's successor, had taken that go-go weapon away from the Sox, and we knew it.

We were facing Early Wynn again, the one who shut us out, 11-0, in the first game. We knew we had to beat their best, and we were ready to do it. But when Wynn set us down without a run in each of the first two innings, you could feel the anxiety build in the Dodger dugout. Not fear, not nerves, just eagerness, a feeling which seemed to say, "C'mon, let's start scoring some runs and get this *over* with."

I came up in the third inning with a man on base, and I knew from my experience that a big blow could light the fire. Once we got started, it would be all over and we'd be champions. But the guy out there on the mound was on his way to winning 300 games and getting himself elected to the Hall of Fame. He wasn't going to give me any batting-practice fastballs.

Wynn threw me a fast ball that was up and away, but Branch Rickey's lessons in Florida 11 years before were still paying off. I hit the pitch to the opposite field, into the left-center-field seats. It was my 11th World Series home run, which is still the National League record, and we had the lead, 2-0.

And my hunch was right. We caught fire. In the next inning we busted loose for six more runs, Moon and Essegian hit home runs, and we won the game and the World Series, 9-3. The date: October 8, 1959, three years to the day after Don Larsen pitched his perfect game against us. Sherry was the man of the hour again. Podres gave up a three-run homer to Kluszewski, so Walt waved Sherry into the game in the fourth inning and the Sox never scored again. Larry picked up the win, giving him two wins and two saves in our four victories. He pitched 12 and two-thirds innings, more than any other pitcher on our team, and had an earned run average of only 0.71. He won the Most Valuable Player award for the Series, with no arguments.

Something else happened in the 1959 World Series. I made the only two errors I ever made in 36 Series games. Wally Moon and I had trouble with a routine fly ball between us. We collided and the ball bounced out of my glove. On the other play, Sherm Lollar hit a line drive to left center with a man on for an apparent double. But Lollar was a slow runner, and the ball got to the outfield quickly, so I made a fast pickup and threw to second. I had Lollar by ten feet—but there was nobody at second. Our first baseman,

226

Gil Hodges, went after the ball but slipped on the wet grass in the infield. Everyone else was expecting a play at third. The throw went through, and I was charged with an error on the best throw I made all year.

Those two errors in one inning added up to a World Series record until Willie Davis, my successor in center field for the Dodgers, took me off the hook in a game against the Baltimore Orioles in the 1966 World Series.

Willie was an excellent outfielder but he had one of those snake-bitten innings against the Orioles in one of the Los Angeles games when Bev and I were in the stands. Bev's favorite, Sandy Koufax, was pitching for the Dodgers and Bev was keeping score, as always, when Willie made three errors in the same inning.

Bev was steaming that somebody—whether it was Davis or someone else didn't make any difference—was undercutting the pitching performance of her hero, Sandy. After having to put down "E-8," the scorer's symbol for an error by the center fielder, three times, Bev handed me her scorecard and pencil and said with disgust, "Do you want a beer?" She never asked me for a beer before.

I said, "Sure, but what am I supposed to do with these? I don't know how to keep score."

Her lips tightened. "Just mark down E-8 in every square," she said, and marched up the stairs.

When Carl Erskine retired voluntarily in mid-June, he was helping the team again by doing it in time for Buzzie to bring Roger Craig up from the minors. Craig, who popularized the split-finger fastball in the 1980s as a pitching coach and manager, had been up and down. Thanks to Carl's unselfish act, Craig was able to rejoin us from the minors in time to win 11 games, a critical contribution in a year when we finished tied for the pennant. It was just like Carl to do something for his team that year.

Art Fowler was another pitcher who made a definite contribution to our success that season. He won three games and saved two more early in the season, but then his arm went dead. He was out of the major leagues in 1960, but was able to come back in '61 and pitch four more seasons. He was finished for '59, but being involved in five wins early in the season was a big help to us.

The closeness of those '59 Dodgers was apparent in what those two pitchers did for us—Erskine and Fowler—and what their teammates did for them. We voted each of them a full share of our World Series earnings.

Time was running out for me too. I knew it better than anyone, but I was fighting it. I had a wife and three children and athletes weren't making a million dollars a year in those days. Besides, like every professional athlete who ever lived, I just knew I could still play.

I was doing everything I could think of to keep the knee as strong as I could. There were diathermy treatments, whirlpool baths, knee rubs, ultrasonic therapy, and cortisone shots—20 of them. During the World Series, Dr. Robert Kerlan, the team's orthopedic surgeon, said, "Duke, that's it. We can't give you any more cortisone. We're finding out more and more things about it, and we just can't give you any more."

Medical people were learning that continued use of cortisone could produce some undesirable side effects, and that you couldn't keep on using the stuff without paying a price.

If I wanted to continue my playing career, I was going to have to do it without cortisone.

Could It Happen Again?

The winds of change were definitely in the air. Although I was still only 33, my playing time was dropping sharply. I was begining to feel forgotten. Don Demeter was being groomed to take my place.

Bev remembers a time during this period when I was feeling overlooked. We were in the Los Angeles airport sitting on a bench—the children, one of their friends, Bev, and me—when an elderly lady came up and told me how much she had enjoyed watching me play over the years.

After she left I said to Bev, "Well at least the old people remember me."

Even though we didn't repeat in 1960, we finished fourth, 13 games behind the Pirates, and in '61 we closed the gap and finished second, only four games behind Fred Hutchinson and his Cincinnati Reds. We were a solid contender, and I was contributing whenever I could. We didn't know it, but fate was getting us ready for another showdown with history—involving our old friends, the Giants.

Playing baseball up to my personal standards of performance was harder, but I wasn't going through the experience with a gloom-and-doom attitude. But knowing you aren't the player you used to be can get to you from time to time if you let it. I tried to concentrate on the positives. I knew I could still help my team. I knew I could still hit, and I showed it in 1961 when I hit .296.

I also acquired that additional incentive almost every athlete has when he nears his September Song. You want to leave the best possible reputation as a player behind you, and the only way you can do that is to post the best possible numbers. You're still helping your team, but you also begin thinking about your personal career goals. When I began to experience success at the end of the 1940s and the beginning of the '50s, people were speculating that I might get 3,000 hits and hit between 500 and 600 home runs. That's more than Hall of Fame numbers. That means you're playing in a higher league than anyone else. Only two other players in the whole history of baseball, Aaron and Mays, ever compiled that combination.

Because the Dodgers always relaxed after winning the pennant and because we didn't pay much attention to our individual numbers, I wasn't concerned during my early and middle years about what my final totals were going to be. I will confess, though, that in my final years I began thinking about them. It wasn't any drive for the Hall of Fame. But it was a desire to leave behind the very best statistical record I could, regardless of my knee. Specifically, I wanted to try my hardest to reach two of the most respected career levels for a baseball player—2,000 hits and 400 home runs.

At this twilight time in my career, the good people of Los

Angeles and our new hometown of Fallbrook held a night for me. It was almost beyond my imagination—that a kid from the sandlots of Los Angeles, from Enterprise Junior High and Compton High, would be given a night, just like the stars he used to listen to on the radio. "Duke Snider Night"—I had trouble believing it.

A caravan of 14 buses with 700 friends and neighbors drove up 100 miles from Fallbrook for my night and a twi-night double-header with the Cincinnati Reds. It was an eventful time for the Sniders of Fallbrook because we were opening the Duke Snider Bowling Lanes the next evening. Georgie Jessel was the emcee and he ran true to form, even announcing Bev's pregnancy to the 51,044 fans in the Coliseum and calling Sandy Koufax "the greatest Jewish athlete since Samson."

The gifts just seemed to keep coming—a new Corvette for Bev and me, a gasoline-powered car for each of the kids, clothes, a TV, a barbecue set, golf clubs, even a boxer dog. The ceremonies were held between games and took 50 minutes.

Our oldest daughter, Pam, remembers, "It went by like a flash of light. I can still see the three cars for us kids, the dog, little Kurt running around the bases, and Mom squeezing into her blue dress, pregnant and hoping it wouldn't show."

There was only one disappointment about that night: We weren't in Brooklyn. I told the crowd, "I can't help but think of another ball park, Ebbets Field in Brooklyn, where I had better years. I was younger then and my legs were better. . . ." I thanked the fans for being so understanding toward me and for cheering me on even though I wasn't able to do all the things I did in Brooklyn. I closed by saying, "I will never forget this night for the rest of my life. I hope I can come through tonight and get a couple of good knocks in the second game."

Walt had asked me which game I wanted to play, since I really wasn't up to playing both halves of a doubleheader any more, and I chose the second. Any athlete who has ever been given a day or a night in his honor holds his breath that he doesn't embarrass himself on that night. They hope to have a night like the one that waited for me.

The Cincinnati pitcher was my old teammate from the Dodgers' wartime training camp in Bear Mountain, New York, Cal McLish. He was the one whose name was longer than his pitching arm—Calvin Coolidge Julius Caesar Tuskahoma McLish. The first time up against him, I hit a home run, the kind of home run you dream about. The ball went over the 400-foot sign in right center field, and the stories in the papers the next day said it cleared the wall by 30 or 40 feet.

On my second time up, I hit a triple to the same spot between Vada Pinson and Gus Bell to drive in a run. We won the game, 2-0, and I drove in both runs. My pal, Don Drysdale, pitched the shutout. Every time I go to the Coliseum now, I look out at that spot. I don't usually say anything about it to the people who happen to be with me, but I always look, and I always remember.

As 1961 arrived, so did Dawna, our "bonus baby," who today is still our loving baby. So too did the rumors about my future with the Dodgers, or the possible lack of one. I had been a Dodger all my life, and I had no desire to leave. If it had to happen, I wanted to go to a contender, to a team I could help win the pennant even if I didn't play every day. One of the rumors was that the Yankees were interested in me. The deal never happened, and it's doubtful the Yankees spent too much time regretting it. That's the year Roger Maris broke Babe Ruth's single-season record with 61 home runs. Mantle hit 54 of his own. Between the two of them they hit 115 home runs and drove in 270 runs.

A ball player who is the subject of trade rumors works under an extra-heavy burden. You're expected to do your job as well as you've always done it, but at the same time you're wondering if you're going to have to move to another city, leave your family, or pull up everybody's roots so the family can move with you. It's a part of being a professional athlete and you're aware of the possibility when you start out, but realizing that it's a part of your profession doesn't make it any easier when you have to live through it.

Ball players do all they can under those circumstances. I worked harder than ever after the 1960 season to get into the best physical condition I could. I took off 20 pounds, strengthened my knee, and reported to Vero Beach ready to have a good season. Things got off to a great start in spring training. I was hitting the ball well and in one case I hit it too well. Larry Jackson, a right-handed pitcher for the Cardinals, threw a slider to me in an exhibition game and when I hit it, the ball and two thirds of my bat went flying straight back toward the mound. Jackson was on the tall side, six-one and a half, and he ducked and turned as fast as he could, but the ball hit him in his backsides and part of the bat hit him in the jaw. I reached first base, but Jackson was still on the ground, seriously injured. His jaw was broken and he was out of the lineup for a month. I felt awful about it, but that's one of the occupational hazards of pitching. To his credit, Jackson came back to win 14 games.

The season got off to a good start for the team, and I continued to hit extremely well. Then I ran up against Bob Gibson, one of the game's premier pitchers, a Most Valuable Player winner a few years later and a member of the Hall of Fame today. He knew I was a hot hitter, and I knew he was an outstanding pitcher. In the third inning, I hit a home run over the screen in left field at the Coliseum.

I knew what would happen next. This was only Gibson's third season but the word was already around the league that he had that mean streak that so many good pitchers have. He was a superb all-around athlete, and a quality player in every way. But in a game situation it's an all-out battle between pitcher and hitter, and the hitter had better work up a healthy dislike for the pitcher because, after all, he's out there trying to keep you from earning a living. He wants to be successful by making you his victim. Not only that, the rulemakers let him stand up on a hill while you have to stand on level ground. That should be enough to make a hitter hate a pitcher while he's in the batter's box. Then, once the ball is released, you transfer your hate from the pitcher to the ball.

It wasn't difficult to work up a healthy dislike for Bob Gibson. He stood out there in defiance, staring you down, and throwing at you from time to time to remind you who's boss.

When I came to the plate after my home run, I had an idea Gibson would throw at me. I said to myself, "If he does, he does. Don't let that scare you off." If a hitter allows himself to be psyched out by circumstances like those, the pitcher has him right where he wants him. I didn't let it happen in the '52 World Series after Johnny Sain hit me. I came up the next time and doubled home the winning run. I wasn't going to let Bob Gibson scare me this time either.

His first pitch was one of his 95-mile-an-hour fastballs, and it came right at me. It was headed for my ribs, and I brought my right arm instinctively to protect my body. The pitch hit my elbow, and the ball dropped straight to the ground. It was no glancing blow. It hit me flush. I shook it off and trotted down to first base, without bothering to start one of those bench-clearing brawls we hear so much about today. As far as I was concerned, I hit my home run, Gibson let me know he didn't like it, and I was on base again, this time hit by a pitch. That's baseball.

When I walked out to the on-deck circle for my third time at bat, I took a three-quarters swing and felt a sharp pain in that right elbow, like someone jabbing a needle in there. I took another swing and felt the same pain. I went back to the dugout and told Alston, "Skip, I don't think I can swing." He lifted me for a pinch hitter and I went into the clubhouse to be examined.

Dr. Kerlan looked at my arm and tried to make a joke out of it. He said, "You might have to drink your beer left-handed for a couple of days." The X-rays the next day showed it wasn't anything to joke about. I had a fractured elbow. I'd be out of action for a month. When he gave me the stunning news, I had tears in my eyes and they started to run down my cheeks. After all that work over the winter, and knowing I had only a couple of seasons left, now this. It's the one thing a veteran athlete lives in fear of—a disabling injury.

Dr. Kerlan tried to console me. "I know how hard you've worked, Duke. But don't let this ruin your season. A month is a long time, but it's only part of the season. You can come back from this."

Alston should have been so compassionate. When my recovery was complete, he sent me in to pinch-hit against Juan Marichal, just about the toughest right-hander I ever faced. He was in the same company with Ewell Blackwell, Gibson, and Drysdale. Campy might have put Blackwell first. He used to tell Rube Walker, "When Blackwell pitches, you get to play because that's the day I get my rest."

Marichal had an exceptional arsenal of pitches—fastball, curve, and slider—and he came at you with his front leg kicked up high. You couldn't see the ball, all you saw was that big foot sticking up in the air.

When Alston sent me in against Marichal, he said, "Let's test that elbow."

I said, "That's going to be a pretty good test, isn't it, Walt?"

When I came back to the bench after being properly disposed of by Mr. Marichal, I said, "Boy, that sure was a wasted five minutes." Even Alston had to grin.

Dr. Kerlan was right. I did come back from the broken elbow, well enough to miss my eighth .300 season by only four points. By this point in my career I was benefiting from my knowledge of the pitchers after 15 years in the league. I also knew you had to bear down extra hard against the great ones like Marichal and company from the right side and left-handers like Curt Simmons, Chris Short, Whitey Ford in the World Series, and Sandy Koufax—if you were unlucky enough to have to face him. Then there was a guy named Johnny Schmitz, who pitched 13 years in the big leagues, mostly with the Cubs. He threw so slow that I once swung twice at the same pitch—and missed both times. No kidding!

Simmons was no bargain for me either. I hit the first two home runs of my career off him and never hit another. Bev was going to see a program at the parish school of our Brooklyn friend Jack McKinney once when I was leaving for Philadelphia. Jack followed baseball closely, so when Bev asked if I wanted her to say anything to Jack for me, I said, "Yeah. Ask him the best way to hit Simmons."

When she did, Jack's answer was, "Sneak up behind him."

Despite the declining years and the knee and the elbow, playing in Los Angeles became fun once I got over the heartache of leaving Brooklyn. Our World Series win in '59 seemed to close the book for good on our Brooklyn days. We were a different team and the letters on our cap were *LA* instead of a *B*. We couldn't change any of that. We could regret it, and I certainly did, but once we made the adjustment, and then won the Series in '59, our conversion was complete.

The kids were beginning to realize their father was a celebrity, and it wasn't always a plus for them. I've never cared much for the word "celebrity," but I've never objected to being a public figure. Baseball has brought me a great life and enabled me to do things for my family that I might never have been able to provide.

However, for the children of celebrities, it can be a different story. When Pam was growing up she knew only that I was a ball player. She was too young to know whether I was achieving any success, just that people knew who I was. She remembers going to a game at the Coliseum with Kevin one night. Kevin had this thing about not letting the fans around him know who he was, but Pam never labored under that burden. When I came up to bat, Pam jumped up and screamed, "C'mon, Dad!"

Kevin shoved her down into her seat and said firmly, "Don't you ever say that!"

Pam said innocently, "But he *is* my Dad."

Pam's way of handling the situation as she got older was more inventive. One of her coworkers in San Jose introduced her to a friend and said, "This is Duke Snider's daughter." He didn't even mention her name. Pam was seething, but she didn't say anything. She just filed it in the back of her mind, and swore she'd get even.

The opportunity came a few months later, when she was about to introduce the coworker, Jerry Carp, to one of her friends. "This is Joe Carp's son," she said.

Jerry knew immediately what was going on. "You got me," he said. "I'll never do that again."

Children of celebrities pay another price too. The celebrity is often away from home for long periods of time, especially athletes and entertainers. "You accept it after a while," Kevin remembers, "but in the early stages I missed you a lot. Mom was strict, but she was good. I realize how hard it was for her, raising us by herself most of the year. She had to be the heavy, even with money. We soon learned if we wanted something extravagant, we'd have to wait until you got home. Pam and I would be down at the stationery store and we'd see a pen we wanted and Mom would say no. We'd look at each other and say, 'Wait till Dad gets home.' Sure enough, we'd get that pen."

Kevin went on to become an excellent high school baseball player, and Kurt had a successful high school football career—the first Snider to score a touchdown. Dawna was too young to remember my playing career, but when she was about to enter Fallbrook High School, Kurt and Kevin took her aside. They said, "Now don't go around school telling everyone you're Kurt and Kevin Snider's sister. Get known for yourself." It sounded familiar. Only the names were different.

While Bev was doing double duty—my job at home as well as hers—with our four kids ages one to 13, I was out making a living for all of us. After my topsy-turvy 1961 season and the broken

237

elbow, my mood was upbeat for '62. I was ready for another exciting year, ready to try to overtake the Cincinnati Reds and win one more pennant—number seven—before calling it a career.

The Coliseum nightmare was behind us now. We were moving into a brand new ball park, Dodger Stadium, in 1962. Drysdale wouldn't be scraping his knuckles on the left-field wall with every pitch, and I wouldn't be aiming at a right-field wall more than 400 feet away from me. The team was ready to play there, and win there.

We closed the gap on the Reds and passed them in '62, but the San Francisco Giants closed the gap on *us*. History was repeating itself. We finished in a tie with our transplanted enemies. There was going to be another playoff series, the Dodgers and the Giants again, just like 1951.

Everything seemed to be the same, only it was different.

1951 Revisited

Few athletes have been so privileged to be in as many showdown situations as I was during one playing career—six pennants and World Series, three ties which forced playoffs, and the to-the-wire race against the Phillies in 1950. And no professional athlete would complain about it. I would have loved to have finishes like those in every one of my 18 years as a major-leaguer.

The 1962 season was another of those pressure years, and it seemed to be coming from every direction. The Reds were defending champions and were a factor to be reckoned with. Any team with an outfield of Frank Robinson, Vada Pinson, and Wally Post had to be a contender, and they got a lot of help from Gordie Coleman, Don Blasingame, and our old pepperpot, Don

Zimmer, plus two 20-game winners on their pitching staff—Bob Purkey and Joey Jay. Pittsburgh was a definite threat with Roberto Clemente, Bill Mazeroski, Dick Groat, Bill Virdon, Bob Skinner, and Smoky Burgess and pitchers like Bob Friend, Harvey Haddix, Vernon Law, and fork-baller Roy Face.

Our crosstown opponents from the old New York days hadn't been standing still either. The Giants hadn't won a pennant in eight years, but they were solid in 1962 with Orlando Cepeda, Willie Mays, Willie McCovey, Harvey Kuenn, Jim Davenport, and the Alou Brothers, Felipe and Matty. Add hitters like that to a pitching staff which produced 16 wins by Billy Pierce, 18 by Marichal, 19 by Billy O'Dell, and 24 by Jack Sanford, plus 19 saves by Stu Miller, and you have a team to be reckoned with.

All that competition could only bring out the best in us Dodgers. And we had some pretty good guns of our own. Tommy Davis had established himself solidly as our left fielder and would lead the National League in hitting that year with a .346 average and in RBIs with 153. He had 27 home runs, and Frank Howard, a major-leaguer for keeps, added 31 homers of his own, another 119 RBIs, and a .296 average. Campy's successor behind the plate, Johnny Roseboro, was continuing our tradition of strength in that position by leading the league in putouts with 842, a tribute to his own skill and to our pitching staff led by those strikeout artists, Koufax and Drysdale. We led the league in strikeouts that year, and Drysdale topped the league in wins with 25.

Then there was Maury Wills. He was the backup behind Don Zimmer until the middle of 1959, when he became our starting shortstop. The first thing he did was lead the National League in stolen bases with 50 in his first full season. The second thing he did was lead the National League in stolen bases in his second season with 35.

And the third thing he did was break Ty Cobb's record for stolen bases by stealing 104 in the next season, 1962. He led the league for three more years in a row—six straight years as the stolen-base king.

What Maury Wills did in 1962 was hard to believe, even for his teammates who watched him every day. Pitchers kept throwing over to first base to hold him close, catchers kept calling for pitchouts to try to nail him attempting to steal, and the other teams in the league must have set a record, if there is such a thing, for most fastballs thrown in one league in the same season. He had bruises all over his arms, legs, and back from so much sliding. Our hitters behind Wills were loving all those fastballs, and still the opposition couldn't stop him.

Wills had that unbeatable combination of speed, smarts, and nerve. He knew just how far to take a lead off first because he studied each pitcher's motion, and he knew when he could break for second against each one, because he had the guts of a burglar. He was half of our offense, between the bases he stole and the errors he forced our opponents into making.

Buzzie Bavasi paid me an honor at the begining of the '62 season. He appointed me the team captain, the same position Pee Wee had for many years.

Deep down inside, I felt sure I had one more good year. Every aging athlete feels that way, but I was sure of it, even though I was an occasional starter and a pinch hitter, I wasn't going to be a starter any more on a team with young players like Tommy Davis, Willie Davis, Ron Fairly, and Frank Howard, but I knew the team had a chance to win the pennant, and I knew I could help.

Buzzie told me, "I want you to help the young players. I want your experience to rub off on them." I was happy to do it, but I must admit I became preoccupied with extending my own career and didn't devote as much time and attention to being captain as I should have—until the last game we played that year, which became my last as a Dodger.

There was an ominous development with one week to go in the season. We were in St. Louis for a series with the Cardinals. Mr. O'Malley made the trip with us, and he called a meeting that included Alston, his coaches, our PR man—Red Patterson—and me as team captain.

O'Malley laid things right on the table for all of us: "Gentlemen, if we don't win this thing, some heads are going to roll."

I didn't understand why he was so uptight about our chances. I spoke up and said, "Don't worry, Mr. O'Malley. We're going to win it." I couldn't imagine anyone in the organization having any doubts about it. The players certainly expected to win. Why wouldn't the rest of the organization, especially our president, feel the same way? The history books show, of course, that we didn't win it—and the only head that rolled was mine.

We were playing well in September because we had already been through our slump. Every team, even one headed for a pennant, will hit a snag at some point during the season. Ours came in August, and it was a strange time. Wally Moon and I, two of the most experienced players on the team, were being used mainly as pinch hitters, and then only against a right-handed pitcher. I went through one stretch of seven weeks without playing even one out on defense.

Toward the end of that spell, we were playing a game against the Cubs and Walter Alston had used everyone except pitchers and me. He turned to me and, not surprisingly, said, "You'll be the hitter if they bring Barney Schultz in." That's what happened. The game went into extra innings, we loaded the bases, and in comes Schultz—and Snider.

"Okay," Walt says, "win it for us." I got a single and won the game.

After the game I told Alston, "I was beginning to wonder if I should just go in and shower and use some deodorant. I haven't gotten too many calls lately."

Alston said, "I'm waiting for the right spot."

When the team hit its snag in late August, Moon and I found ourselves in the lineup more often. Both of us started hitting, and the team started winning again. Both of us knew Alston had to take a certain risk defensively when he put Wally and me in the starting lineup. Neither of us was a kid any more, and we couldn't cover the ground that the younger outfielders could, but we could "cheat" a little on defense with our knowledge of where to play certain hitters, and we certainly had more experience than the kids in playing under the pressures of a September pennant drive.

Buzzie Bavasi didn't help the cause any with a remark he made to Maury Wills, although I'm sure Buzzie didn't mean it to sound the way it did. In September Maury broke Cobb's record, and a few days later Buzzie said to him, "Now that you have the stolen-base record, maybe we can concentrate on winning a game or two and win the National League pennant."

The reason I'm sure Buzzie didn't mean anything by it is that when Wills stole bases, we won ball games. He'd walk, steal second and score on a single to the outfield, or he'd get a hit, steal second, get bunted to third, and score on a fly ball or a ground ball. His stolen bases were a key part of our offense, and Buzzie certainly couldn't have been telling Wills to stop stealing bases now. You could see we were winning by looking at the standings. You could see *how* we were wining by looking at Maury, with those scratches and bruises and strawberry marks all over his legs and hips.

Whatever Buzzie's reason was, he made the remarks a few minutes before game time one day in late September and Wills immediately went straight into the trainer's room. He wasn't going to play after what his general manager told him.

Jim Gilliam came to me with the problem, which I hadn't known about, and said, "Duke, Maury is so mad he says he's not going to play."

At about the same time, Alston handed me the day's lineup card. Moon and I were starting again. Maury wasn't. I had to speak up as captain and lay it on the line this time.

"Walt, as much as I want to be in this lineup, and as much as Moon wants to, Wills *has* to be in there. He can get on, steal a base, and win the game for us."

Alston said, "Don't make any rash decisions. I'm working on a couple of things here."

One decision I made, rash or not, was to send Gilliam into the trainer's room to talk to Wills. I told Jim, "You have to talk Wills into playing. Tell him to just forget what Buzzie said, that he didn't mean it the way it sounded. We need Wills in there, Jim. We've *got* to win this game."

Gilliam's pleadings were successful. Wills listened to reason, put the whole thing behind him, and went back into the lineup. This was no time to lose the guy who was so important to our offense and was our starting shortstop too.

The scene shifts now to the last inning of the last game of the playoffs in 1962. We finished tied with the Giants again, just like 1951, and we split the first two games, just like 1951, and we're leading in the ninth inning of the final game, just like 1951, against the Giants, just like 1951. The score was 4-2. In 1951 at this point the score was 4-1.

I came out of the game in the eighth inning with a pulled thigh muscle, and was sitting on the far end of the bench. It looked all too familiar. There was too much 1951 in all this. I was the only player left from that team and I didn't like the symptoms. I didn't say anything. I just sat there at the far end of the bench and hoped. At the other end, Alston was plotting strategy with Leo Durocher.

Our pitchers were worn out by this point—Koufax, Podres, Ron Perranoski, Stan Williams, Ed Roebuck—all of them—except one, Don Drysdale. Roebuck was pitching. Big D was sitting next to me when the ninth inning started and I said to him, "Don, go down there and tell Alston you want to warm up. We could still lose this thing if we're not careful. It's only 4-2. In '51 it was 4-1 and we lost."

Don says, "I already told him."

"What did he say?"

"He said he's saving me for tomorrow." That would be the first game of the World Series, against the Yankees.

"Do you realize there might not *be* a tomorrow? Our staff is tired. Go down there and tell him again."

He came back a minute later and I asked him the same question: "What did he say?"

"He said I'm pitching tomorrow against the Yankees."

Durocher told me recently that he also tried to convince Alston to get Drysdale loose in case Roebuck ran out of gas. Alston told him, "Roebuck's my man." Leo told him he was crazy.

A few minutes later, Leo tried again. Alston said again, "Roebuck's my man." When Leo then questioned Alston's sanity in more candid terms, Alston said, "Well, then, you're fired."

Durocher said, "I can get a job tomorrow, but you're still wrong if you don't get Drysdale ready."

Finally Alston did make a change, but it wasn't Drysdale, it was Williams. Alston sent Leo to the mound to make the change. Leo was the winning manager in the '51 playoff game. He was about to become a losing coach in '62.

The Giants got a couple of men on base and up comes Harvey Kuenn, one of the best hitters in either league and a tough man to defend against because he hit the ball to all fields. Alston thought he would hit to the right side, so he waved our second baseman, Larry Burright, more toward first base and Wills was waved over from the normal shortstop position toward second. Our end of the bench started calling to our third baseman, Gilliam, telling him to move Burright back toward his normal position closer to second, not to be so far over toward first.

Jim called in to us, "I can't tell him. They want him over there where he is."

In the dugout we didn't think Kuenn would hit to the right side. We were expecting him to hit the ball to short or up the middle. The managerial staff obviously expected otherwise—that Kuenn would hit the ball to the right side.

Unfortunately, we were right. Kuenn hit a ground ball to the left side, straight to Wills—a routine double-play ball, especially against Kuenn, who did not run well. Maury made the quick pickup, but then he had to wait for Burright to get to the bag because he was playing so far toward first. Burright got the throw from Wills, pivoted, and made a jump throw to Ron Fairly at first.

Kuenn beat the throw by half a step. The Giant rally continued and the Giants won the game and the pennant, 6-4.

The scene immediately became ugly. A couple of our players coming off the field, knowing they had just lost thousands of dollars as their share of the World Series money, screamed at Alston, "You stole my money!"

I jumped on them right away, even though I had disagreed with so much of Alston's strategy. I told them, "Shut up! Just shut up!"

In our dressing room the atmosphere was somber, just like 1951. That's when being team captain is no fun at all. I knew how Pee Wee felt in 1951. I had told the team the day before to bring some bubbly to this game if they wanted to, because win or lose, we were going to celebrate a great season. So in the gloom and despair, slowly the corks started to pop. Alston was in his office, and the coaches were not in with us either. It was just us players. I said to my teammates, "I'm not going to let the press in for a few minutes, fellows."

I opened the door slightly and told the reporters waiting on the other side, "Let's wait a few minutes before you come in. It's pretty grim in there."

They said, as I knew they would, "But we have deadlines to meet."

"I know you do, but it's not a pretty scene right now." Then I closed the door and kept them out.

Wally Moon, who was the team's player representative, said a few words of consolation, especially for the sake of the younger players.

Alston came out of his office and asked me to let the press in, but I refused for the same reasons I gave the reporters. "Duke," he said, "you're violating club policy. You know it's our policy to let the reporters into the clubhouse right after a game with no waiting period."

I knew that. I also knew this was an extreme case, and because of '51 I had a special understanding of the depression in that room. I refused Alston's request. He reminded me again that I was disobeying the club's policy, but nobody was going to talk me out of it, not even Mr. O'Malley himself. I was their team captain.

A few minutes later I told the team, "I'm going over to congratulate Alvin Dark and his players. But as soon as I come back, I'm going to have to open this door, so get ready because the vultures are going to come in."

I went across the way to the Giants' dressing room and found Alvin in all the chaotic celebrating, with champagne shooting all over the place. I would have congratulated the opposing manager in a situation like that anyhow, but there was an extra reason to seek out Alvin. He was the Giants' shortstop in 1951 when Bobby Thomson's home run beat us. He and I had been through this before. Both times Alvin was with the Giants. Both times I was with the Dodgers. And both times Alvin won.

He could not have been more gracious when he spotted me. He gave me a big hug and said, "Duke, you're the one guy I feel sorry for in all this, and that's because it's happened to you twice."

Then I went back to our own dressing room, opened the door, and 15 to 20 reporters blew in. Half of them left right away. There didn't seem to be a story for them after all. Nobody felt like talking, so the reporters went over to the Giants' dressing room, where people were in a more talkative mood. If the writers had listened to me in the first place, they could have been over there a lot sooner. The media crisis passed.

I've since thought a lot about what I did that afternoon. If I had to do it over, I'd do the same thing. I don't think it was wrong to keep the writers out for a few minutes in that unusual situation. There would have been some nasty quotes about our strategy and we would have had a far worse team problem than we did with a few writers grumbling about the First Amendment. I told Alston I was willing to take full responsibility for my actions. I would tell Buzzie or Mr. O'Malley or anyone else that Walt had tried to talk me into admitting the reporters, but I had refused, for reasons which I thought were in everyone's best interests.

247

In the spring of 1963, Alston spoke to us. He said we could make something positive out of the defeat, as crushing as it was. He said we were an outstanding team and we could convert this defeat into a determination to come back and be even better.

When he was finished, I said, "Walt, can I say something?"

He gave me the floor.

I told my teammates, "This same thing happened to the Dodgers in 1951. Right after that game, Mr. O'Malley came into our dressing room and told us we could make our loss a positive experience. We could go to spring training in '52 knowing that we were good and feeling more determined than ever to win the pennant.

"The same thing can happen here. We can commit ourselves to making this defeat a 'positive negative' and winning the pennant."

I'm sure nobody was eager to agree with me. I certainly didn't get any standing ovation for my motivational message. Neither did Mr. O'Malley 11 years before, but after the Giants beat us in the '51 playoff we won the pennant in four of the next five years. And after the Giants beat us in the '62 playoff, the Dodgers won the pennant in three of the next four years.

We had a saying on the team that spring in Vero Beach—"Who moved Burright?" I should have squelched that, but I didn't. All of us were still smarting over what we considered was a giveaway the year before. We were more convinced than ever, six months later, that we were better than the Giants and that we would have beaten the Yankees in the World Series. The Giants lost to them in seven games in '62. The Dodgers would sweep them in four games in '63.

We were also still convinced that Drysdale would have slammed the door in that ninth inning without giving up the four runs that our tired pitchers did. It did no good to argue that Drysdale would pitch against the Yankees the next day in the opening game of the World Series. The next time Drysdale pitched against the Yankees was six months later. It wasn't the World Series by then. It was only spring training.

Many years later Walt Alston and I were talking about our years together with the Dodgers. He's one of only 11 managers in the Hall of Fame, and goodness knows he deserves it, but as we were reliving our times together, I asked, almost with hesitation, "Walt, what about the '62 playoffs?"

Walter Alston was a strong and direct man. "Duke," he said, "out of my whole managerial career, I'd like to have back the last week of the '62 season, and the playoffs."

He had gone to our defensive lineup, starting the kids again and putting Wally Moon and me back on the bench. I knew what Walt was thinking, that we only needed to win a couple. But we lost our momentum when he switched from an offensive lineup to a defensive one, and the Giants got hot at the same time.

"I made a mistake going to our defensive lineup," Walt went on, "and I should have had Don Drysdale warming up in that last game. I made a mistake there. I know about the second-base situation with Burright too. We knew about the conversation down at your end of the bench."

Buzzie Bavasi has told me that Mr. O'Malley gave him the authority to fire Alston after the '62 playoffs, but Buzzie refused even though he was extremely upset about the loss. His defense of Alston: "Every manager is entitled to one mistake, one bad playoff, or one bad World Series." Buzzie knew what he was talking about. Walt won seven pennants for the Dodgers, four of them after 1962, and his teams won the World Series four times.

In spring training six months later, I began getting those telltale signals, the little messages that players recognize. I was left behind when the Dodgers played games in other parts of Florida. I was called at 8:30 in my room and told to report to the minor-league game at 9 that morning. When I played on the major-league team, I was playing only in the late innings.

I knew the message: "They're telling me that I'm gone." The whole team, including me, flew to Albuquerque for one of our last spring exhibition games before flying back to California for the start of the season. Some of my teammates told me before we boarded the plane that I had been sold.

Sold? Not even traded for another player? You mean the Dodgers thought so little of me that they just sold me? It was a long flight to Albuquerque.

When we landed, I was still a Dodger, or so I thought. Mr. O'Malley called me aside and said, "Duke, it's official. You've been sold to the Mets." I didn't ask, but I wondered: Did my stand against the press in the clubhouse door have anything to do with it?

Being sold was humiliating enough, but being sold to the New York Mets in those days seemed like the ultimate humiliation. They were the worst team in baseball. I wasn't going to a contender. I was sold. And to the Mets!

Buzzie Bavasi was so upset at my leaving that he couldn't bring himself to tell me, which the general manager should do. He had to ask Mr. O'Malley to tell me. I wasn't angry with Buzzie about that. We were friends, and we still are. In fact, I felt as sorry for Buzzie as I did for myself, almost. He obviously felt the same way. The price of the sale was $40,000. At the end of the season, he gave me $10,000 of it.

I called Buzzie as soon as Mr. O'Malley gave me the word and told him I was thinking about retiring. "Don't do it," he said. "Go to New York and get your 400 home runs and 2,000 hits." Buzzie's advice was right on the money again. That's what I did.

My teammates found me in the hotel where we were staying—where *they* were staying—and said they wanted to throw a party for me. It turned out to be more of a wake than a party. Don Zimmer was there, and Ron Perranoski, Bill Skowron—who had just come over to the Dodgers from the Yankees, Don Drysdale, Sandy Koufax, Ron Fairly, Johnny Podres, Don Zimmer, and others—12 to 15 of my friends. There were a lot of tears shed, real tears. With all the defeats and disappointments over 16 years as a Dodger, this was my saddest day.

After I left the team—my team—Bob Hunter of the *Los Angeles Herald-Examiner* wrote a touching column about the sorrow of it all. Bev still has the article, in her scrapbook for 1963:

> . . . as did the wagon trains of long ago, baseball made an overnight stop here on the shifting sands of the New Mexico desert. When baseball left these wastelands, it left without Duke Snider.
>
> And not even a wooden cross marks the lonesome spot they picked for the obituary of a star.

One Last Chance

That nightclub act with Milton Berle in the off season between 1962 and 1963 turned out to be good preparation for joining the New York Mets. On one hand, you had to be able to make people laugh. And on the other, you had to be able to laugh yourself.

I went to the Mets despite Charlie Dressen's efforts to get me for his team. He was managing the Detroit Tigers, who were not exactly a contender themselves in 1963, but at least they won 28 more games than the Mets did. The Tigers and the Dodgers weren't able to agree on a deal so I went to the Mets and immediately joined what amounted to the Dodgers Alumni Association. The Mets had Gil Hodges, Larry Burright, Roger Craig, Charlie Neal, Larry Sherry's brother Norm, and Tim Harkness.

I was self-conscious about what the baseball fans of New York might think of me because I was not nearly the player they remembered from my Brooklyn days. But the fans, and the writers too, were great about it. I even asked the writers, "Make sure you tell the fans that I'm not the player I was."

When I walked through the door of the dressing room in center field on Opening Day, I was still thinking about the strangeness of dressing in the home team's clubhouse at the Polo Grounds, the one used by the Giants until both teams moved to California. As I was thinking about that, I came out onto the outfield grass and started walking toward the infield. The first few fans who saw me started applauding, and the noise seemed to build with each step I took. I was getting goose pimples. Everyone was being nice to this old Dodger.

I looked around and touched the beak of my cap to acknowledge the nice welcome I was hearing. As I looked I saw banners hanging from the stands saying:

BEDFORD AVENUE, DUKE!

**IT'S WORTH THE LOOT
TO GET THE DUKE**

**WELCOME HOME, DUKE—
WE STILL LOVE YOU!**

I went 0 for 5 on that first day, but I made a great catch to contribute something to the team. A few days later in a game against the Braves, the pitcher was Warren Spahn, the Hall of Fame left-hander. He threw me his slider. I hit it for a home run, my first as a Met.

Some nice things happened to me while I was with the Mets, with the compliments of the Cincinnati Reds. I hit the 400th home run of my career against the Reds in Cincinnati, off Bob Purkey. It was a long shot, not a cheapie, and I was proud of reaching that milestone. The ball is now on display at the

Baseball Hall of Fame in Cooperstown. I also got the 2,000th hit of my career in Cincinnati, against Jim Maloney. Once again, Buzzie Bavasi had been right. He advised me against retiring after the '62 season. I went out and reached that double milestone, just as he said I would.

I got a telegram from Los Angeles after getting that 400th home run, from Dr. Kerlan, the Dodgers' physician who had helped me through my knee troubles so much during my years with them. The wire said:

CONGRATULATIONS ON 400TH HOME RUN, A TESTI-MONIAL TO MEDICAL SCIENCE.

There wasn't a whole lot of publicity about the 400th homer. I was playing with the worst team in baseball and we were on the road anyhow, so it didn't get much notice. My new teammate Jimmy Piersall needled me about it. "I bet I'll get more ink when I hit my *one* hundredth than you got with your *four* hundredth," he said.

Piersall had a reason for his confidence. He hit number 100 back in New York, the top media town in the country, but he wasn't going to let it go at that. He rounded the bases backwards, and slid into home plate head first. That picture was used in papers and on TV stations all over America. That's why he knew he'd get more ink than I did. He'd planned the stunt all along.

With characters like Jimmy Piersall and "Marvelous Marv" Throneberry and a manager like Casey Stengel, you expected such things from the Mets in those early years. They were the worst team in the history of baseball the year before, losing 120 games— a new team stocked with the rejects from the older teams. In my year with them, we lost 111. Throneberry has said that the Mets weren't all that bad, that they had a lot of bad luck. There isn't enough bad luck in the whole world to make you lose 120 games. That takes a team effort.

255

Stengel was the best commentator on the state of the Mets. Here was the man who had managed the New York Yankees for 12 seasons and won five straight pennants and World Series in his first five years on the job. He was with the Yankees for 12 seasons and won ten pennants and seven World Series. Then he was fired after the 1960 season. The reason announced by the Yankees was that Casey had reached the mandatory retirement age of 70—something you could never get away with today—but everyone knew the real reason was that he lost the World Series that year, to the Pittsburgh Pirates, and the Yankees had a habit in those years of asking their players and managers, "What have you done for us lately?"

When the Mets were born two years later, they grabbed the "retired" Stengel in a hurry as a drawing card against their city rivals, the Yankees. Then they went one better than that and hired George Weiss, the Yankees' general manager during those glory years, who was fired with Stengel for the same announced reason.

Stengel knew what he had with the Mets, and what he didn't have. He looked around at his crop of rejects one day and asked the world at large, "Can't anybody here play this game?" Then, converting a negative into a positive, he wrote a book by that title.

When I joined his team in '63, Stengel told the writers, "We'll be all right. All we need are ball players."

It was a miserable experience, playing for a team losing 111 games. If you think it hurts to be defeated, try having it happen to you 111 times in six months. It was as much my fault as it was anyone else's too, because I couldn't do the things I used to be capable of. Casey Stengel made that year bearable for me. He accorded me respect because of our years of competing against each other in those World Series, and he liked the way I was serious about the game. He saw how much all that losing got to me, and he tried to help me through it.

Losing is difficult to take for someone who has the pride of a professional athlete, but losing is like anything else—it can become a habit. And when you find yourself getting used to it, you've got a big problem. You'll never pull yourself out of it once you start feeling: "There doesn't seem to be anything we can do about losing, so let's just relax and not worry about it."

That was the feeling of the New York Mets in 1963, and I had trouble accepting it after 16 seasons with a consistently winning ball club. Stengel went out of his way to help.

We were sitting next to each other on the bench one day in a game against the Reds when Casey said, "Hey, kid, I'm going to grab a few winks. You're managing the team." He often called players "kid," just like Babe Ruth.

When Stengel decided to rest his eyes for a while, we were losing, 3-1. When he woke up it was 9-1. I told him, "Casey, I hate to tell you this, but now we're losing by a lot more. It's 9-1."

Stengel gave me one of his infamous winks and said, "Don't worry about it, kid. It's not your fault. You look over there into the Cincinnati dugout and what do you see? All mahogany. Then you look at our bench and all you see is driftwood."

We were in Chicago for a series with the Cubs when I walked through the lobby of the Conrad Hilton Hotel, Pee Wee's favorite hotel, heading toward my room. It was 11:30 and I wanted to get to bed because we had a day game the next day, but as I passed the bar a familiar voice called out, "Hey, kid! C'mere!"

Casey was in there talking baseball with the bartender. I went in and Casey invited me to join him for a drink. I told him I wanted to get to bed because we had a game the next afternoon, but he told me, "Don't worry about it. You're not in the lineup anyhow." I overlooked the remark and joined him.

The man's endurance was hard to believe, for someone in his 70s or even his 40s. We closed the place up at 2 A.M. Then this 73-year-old man says, "Come on with me. I know a place that's open till four."

We closed that place up too.

The next morning we got on the team bus to go to Wrigley

Field and I'm really dragging and there's Stengel, almost 40 years older, just as bright-eyed and bushy-tailed as you please, ready to take on the world.

On the bus to the ball park he says, "Sit next to me on the bench today. We'll talk about the '52 Series." He always wanted to talk about those great times, but it was always the '52 Series, or '49, or '53. It was never '55, the year we beat him.

I said, "When are we going to talk about '55?"

"Later."

We never did.

Despite Stengel's clowning ways, you always knew he was the manager. He ran things, and he ran them his way. In spring training he took the whole team through an all-day lecture out on the field. He got us all around home plate and then went over every possible thing that can happen at home plate. Then he led us down to first base and did the same thing there. We went to every infield position, the mound, and the outfield. We didn't do another thing that whole day, not even batting practice.

He seemed to notice more things than the rest of us, even suggesting to one of our pitchers, Alvin Jackson, that he wear the beak of his cap lower when he had a runner on first base. Stengel told Jackson he was tipping off his throws to first base with the movement of his eyes. Casey's solution: Make it harder for the runner to see your eyes.

Casey had that habit of dozing off on the bench. Once when he did, Charlie Neal slipped him a hot foot, a popular stunt in dugouts in those days. It's almost impossible to tell who the culprit is when you're rudely awakened by a match burning a hole in your shoe, but somehow, Casey knew.

Neal was traded to Cincinnati shortly after that. When Stengel gave him the news he added, "And you can take your matches with you."

He tried never to miss a trick, even where he was involved himself. I went into his office after a game one Saturday afternoon and there he was putting Shinola liquid shoe polish—light brown—on his hair. I asked him what he was doing and he said, "Edna and I are going out to dinner with some friends tonight and I don't want them to think I'm as old as I am."

"But, Casey—that's *shoe polish!*"

"I know it—but it's the right color."

Casey Stengel was serious about his American heritage. The story is told that a few days before he died, a baseball game was about to begin on the television set in his hospital room. Stengel, knowing he was a dying man, struggled out of his bed, stood up, put his right hand over his heart, and sang the National Anthem with the crowd—every word of it.

The longest disagreement I ever had with an umpire started in 1963. It lasted several years into my managerial career in the minors.

Frank Walsh was umpiring a game we were playing against the Giants at Candlestick Park in San Francisco when a Giant hitter sent a long fly ball down the left-field line. I was playing left and hustled over, but the ball curved foul and landed in the seats, only Walsh didn't call it foul. He called it a fair ball—a home run off Roger Craig. I ran into the infield and argued the call, but he wasn't about to listen. Someone else was so mad at the call he kicked in the door to the umpires' dressing room, and the next day all the Mets resumed the argument. That's how bad the call was, but it stood. We lost the argument and the game.

Frank Walsh lost more than that—his job. There were so many complaints about that decision, and maybe other things we didn't know about, that Walsh's contract was not renewed for the 1964 season.

A few years later I was managing the Dodgers' Albuquerque farm club and we were playing a game in Little Rock. I was talking to Joe Medwick, who was with Little Rock, when we heard this voice from the grandstand holler, "If you don't break up that conversation down there, it's going to cost you. You're going to get fined for fraternization." That is the rule that says you can't get too chummy with the opposition before a game.

I turned and saw Frank Walsh up in the stands. He was going to be our umpire that night. I bowed slightly and said with mock respect, "Yes, sir, Mr. Walsh." When it came time for me to present my lineup card to him at home plate just before the start of the game, he said to me, "That ball was fair in San Francisco."

I said, "Frank, did you ever stop to think that's why you're umpiring down here in the Texas League?"

"I don't have to take any guff from you," he snapped. "You give me any and I'll throw you outta this game before it even starts."

"Yes, sir, Mr. Walsh."

"And don't keep calling me 'Mr. Walsh' either."

"That's not what I'd like to call you, Frank, but I'm not going to use any profanity."

"Good. Now let's get this game started."

It was a hot night and in the late innings my pitcher began to run out of gas. I went to the mound and began to stall for time, so my relief pitcher could get warmed up. Walsh comes out and says, "I'll give you fifteen seconds to finish your business out here or this game belongs to Little Rock."

I told him, "Mr. Walsh, you've got a big chip on your shoulder."

"Don't call me Mister."

Ted Sizemore, my catcher, was loving every minute of it. He used to run to the mound whenever Walsh and I got into it so he wouldn't miss a word.

Walsh says, "You better make your decision," and when he said it he spat the words out—maybe accidentally, but I was getting a saliva shower.

"Frank, please don't spit at me."

Then I waved in my relief pitcher from the bullpen. But Walsh

260

doesn't leave it at that. He runs all the way out to the new pitcher and starts cussing at him and yelling to him to hurry up and get to the pitcher's mound.

I thought that was a bit much. "Frank," I said, "if you're going to cuss anybody, cuss me. Leave my pitcher alone."

That was the end of that particular episode, but not of the story.

We got him again in Amarillo later that month, and, naturally, trouble erupted. My shortstop, Donnie Williams, was called out by Walsh on a close play at home after I waved him in from third. Donnie starts to argue with Frank and I ran down to the plate to stick up for my player. Frank, so help me, starts to swing at Donnie with his mask. He had already done that once in the Pacific Coast League, and I knew it. This time somebody grabbed him, I grabbed Donnie, and we were able to avoid something much worse than just an argument at home plate.

A few weeks later, we were playing El Paso, managed by my old Dodger pal, Rocky Bridges, when the same thing happened. Donnie Williams got called out by Frank on a close play at the plate. Donnie said something and then walked toward our dugout. Walsh stares at him and follows him with his eyes. From my third-base coach's box I call into the plate, "Don't stare him down, Frank. Get the game going."

"Don't tell me what to do."

I walked to the plate slowly and started talking calmly when Frank tries the same thing—he starts to swing at me with his mask. I wrapped my arms around him, picked him up, and slammed him down to the ground on the first-base side of home plate. Rocky then grabbed me, and some of the players grabbed Walsh.

Rocky says, "He's not worth it, Duke."

I was thrown out of the game, to the surprise of no one. The next day, fans kept calling me and telling me they were witnesses, that they saw that Walsh was going to hit me with his mask. Rocky said he would testify in my behalf, if something came of it. What came of it was that we were both punished. I was suspended, and Walsh was fined, almost an unheard-of development involving an umpire.

A couple of months later I was managing a game in Dallas-Fort Worth when Walsh called to me from the umpire's room.

He asks, "Can I talk to you for a minute?"

"Sure, Frank."

"I want to apologize. The thing in San Francisco might have cost me my job, and I've been taking it out on you. You've needled me pretty good all this time, but I asked for it. It's been my fault, and I want to apologize."

I said, "Frank, that's fine with me. We all make mistakes. No umpire in the world has gone his whole career without making mistakes." We shook hands.

My team got every close call that day. Later in the Dixie Series against Birmingham, which had Reggie Jackson, Joe Rudi, and Dave Duncan on their way up to the A's, Frank was umpiring and every close play he had seemed to go our way.

Not long after that, Frank Walsh retired and moved to San Antonio. I was managing the Alexandria ball club by then, and every time we came to San Antonio for a game, Frank would come down to the field and we'd have a little visit. During one of those chats, several years after the incident in San Francisco that started it all, he said, "You know, Duke, I think it's really nice that you and I became friends."

I felt the same way.

I received two honors in one day in New York in 1963. They gave me a night at the Polo Grounds—imagine, an old Dodger being saluted at the Polo Grounds!—and the Sky Island Club of Long Island roasted me in a luncheon at Roosevelt Field.

The luncheon was attended by 350 Long Island executives and government officials plus celebrities like Richard Nixon, Eddie Arcaro, Guy Lombardo, and Whitey Ford. There were wires, as always, from Pete Rozelle and Pee Wee, and one from Don Zimmer saying:

NEVER THOUGHT I'D SEE THE DAY WHEN THEY WOULD HONOR YOU AT THE POLO GROUNDS.

The night for me was one of the last baseball games played at Polo Grounds before the Mets moved to Shea Stadium. I wished the family could be there, but school was in session and Bev and the children were back in California. I was the last player to be given a night at the Polo Grounds. Lindsey Nelson was the emcee and he introduced many of my teammates—Jackie, Newk, Gil, Skoonj, "Oisk," Campy, Ralph Branca, and Cookie Lavagetto. It was an All-Star lineup, only we had all played on the same team.

They gave me a lot of beautiful presents, including a new Thunderbird. Another was a two-week trip for Bev and me to anywhere in the world. Instead we took only a one-week trip to Coco Palms in Kaui, Hawaii, with the four children, a vacation none of us will ever forget.

Alvin Dark, the Giants' manager, gave me a nice present too. He gave me Juan Marichal to hit against. I went 0 for 4.

The people of New York, the writers and the Mets management were great in their friendship with me that year, but the experience of losing 111 games was more than I could bear for a second year, so I asked the Mets if they could please make a deal that would send me to a team which might be a contender for the pennant. They obliged by selling me to the Giants. The Mets had honored my request by sending me to a contending team, and San Francisco was a lot closer to my home in San Diego than New York.

Maybe I wasn't upset, but Buzzie Bavasi was. He told me later he made the Mets agree to keep me for two years when he sold me to them. If they didn't, Buzzie was to get the opportunity to buy me back. "I knew I'd want you back," he said, but his counterpart with the Mets, George Weiss, made the deal with the Giants just after spring training was over, on the last weekend before the season started.

On the plane west to join the Giants, I was still remembering spring training at the Mets camp in St. Petersburg, the only training camp I was ever in which wasn't a Dodger camp. It was the weirdest camp of my career. Everything was a picnic. Nobody was going to take anything too seriously. It was the complete opposite of the environment in Dodgertown at Vero Beach, where everything was regimented and run on a detailed schedule. With the Mets there was a lot of standing around during practice. Off the field, you were on your own—no curfew. We went five straight days without batting practice.

When I reached San Francisco Opening Day was over, and the Giants had won. The Giants' front office called the next day to say it was sending over a uniform shirt and a photographer so they could get a publicity shot of me for the papers. I put the shirt and cap on, the orange and black, and checked myself in the mirror to make sure everything was straight. Then it hit me. What a sight—Duke Snider, the Duke of Flatbush, wearing a Giants' uniform.

No matter how you might justify it, I couldn't get used to the sight of myself wearing that uniform. But the Giants wanted me, and I wanted to help somebody win just one more pennant.

Chub Feeney, the Giants' president, apologized for not being able to give me number 4, but I already knew that wouldn't be possible. The Giants had retired that number years before in honor of the great Mel Ott. They gave me number 28 and Feeney said, "It doesn't matter what number you wear as long as you drive in some runs for us." I drove in only 17 and hit only four home runs, the first one against the Dodgers at Dodger Stadium off Joe Moeller, who played for me the next season when I managed in Spokane. Willey McCovey was on base when I hit it. The homer tied the game and the Giants eventually won.

I appeared in more games as a pinch hitter than as an outfielder. My manager for that final year, my old friend Alvin Dark, told me near the end of the season, "You won nine games for us, Duke— eight with your bat and one with your glove. You don't have anything to apologize to us for."

I was glad to hear him say that because I wanted to help Alvin as much as I could. He had a strong lineup, including most of the guys who had beaten us in the playoffs in 1962. We finished fourth in '64, but we were only three games behind the first place team, the Cardinals of Lou Brock, Curt Flood, Ray Sadecki, and Bob Gibson.

The Giants still had Mays, Cepeda, McCovey, the Alou brothers, Marichal, Gaylord Perry, Jack Sanford, and Bob Shaw. The only thing wrong with a lineup that strong was the equally strong egos and personalities. As the season wore on I could see the problem clearly. Professional jealousies kept that team from winning another pennant, and it's a tribute to Alvin Dark's ability as a manager that the Giants finished as high as they did.

Mays asked for a day off in May and Dark gave it to him. To Willie's credit, he came to the ball park, put on his uniform, and was available in the clubhouse if Alvin had needed him to pinch-hit or if someone got hurt. Not long after that, Orlando Cepeda said he wanted some time off too, and not just one day but two. Alvin granted that request too. The difference was that Cepeda never came to the park. He was gone for two days. We won the first game he missed, but we lost the second. If Cepeda had been available, he might have helped us with a pinch hit or some late-inning defense in that second game. That's the way it was with the Giants that year. A lot of talent, but too many factions and personalities. There's a difference between having nine guys on the field and having a team out there. The Dodgers proved that, especially the *Brooklyn* Dodgers. I wish we, the Dodgers, had known in '62 what I learned that year about the Giants. It might have helped us win the pennant.

In the last week of the season it was still a horse race. The Reds, Phillies, Cards, and Giants all had a shot at the pennant. Anything was possible—even a four-way tie. Out of fairness to the San Francisco management, Billy Pierce, a good left-handed pitcher who spent most of his career with the Chicago White Sox, and I told Chub Feeney we were retiring after the season. We wanted them to know early so they could decide on replacements. The Giants' front office then notified the National League that we were being put on waivers for the purpose of our unconditional release, and therein lies a story.

Pierce pitched three shutout innings on Saturday and I got a pinch-hit single and scored on a home run by Mays. We lost, though, and we were eliminated from the pennant race. The next morning, I packed my car and drove to Candlestick Park ready to leave right after the game for Fallbrook and Bev and the kids. I couldn't wait. The ordeal of finishing my career and just getting it over with was almost complete. In fact, it already was over, but I didn't know it.

When I got to the park, Alvin called Billy and me into his office and said we couldn't suit up for the game. The front office goofed. We'd been accidentally put on waivers on Friday, but no one had realized that made us ineligible immediately.

"In fact," Alvin told us, "you weren't even eligible yesterday or Friday."

Pierce was ineligible when he pitched those three shutout innings, and I was ineligible when I got my pinch single.

Billy asked the most pertinent question of all: "What would have happened if we'd won yesterday's game—with two ineligible players?"

Alvin said with a smile, "We'll never know."

I said my goodbyes and headed for my car. While my Giant teammates were playing their last game of the season, I was driving down the highway along the Pacific Ocean. Then it dawned on me: When I got the last hit of my major-league career, I was an ineligible player.

19

Who Goes Up
Must Come Down

Seeing your income plunge from $40,000 one year to $12,000 the next is not an experience I would recommend. That's what happened to me when my playing career ended. The most I ever made as a player was in the mid-five-figure range, and I was still hanging around that neighborhood when I retired at age 37.

I could handle the emotional adjustment of missing the only life I'd ever known, I could handle not seeing my teammates, the end of first-class travel across America, and the end of all the hero-worshipping. What Bev and I had trouble handling was the steep plunge in income. We were still feeding, clothing, and housing our family and paying for the education of four children, on an annual salary of $12,000. I wouldn't even have had that except Buzzie Bavasi had always promised me there would be a job for me in the Dodger organization when my playing days were over. When the time came, Buzzie kept his promise.

He hired me to do some advance work for him, plus some scouting and work as a hitting instructor, for $1,000 a month. Becoming a hitting instructor required me to go through a learning process. I had always been the student, but now I was the teacher. I applied some of the techniques that Branch Rickey and George Sisler used on me in 1948. Al Campanis talked to me at length every day about it. I talked to Charlie Lau and other successful hitting instructors, including Wally Moses, whose advice about pointing my front shoulder toward shortstop helped me so much in 1952. I wanted to be a good instructor.

Bev and I were getting by, but only because of some investments I made as a player. We sold our avocado ranch because the bowling lanes went bankrupt and I didn't have the time to work the ranch anyhow. After that, the only guaranteed income we had was my Dodger job, which worked out to $250 a week. It made for a lot of sleepless nights staring at the ceiling. That's when Bev instituted "the envelopes," her own system of finance which is now a legend in the Snider family. We weren't exactly on food stamps, but the days of free spending were obviously gone, at least for the time being, so we needed to control our expenditures. Bev made up a set of envelopes and wrote a specific purpose on each— clothes, gas, entertainment, and other "extras." On the first of each month she put money into each envelope. When the envelope was empty, that was it for the month. All four of our children still remember "Mom's envelopes." It was Bev's homemade system of accounting, and it worked. She got us through our private recession.

Fate brought Pete Reiser and me into each other's lives a second time a year after I retired as a player. Almost 20 years after being tapped to succeed him as the Dodgers' center fielder, I was tapped again, this time to succeed him as the Dodgers' manager of their farm team at Spokane.

Buzzie called me at home one morning early in the 1966 season and said, "Pete Reiser has just had a heart attack. I want you to go up to Spokane and manage the club for us. You'll be the acting manager until Pete comes back." Peter O'Malley was the general manager there.

Life in the minor leagues is difficult for everyone. The travel is hard—by bus many times—and you don't have any money. I remembered all this from my own days in the minors at Newport News and Fort Worth. On the other hand, maybe I could some day become a manager in the major leagues. This might be the break I needed.

I was pleased to be starting at the top of the minor-league structure, the AAA classification, but I didn't realize that Triple-A is the most difficult level for a manager. You have four different kinds of players in minor-league baseball—players who are going to make it eventually to the major leagues but are frustrated that they're not there already; those who know they'll never make it but keep hoping anyhow; those who have just been sent down for more experience and are angry; and the ex-major-leaguers who are just hanging on. At the Triple-A level, you have all four types, the only level where this takes place.

Some are trying hard and some are not. Some are a joy to work with and some are a royal pain in the neck. Some want advice and some reject it—they're going to hit .240 their way. In addition to having all four categories of minor-league players, Spokane now had a manager who was thinking he could still play in the majors—me.

Spokane was in last place when I took over and I didn't improve it much. The team was at the .500 level when Pete came back. I prepared to head back down the Coast to Fallbrook and was spending my last night as manager when the phone rang at 4 A.M. It was the Spokane trainer, Doc Mattei, saying, "Unpack your bags. Pete just had another one."

Things weren't going to improve a whole lot on that team. We had a weak pitching staff that got even weaker the night when our best relief pitcher, Thad Tillotson, got mad at an umpire's call and rammed his fist into a wall, breaking a finger on his pitching hand.

Even though we were not that successful as a team, five players made it to the big leagues—Bill Singer, Joe Moeller, Lou Johnson, Bart Shirley, and Al Ferrara.

We finished last. When I got back to Dodger Stadium after the season ended, I told Buzzie, "The players may not have learned much, but I learned an awful lot."

Despite the inauspicious beginning to my managerial career, Buzzie asked me to manage again the next season, at Tri-Cities, a small area in the desert on the Snake River in Washington, composed of the communities of Pasco, Kenniwick, and Richland. New York it wasn't, but the people were great.

I managed for four years in the minor leagues, and after that last-place finish in my first season, I managed nothing but first-place teams, and it started for me at Tri-Cities. The league itself made Spokane and Triple-A ball look like the big leagues. Far from being AAA, it was all the way at the bottom of the minor leagues—a rookie league for kids playing their first year of professional baseball, mostly kids right out of high school. You get an idea of how fundamental it is at that level when you hear this: On my first morning at Tri-Cities, I had to conduct a class on how to put on a baseball uniform and wear it properly.

One of the delights of managing young players in the low minors like a rookie league is their determination and their willingness to put up with almost anything in their burning desire to move up the ladder and into the big leagues. Ray Lamb, Ted Sizemore, and Billy Grabarkewitz were three such guys.

Lamb was a right-handed pitcher, 6-1 and 170 pounds, a California boy from Casey Stengel's adopted hometown of Glendale who made it up to the Dodgers and also pitched for the Cleveland Indians. He was an excellent pitcher in college for the University of Southern California, but he was overshadowed by another pitcher on that staff, a pitcher named Stewart, who was pitching for Yakima in our league. We had a doubleheader with

Yakima and I asked Lamb if he had any preference as to which game he would pitch. He certainly did. He wanted to start the second game, the one when he knew his former pitching teammate would be his opponent.

Lamb won the game on a shutout, 7-0. The two hooked up again later in the season. Lamb won that one too. By then he felt he had proved his point about just who was the better pitcher.

Just to make sure his old coach at USC, Rod Dedeaux, got the message, Lamb sent him the box score of each game.

Sizemore was just as competitive as Lamb was. I met the players on the first day of practice and had a little chat with each one. When I came to Sizemore and I asked him his position, he said, "I'm a catcher." I was surprised. The guy was 5 feet 10 inches tall, which isn't big for a catcher, and was definitely on the light side—165.

I said, "A skinny little guy like you and you're a catcher?"

Sizemore looked at me with determination suddenly written all over his face and said, "I'm a tough kid from Alabama and I can catch." He played college ball at Michigan State.

Well, he was a tough kid all right, and he made it to the big leagues for 12 successful seasons with the Dodgers, Cardinals, and Phillies, but not as a catcher. He became an infielder, mostly a second baseman. Out of 1,411 games as a major-leaguer, he caught four times.

But you couldn't tell him that at Tri-Cities. He was ready to take on anybody who doubted his ability to make it as a catcher. Another thing I loved about the guy was his enthusiasm for the game. He was always talking baseball, a throwback to the players we had on our team in Brooklyn, the old-fashioned kind who talked about his sport with as much zest as he showed as a player. Sizemore was my kind of guy. That's why he always rode with me on our road trips, sitting next to me in my Mustang. I did all the driving, and we talked nothing but baseball.

Grabarkewitz was just as hard-nosed and old-fashioned as Sizemore, and maybe for the same reason. He had the same dimensions—5-10, 165. He too made it to the big leagues, for seven good seasons as an infielder.

With competitors like Lamb, Sizemore, and Grabarkewitz we won the league championship. We had come a long way from that first morning when I had to show some of my players how to put on a uniform.

When Buzzie moved me up, to Albuquerque, I asked him to let me have all three of my favorites from Tri-Cities. I got two— Sizemore and Lamb. This league was more spread out, so we travelled by plane, one of the old classics, a chartered DC-3. The airline had several of them and we flew to Little Rock, Amarillo, Dallas-Fort Worth, San Antonio, and El Paso.

We repeated the Spokane success in helping to send players up to the big leagues—six this time—Sizemore, Lamb, Willie Crawford, Bill Sudakis, Bob Stinson, and Mike Kekich. We won our league championship again, and we did it our way. We played Amarillo three doubleheaders in the last week of the season, swept all three of them, and finished on top. Then it came time for the annual Dixie Series with the winner of the Southern League championship, Birmingham. We won the first two games of that series, a best of seven, and we were winning by three runs in the last inning of the third game. Our grip on the Dixie Series championship was getting firmer.

Ray Lamb was getting loose in the bullpen for the fourth game and was really popping the catcher's mitt. One of our relief pitchers, a fellow named Dermody, was in the game for us. He was a sinker-ball pitcher, and with men on first and third, he got the hitter to send a ground ball to Donnie Williams at short. The ball hit a pebble and bounced over Donnie's head. Then Dermody hit the next batter.

I looked out at the bullpen and Lamb was popping that catcher's mitt louder than ever. I was toying with the idea of bringing him in, even though he was a starter. He was a strikeout pitcher, and the next hitter, Dave Duncan, struck out a lot. If we won this game we'd be way out in front, three games to none, needing only one more win for the Dixie Series championship. But I decided against the move, feeling it was best not to fool with our pitching rotation at that point. Duncan hit a home run over the scoreboard and we lost, 9-8. I should have turned that decision over to my first-base coach, Joe Behl, who was a great help to me that year. He ran the team while I was suspended for three days after the Frank Walsh episode, and Joe won all three games.

Maybe the loss was my fault—I felt that way. But I knew I had made the right decision anyhow. Ray Lamb was my pitcher for game number four.

What I hadn't counted on were the birthday boys. When we arrived at the Albuquerque airport to fly to Birmingham, my players looked like the guys in the painting of the Spirit of '76. Willie Crawford and Ted Sizemore had birthdays around that time, and after the third game their thoughtful teammates had decided to throw a birthday party, right in the middle of the Dixie Series, at a bar. That was Misjudgment Number One. Misjudgment Number Two was their decision to pick a fight with the members of the New Mexico University football team. Lamb showed up with 14 stitches over his mouth. My third baseman, Bill Sudakis, had cracked ribs. My center fielder, Bob Stinson, had a concussion, the result of being hit over the head with a beer bottle. Sizemore and some of the others had assorted ailments, including a lot of swollen knuckles. That brawl was the only thing the New Mexico football team won all that year.

I called a team meeting to discuss our alarming physical condition and the need to play as hard as we could. It didn't matter now that the guys had done what they had. It couldn't be undone. The thing to do was put that behind us and go out and give it everything we had, remembering that we were still up in the Series, two wins to only one for Birmingham.

I said all the right things. We lost the next three games and the Series.

*   *   *

Next stop: San Diego, only an hour from our family home in Fallbrook. I was still working for Buzzie. By now the city had been awarded an expansion franchise in the National League and Buzzie was its president and part owner. He hired me to scout the minor leagues for the player draft which would stock the Padres' team. Then he appointed me as one of the Padres' radio and TV announcers, a job which didn't prove to be as enjoyable as I had first expected. I told Buzzie I wanted to manage again, and there was some solid reasoning connected with my request.

I asked for the Padres' farm team at Alexandria, Louisiana. I knew the personnel on that team, and I saw a chance down the road to become a coach in the major leagues for the Padres, and maybe even become a big-league manager for the Padres or some other team. Buzzie went along with the request, and when the 1972 baseball season opened, I was the manager of the Alexandria team. My boss was Buzzie's son, Peter, who now was the head of the Padres' minor-league system.

It was an exceptionally talented minor-league team. Of the 25 players 15 made it to the big leagues. However, no minor-league manager has really experienced it all until he has a showdown with the front office of his parent team, and that was the year when I had mine.

Mike Ivie preferred to play first base even though he had been signed as a catcher, so I put him at first and moved Randy Elliott to right field. This was in response to instructions by Peter not to talk to Mike about catching—just find a position for him and play him every day. Then all of a sudden Johnny Podres, my old Dodger teammate who had been hired by Buzzie as the Padres' minor-league pitching coach, came down from San Diego and conned Ivie into warming him up one day, all of it looking very innocent. Then he talked him into making a few throws down to second from behind the plate. Maybe the Padres had changed their minds about where to play Ivie, but nobody bothered to tell me about it.

I walked over to Podres and said, "How much did Peter offer you if you could get Ivie to catch?"

Podres looked stunned and said, "How did you know?"

I answered, "You can't fool me. We've been together too long, John." Podres stopped working with Ivie.

Mike played 11 years in the majors, his first five with the Padres. Out of 857 games, he played first base 602 times. His managers made him their catcher in only nine games.

I had another disagreement with Peter, this one the same kind of issue—where to play a certain man. He wanted me to move Dave Hilton from third base to second. He reached me one afternoon at the ball park to tell me about it, but first he complained that I had no phone in my apartment and wanted to know why.

"With the salary you're paying me," I told him, "I can't afford one. If you want to call me, you'll have to get me here at the ball park at three in the afternoon."

Then he told me he wanted me to move Hilton over to second. I worked Hilton out at second and immediately saw he was not agile enough to play there. Coming after Peter's efforts to move Ivie back behind the plate, I thought this was just about enough. I told Peter, "We're leading this league by fourteen games. Suppose I just send you some lineup cards and you can make them out and just mail them back. I'll play your lineups and I'll explain everything to the players."

He hung up.

Peter made one more effort to make a second baseman out of Hilton. He sent Donnie Williams, a former player of mine who had become a Padres scout, to Little Rock when we were playing there, to get a look at Hilton at second base in an afternoon workout. It was just the three of us—Donnie, Dave, and me.

Donnie showed Dave all the tricks of the position, then worked him out with ground balls for what seemed like forever so he could get a good, accurate estimate of Dave's potential at second. Finally he walked over to me and said simply, "He can't play second base."

I said, "Don't tell me. Tell the man who sent you."

That was Peter's last try with Dave Hilton. I wasn't always

right. I told the Padres Randy Jones had the potential to be a big-league pitcher, but only as a reliever. I told them he didn't have the stamina to be a starter. He was a major league pitcher for ten years—as a starter—and won the Cy Young Award in 1976 as the National League's best pitcher.

But I was right about Hilton.

Hilton's experience was just like Ivie's. He made it to the big leagues too, to Peter's parent team, the Padres. He played for them for four years—at third base.

I was able to solve one problem without any help. My family was with me for the summer, and one night while I was coaching third base I looked out and saw Kurt, by now a high school student, tossing hot dogs, peanuts, and other snacks over the bullpen fence to the relievers. They saw me looking in their direction and told Kurt, "Don't throw any more over—your father's watching."

I had to admire their nerve—using the manager's son to break a basic rule like that. Kurt was just trying to be a good guy, but the players knew what they were doing.

I sent word to Kurt to rejoin the rest of the family in the grandstand.

That team was a happy experience, even with the occasional unsolicited suggestions from San Diego. I had the players circulate in the stands before each home game and mingle with the fans during the visiting team's batting practice. I did the same thing. We'd explain things about the game of the night before and talk about what we thought might happen in the immediate future, and everyone got to enjoy everyone else—the fans enjoyed the players and vice versa.

We won the championship too.

I had been retired as a player for more than the five seasons required to be eligible for election to the Baseball Hall of Fame. I wasn't really expecting to be elected, but I picked up a few votes in my first year, and people began telling me I'd had a Hall of Fame career. The question began to occur to me: Will I really get elected to my sport's Hall of Fame?

It was to become more than a question. It was to become an obsession. Now that I didn't have to worry about strikeouts, I had found something else to be overly concerned about.

At that same time, my career took another unexpected turn. There was a vacancy for a coach on Don Zimmer's staff at San Diego, the kind of a job that I had prepared myself for as a manager in the minors. I was ready and qualified, but the Padres said they wanted me to manage Alexandria again. I felt I had earned my letter there, so I left the Padres organization. There I was again—no salary, a man without a job.

I shopped around, approaching various teams including the Dodgers. Nothing. I bought an interest in the Red Dog Saloon at the Valley Fort Steak House at home. I was tending bar there when I got a surprise call from John McHale, the general manager of the Montreal Expos. He knew I had announced the Padres games on TV for three seasons, and he wanted to hire me as his TV analyst.

I grabbed it. I teamed up with Dave Van Horne for 14 seasons. The job was great, and so were the Canadian people and the Expos' organization. John and his owner, Charles Bronfman, were major-league in every way. Dave Van Horne helped make me a broadcaster and was the perfect broadcast partner for me.

The Montreal TV job was a much bigger job than the one in San Diego because the Expo games were televised throughout the Dominion of Canada, and even into some American cities on the border like Buffalo, Cleveland, Detroit, and Seattle.

I learned in my first year with the mike and the camera, at San Diego, that you have to be careful what you say and, more importantly, how you kid people. Preston Gomez was the San Diego manager and he had an expansion team that wasn't giving the fans much to cheer about. The team was struggling to get off the ground, but on one particular night there was reason to get excited about the Padres. Their pitcher, Clay Kirby, was pitching a no-hitter after eight innings, even though San Diego was losing to my friend, Gil Hodges, and his Mets, 1-0.

Gomez then shocked the fans by lifting Kirby for a pinch hitter. He didn't just shock them—he infuriated them. A few fans came onto the field and had to be restrained by security officers. The next night there were the usual banners hanging from the upper deck, but one of them called for an act of terrorism. It said:

HIJACK GOMEZ

I was talking to one of my other broadcast partners, Gerry Gross, who combined with Frank Simms and me to form the Padres' broadcasting team, and I said—with a straight face, "Hey, Gerry, Gomez has a brother at the game tonight."

Gerry said, "That's nice. How do you know?"

"Well, some of the fans made a nice banner to say hello to him and it's hanging from the upper deck. It says, 'Hi, Jack Gomez.'"

Gross went on the air, and after several innings he said, "I see we have some of our usual creative banners from the fans here tonight. And there's one especially nice one out there in the outfield saying hello to Preston Gomez's brother, who is here at the game tonight. It says, 'Hi, Jack Gomez.'"

During the commercial break between innings, I had to explain it to him. "No, no, Gerry," I said patiently, "that banner doesn't say, 'Hi, Jack Gomez.' It says, *'Hijack* Gomez.'"

It used to be I had to watch what I said to umpires and the media. Now I had to be careful about what I said to announcers.

20

Cooperstown And Flatbush

The talk about the Hall of Fame was getting serious by the mid-1970s. I became eligible for election in 1969 after the five-year waiting period, and when I wasn't elected in my first few years of eligibility, some people seemed worried. I wasn't concerned about it at first, but when others started getting bothered by it, so did I.

I had been to Cooperstown twice, once as a Brooklyn Dodger and once with the Los Angeles Dodgers. The L.A. Dodgers played an exhibition game there against the Baltimore Orioles in the game the Hall of Fame people put on every year as part of the enshrinement weekend. I didn't remember that much about the Hall of Fame itself, but I did remember the swimming pool by our dressing room.

Brooks Robinson, Don Drysdale, and I were in the pool—not

knowing that one day all three of us would be members of the Hall of Fame—when another Dodger, Norm Larker, came out to the pool and climbed onto the diving board. He wasn't wearing a bathing suit. He was wearing a real suit—coat, tie, and dress shoes—and he was holding a cigar in his mouth and a can of beer in his hand.

As he stood there on the diving board, he asked us how much we'd give him if he jumped in. We offered him $20 from each of us to jump into the pool fully clothed. He said, "My shoes alone cost more than that."

While he was attempting to negotiate a higher price out of us, Maury Wills sneaked up behind him and pushed him in. As he was heading toward the water feet first, he held his beer up over his head. The can of beer was the last thing to go under. When he bobbed back up to the surface, the cigar was still in his mouth.

In my first couple of years in the balloting, I received only a few votes, so I began to think it just wasn't in the cards for me to become a Hall of Famer. Then the votes for me began to increase, and I started to want it badly—too badly. I began to wonder if it was just a popularity contest and whether some of my controversies with the media as a player were coming back to haunt me.

That's when it became an obsession. Each year I got a lot of votes, but each year I missed being elected. The vote total kept increasing, but even that made me wonder. How come I got more votes each year? I wasn't a better player this year than I was the year before. I was retired, so how could I be getting better? I didn't understand how my qualifications could change from one year to the next. Either I belonged in the Hall of Fame or I didn't.

The whole thing began to eat away at me, just like my strikeouts. In a way it was the same thing. I was striking out again. It was only once a year instead of 90 times, but I still was striking out.

One Sunday night, I was in my hotel room in Montreal when Bev called from home. She had news that she couldn't wait to share. "I had the most wonderful experience today that I've ever had in my life," she said. "I visited a church called the Neighborhood Church. Pastor Bob Hobson preached a sermon right out of the Bible and I got so much out of it that at the end of the service I invited Christ into my life."

All I could say was, "Oh?" I was skeptical, but listening to Bev, I was intrigued. She added, "I can hardly wait for you to get home to hear him."

The first Sunday I was home, we went to hear Pastor Bob. Going to church wasn't a new thing for me. I had been a pretty regular churchgoer most of my life. When we moved the family to Fallbrook, we became members of the Methodist church there. Much of what I heard coming from the pulpit went in one ear and out the other but it wasn't the minister's fault. For Bev to sound as she had on the phone, I knew there was something different about the service she had attended.

I went to the service not knowing what to expect. Pastor Bob was a tall, slender, good-looking guy with blond hair, about my age, full of energy. He was a dynamic speaker and knew the Bible like the back of his hand. He had a knack for talking about spiritual things in a way that made sense. He was not a man you could ignore. At the end of the service, he said, "If you've never invited Christ into your life, now is the time to do it, but be careful because He's listening. If you ask Him to come in, He'll come in."

That Sunday I asked Christ to come into my life and live in and through me. I walked out of there feeling that for the first time ever, I'd gotten something out of church. During the winter Bev and I attended church every Sunday and went to Thursday night Bible Study. I played golf with Pastor Bob, and it seemed he always left me with interesting things to think about. He had a way of putting things into perspective. One thing that really hit home was when he said, "You came into this life with nothing and you're going to leave with nothing. It all belongs to God—the

281

money, cars, things. The important thing is knowing Him and having a whale of a time in between."

In the week that the 1979 votes for the Hall of Fame were announced, Pastor Bob and his wife Nina were at our house for dinner. He said in a lighthearted way, "Well, Duke, I see you missed it again."

He immediately noticed he had struck a raw nerve. He said, "This really bothers you, doesn't it?" When I admitted that it did, he suggested we let God handle it. I thought that sounded like a good idea. "There are several things in life you don't need, Duke," he said, "and one of them is luck. You don't need luck because you have Christ."

It was then that I came to realize I could accept whatever happened, or didn't happen. It was out of my control. If I made it fine. If I didn't make it, that would be fine too.

The next year I was elected to the Baseball Hall of Fame. It had been ten years.

Jack Lang of the Baseball Writers Association of America called me in January 1980 to alert me that I should be ready to fly to New York on a moment's notice because it looked as if this might be it. He called Al Kaline and told him the same thing.

I tried not to get too excited because I knew I could still be disappointed. The Hall of Fame is, and should be, limited to only the very best players in the history of the game. After ten years, I knew it wasn't easy. And I knew the system currently in use doesn't exactly ensure the best decisions anyhow.

Members of the Hall of Fame are chosen by vote of the more than 400 members of the Baseball Writers Association of America. They can list up to ten players from those eligible. It doesn't matter if your name is first or tenth as long as you're on the list. You have to be named on 75 percent of the ballots returned. If all the writers did their homework and also remained impartial in their voting, there would be no problem, but they don't. The fact that men like Gil Hodges, Phil Rizzuto, and Leo Durocher are still not in the Hall of Fame proves that the present system doesn't work as well as it should.

When Jack called again a few days later with the joyous news, Bev and I both cried. Then we kissed. Our youngest child, Dawna, was there, and she joined in on the hugging and kissing and crying. Bev and I called the other kids, then drove to San Diego and hopped aboard the red-eye to New York for the announcement that Kaline and I had made it. We couldn't sleep a wink all night as we crossed the country in the dark.

We landed in New York at 5 A.M. and went to our hotel to wash and change for a press conference with the national media, with a special hookup to the Los Angeles reporters gathered at Dodger Stadium. Back home, Dawna and Bobby Rucci, a school friend of Kurt's who has become like a third son to us, were covering the phones. This was something special to them, to be involved in this excitement. They took more than 50 messages the first day we were gone.

Tom Valenti, our old Dodger friend, and his wife Marilyn took Bev and me to dinner that evening at the River Cafe under the Brooklyn Bridge. It was a lovely setting—candlelight dinner with the lights of the New York skyline twinkling in the distant darkness. The restaurant was full. A Catholic priest a few tables away saw us and started to applaud, softly and politely. Others in the restaurant picked up on it and joined in. Soon everyone in the place was applauding. Someone sent over a bottle of champagne. The people of Brooklyn were still being nice to the Duke of Flatbush.

I had another warming experience that night. As we were leaving the restaurant, we walked past a long line of people waiting to get in. A man stepped out of line, took something out of his wallet, and asked me to autograph it.

As I signed my name, I looked at the wallet item. It was a bubble gum card of me in my Brooklyn Dodger uniform. He'd been carrying it in his wallet for 25 years.

* * *

The August morning in 1980 dawned like one of nature's masterpieces. It was seasonally warm, a pleasant summer day in the Adirondack Mountains of upstate New York where the family of James Fenimore Cooper started a town. Cooperstown, with the giant shade oaks and a lake 12 miles long and Indian names which show up in Cooper's novels, was up early for its biggest day of the year, the induction ceremonies at the Hall of Fame, on the spot where Abner Doubleday is said to have laid out the first baseball diamond.

The Dodgers showed their class throughout the whole event. Fred Claire, the Dodgers' executive vice president, called me in early August to tell me they were going to retire my number, a tradition which the Dodgers follow when one of their players is elected to the Hall of Fame. He also said the team would pay the expenses of every member of the Snider party going to Cooperstown whose trip would not be covered by the Hall of Fame itself.

I thanked him, but I wanted to be sure I didn't accidentally take advantage of the team. "When I get the tickets, should I get 'Y' class or first class?"

Fred said, "You know the Dodgers always go first class."

We flew in from all points on the compass. Bev, Kevin, and Dawna flew out of San Diego to Chicago, where they met Pam and Kurt and Kurt's wife, Kim, who flew to Chicago from their home in San Jose. The two groups landed in Chicago about five minutes apart and flew together to Syracuse, where a van met them and drove them down to Cooperstown. Bev's sister, Elaine, and her husband, Cliff Ditto, came with their children, Brad, Steve, and Pattie.

I was in Montreal Thursday broadcasting an Expos game. "Good Morning America" wanted me to be a guest the next morning in New York. ABC flew one of its private planes to Montreal to pick me up and fly me to New York. I had only a few hours of rest at my hotel, appeared on the show, and then took a commercial flight back to Montreal to broadcast the Expos'

Friday night game. I drove most of the night and arrived in Cooperstown at 4:30 in the morning. Everybody was asleep.

The Sniders weren't the only ones there to see me inducted. Carl Erskine was there, as I knew he would be. Campy and Koufax, both of them Hall of Famers, were there, and Pee Wee, now a Hall of Famer too, remembered to send a telegram when he couldn't make it. My first press agent, Pete Rozelle, was there with my first coach, his uncle, Joe Rozelle, and Bill Schleibaum—all at Pete's expense.

There was a busload of friends from Montreal, plus Dave Van Horne, my broadcasting partner, and my relatives from Ohio, Mildred and Carl Forbeck. Buzzie was there with his wife Evit, and when Bobby Rucci made a surprise trip from Fallbrook, the Bavasis gave him their hotel room because they had to leave right after the ceremonies. My three buddies from Fallbrook showed up—Cliff Dapper, Bob Kruis, and Steve LaFevre.

A man named Frank Taylor was there too. More than ten years before, when I was announcing for the Padres, a man came up to me in Atlanta and said, "You're Duke Snider, aren't you?" When I said yes, he pulled out a bubble gum card of me and said, "My name is Frank Taylor, and they call me 'the Duke of Dixie.' I've been carrying this for years." He had me autograph it and later had it made into a plaque and gave it to me. He was from Memphis, and he knew more about me than I knew about myself, and on that day in Cooperstown, he was there.

The sky was a bright blue, dotted by puffs of white—chamber of commerce weather. For me, it was more like Christmas than a day in August, and Al Kaline surely felt the same way. We were receiving the ultimate honor our profession has to offer. This was a Day of Days.

I was talking to Al just before the ceremonies began. I had jotted down a couple of notes, nothing much, but I saw he had three pages of material, all typed out, word for word. I said, "Gee, Al, I just have these couple of three-by-five cards with a few things jotted down. Don't show me up."

When he gave his talk, Al struggled to keep from breaking into tears, and if he had, he wouldn't have been the first. It's hard for anyone else to imagine what an overpowering emotional experience it is. Al wasn't doing anything to help my own composure. His voice cracked and as he talked about his debt to his parents, who were there, I got a little tear in my eye too, like everyone else. The horrible thought occurred to me, "If this happens while I'm listening to Al talk about his parents, what's going to happen to me when I get up there?"

I sort of looked toward the sky and said silently, "Mom and Dad, I'm not going to talk too much about you today." I'm sure they understood and approved.

Ted Williams was also on the platform behind the red, white, and blue bunting to represent the Boston Red Sox and the family of Tom Yawkey, the owner of the Red Sox for four decades, who was being inducted posthumously.

That was an extra touch for Bev. Ted was always at least her second most favorite player in either league, although at times I'm sure he was first. I'd come home from our game and say, "Hi, honey—I hit a home run today."

Bev would smile and say how happy she was at the good news. Then she'd say, "Ted hit two today."

After he finished his remarks, Ted turned toward Al and me, both of us a few seats away from the lectern. He had some nice things to say about Al and his outstanding career with the Detroit Tigers, starting when Al won the American League batting championship at age 20, the youngest player ever to do it.

Then Ted turned to me in full view of ESPN's cable TV cameras and the rest of the news media and said, "And the Duke. I wanna tell you, buddy—you are the perfect example of what I've said about the writers for a long time: They're not always right, because in your case they were ten years late getting you here where you rightfully belong."

When Al was introduced by Bowie Kuhn, who was then the Commissioner of Baseball, the crowd had chanted his name, and the same thing happened when the Commissioner introduced me. I heard, "Duke! Duke! Duke!" from the fans gathered on the green lawn under the oak trees.

I looked toward my family. I was just as proud of them as they were of me, and I made sure I introduced each of them. After thanking everyone, starting with Bev and including her hero Ted, and without crying, I closed by saying, "I'd like to thank God for including me in His master plan—allowing me to be in the Hall of Fame and be a Brooklyn and Los Angeles Dodger."

Now I was in the Hall of Fame, and with people who meant a great deal to me during my career. So many Brooklyn Dodgers are enshrined there—Jackie Robinson, Roy Campanella, Sandy Koufax, Don Drysdale, Pee Wee Reese, Walt Alston, even our president, Branch Rickey. Others from our time belong there with us—Gil Hodges and Leo Durocher—and some of our autumn opponents like Roger Maris and Phil Rizzuto.

Being allowed to be a major-league baseball player for 18 years was more than a piece of cake—it was the *whole* cake. Getting to play as a Dodger was the icing on the cake. Being elected to the Hall of Fame was the cherry on top. As the kid from the ethnically mixed neighborhood on the east side of Los Angeles, the one with cardboard from his mother in his tennis shoes, whose father made him bat left-handed and called him "Duke," I was given one of life's greatest blessings—to do what I wanted. For such good fortune, anyone would be grateful.

Over my more than 40 years as a player, scout, hitting instructor, manager, and broadcaster, the sport to which I owe so much has undergone profound changes. Baseball isn't played in the sunshine much any more. Most of its games are at night. It's not an all-white sport any more. Every team has black players. There never used to be a team west of St. Louis. Now there are ten. We used to travel by train. Now it's jet airplanes. The fans used to follow the games on the radio. Now it's television—they can sit right there in their own homes and watch the games, free and in living color, and even make their own video tapes. The new scoreboards are full of colored lights and magic messages and fireworks that explode when the home team hits a home run. The uniforms have the player's number on the front as well as on the back, and the back has his name on it too. They play baseball indoors now, and on grass that isn't even real.

But it's still baseball. Kids still imitate their heroes on playgrounds. Fans still ruin expensive suits going after foul balls that cost five dollars. Hitting streaks still make the network news. And the hot dogs still taste better at the ball park than at home.

It says something about the Dodgers, especially the Brooklyn Dodgers, that to so many people we remain a symbol of baseball, and of America itself, in the 1940s and 1950s. Those of us lucky enough to be young in that special time can still see that special team—

Johnny Podres is still asking for only one run . . . Bobby Thomson is still leaping his way toward first base . . . Don Larsen is still perfect . . . Jackie is still stealing home while Yogi screams . . . Campy is still chirping, "Same team that won yesterday is gonna win today" . . . Skoonj is still throwing out runners at third base . . . I'm still floating down the first-base line past Allie Reynolds . . . The fans still holler out to "Oisk" . . . Leo is still getting kicked out for arguing with the umpire . . . Newk still has sweat dropping from the beak of his cap and rolling off his nose . . . Pee Wee is still throwing to Gil for the last out . . . And the advertisement on the outfield fence still says, "Hit Sign, Win Suit."

Ebbets Field still stands.
The Brooklyn Dodgers still live.